The Figure of

The Figure
of the Detective

A Literary History and Analysis

CHARLES BROWNSON

McFarland & Company, Inc., Publishers

Jefferson, North Carolina

LIBRARY OF CONGRESS CATALOGUING-IN-PUBLICATION DATA

Brownson, Charles, 1945–
    The figure of the detective : a literary history and analysis /
Charles Brownson.
        p.   cm.
    Includes bibliographical references and index.

    ISBN 978-0-7864-7769-2
    softcover : acid free paper ∞

    1. Detective and mystery stories, English—History and
criticism.   2. Detective and mystery stories, American—
History and criticism.   3. Detectives in literature.
4. Crime in literature.   I. Title.
    PR830.D4B76 2014
    823'.087209—dc23   2013048600

BRITISH LIBRARY CATALOGUING DATA ARE AVAILABLE

Front cover: Pondering private eye © 2013 Shutterstock

Manufactured in the United States of America

McFarland & Company, Inc., Publishers
    Box 611, Jefferson, North Carolina 28640
        www.mcfarlandpub.com

Contents

Preface

The origin of this book lies in a question about Sherlock Holmes. It is a common assertion (made by Conan Doyle and even Holmes himself as well as many critics and readers since) that Holmes was both a superlative reasoner and a *cold* man. He was (and is) distinguished from the warm and emotional *unreasonable* artist. Two things about these assertions intrigued me as being obviously false—first, that Holmes was a cold man, and second, the association of reasoned or "logical" knowledge with coldness.

My interest expanded rapidly from this kernel. What I saw in the detective story (and not in the literature on it) was how complex the figure of the Detective was. By a "figure" I mean a cultural icon that grounds our views of life and its possibilities and at the same time validates them. Throughout the book I shall capitalize this word when referring to this figure and use the uncapitalized word when referring to specific detectives.

The Detective is, and was from the beginning, a figure of iconic status, drawing to himself many psychological and cultural desires and fears, thus becoming a nexus through which such issues could be understood, studied, accommodated, and perhaps ameliorated. As I began to understand this, I grew curious to know more about how the figure of the Detective arose and what has happened to it since. This is the subject of this book.

In order to answer these questions about the cultural importance of the Detective I found that, although I was dealing with literature and, to some extent, film, what I sought was not literary, but rather philosophical, historical, and socio-cultural. A certain amount of critical theory was required, but a thorough survey of fictional detectives and of the literature of the detective genre would be a distraction and indeed superfluous. What interested me were the reasons for the existence and persistence of the Detective as a cultural icon, which would require an inquiry into the nature of the Detective himself—that is, a typology. Particular detectives would be of interest only insofar as they advanced the developing analysis.

This book is thus neither a critical work of genre theory nor a detailed

1

history of the genre. It is based on the assertion that literary formulas (genres) are not arbitrary constructs but come into existence out of the needs and fears of their readers, and so any change in the formula must be driven by social changes. Much more than literary (that is, non-formulaic) fiction, genre writing is an index of social change. A history of the genre written with this in mind would treat it as a living thing and perhaps uncover new connections and explanations not noticed before.

It was soon obvious that the sporadic culture wars over the detective story are irrelevant to my aims. Whether these stories are worthy of attention by readers and critics, or are simply lowbrow entertainment, has nothing to do with the cultural work that the Detective does. But at the same time, that there are such controversies at all is indicative of some cultural need. What is it? Why, at particular times of hegemony and change, does the detective story have such a popular appeal, impervious to intellectual disparagement? Of the needs that the reader is hoping to satisfy, entertainment is likely one of them, but the desire to be entertained is not confined to the detective story. The question is rather *why* we are entertained by reading stories about detectives, and sometimes needful beyond simple entertainment. It seemed to me that the resonance and endurance of the Detective as a cultural and literary figure implies some importance that has nothing to do with whether or not detective stories are bad for us.

In my reading for this book I have largely ignored the standard genre histories and most of the critical literature in favor of a few works that pick apart the structure of the detective genre as it has existed at various times since the nineteenth century, and in favor of works outside the field of literature that address the social, historical, and philosophical issues that I felt were important to my intentions.

Nevertheless, this book is a literary one after all, not a systematic social history. Being concerned with a detective's work of getting and deploying knowledge, it has a philosophical inflection. But finally it is based on my reading of a great many novels, out of which I have chosen those that seemed to add something important to a slowly growing understanding of how this very popular, long-lived, and important sort of fiction works.

Of works of scholarship, this book is indebted to John G. Cawelti's 1976 groundbreaking genre analysis *Adventure, Mystery, Romance*. I hope I have been able to extend his insights into new territory. I began by saying that the origin of this book was a question about Sherlock Holmes. That is not the whole truth. Underneath all the critical theory and literary history and the talk of social work I hope the reader will discover my fondness for detective stories of all sorts. The origin of this is a detective story I read at the age of seven or eight about Freddy the Pig. For those who don't know, there were twenty-five of these, written between 1927 and 1958 by Walter R. Brooks, illustrated by Kurt Wiese. I had to look that up — I remembered the stories but not the name of the man who wrote them, as it so often is. I find out now that there was a twenty-sixth book, a collection of poems. My childhood public library seems not to have bought that one. Who knows what might be if it had? Perhaps ... but whereof what one cannot speak, thereof one must be silent. Holmes, I think, said something of the sort also.

Introduction

The detective genre has been variously subdivided. One category that always stands outside any typology of the genre is crime fiction, to which we may in this case annex true crime, as it is called. The ordinary reason for differentiating crime fiction is that it either does not contain a detective or it does not follow the rules of the genre.

This label might be useful to publishers as a signal to readers, but it is immediately obvious that if we are investigating the always-changing content and boundaries of the genre we will have to concern ourselves with crypto-detectives of just the sort not supposed to be present in crime fiction, and with various rule-breaking modifications of a genre that has not been limited by rules since the days of Agatha Christie. Other labels such as mysteries, murder mysteries, and so forth do not help much. I will call all of this detective fiction. I will also use the word *genre* somewhat loosely to mean at times the field of writing about detectives and at other times to mean a genre as found in critical theory. I trust the reader will be able to distinguish these uses. Finally, in distinguishing the various forms that detective stories may take I will prefer such words as formula or tradition, recognizing that these stories are intended first to be like each other, for that is the way of a genre. Each is one more of the same.

The origins and history of the detective story are not entirely agreed upon. It seems clear enough that the Detective arose from English, French, and to an extent American culture but was never the exclusive property of those three. Anyone can write a detective story, and detective stories are in fact enhanced by exotic locales, outré characters, and unusual villains. A good detective story might also be just the opposite — the sort of meticulous realism that pays close attention to everyday details and ordinary experiences. But although anyone could write such a story, in fact only a particular few actually did. Why should the origins of the genre be so constrained by time and place?

It is not so now. During the last twenty years there has been an explosion of detective stories worldwide that has added a great deal to the stock of interesting books. Likewise, we have been treated to many new sorts of detective of different ethnic and social origins. Why is that? I will not be able to deal with this in any detail. My plan is instead to develop an analysis of sufficient generality as to make it a tool for an extended discussion. We may ask, for example, why the Swedish detective Martin Beck appeared when he did, and why he was part of a team of fully realized people — characters — who shared the work. Did it have anything to do with Sweden's social ideals at a time when allegiance to those ideals was felt to be breaking down? Beck thought so. I hope to provide the means to engage in this discussion.

All of my arguments orbit a fundamental dichotomy between what I call warm and cool knowledge. The distinction is simple. Cool knowledge is rational, acquired by thinking and observation, subject to logical analysis. Warm knowledge is instinctual. I use this word here and throughout not as a psychologist or a biologist would — not as scholars and scientists who rightly dispute whether there is such a thing as instinct — but to mean in the ordinary way the sort of knowledge about the world that arises from the non-verbal, non- or pre-rational consciousness, the most ancient, limbic core of the brain. We are accustomed to call this sort of knowledge emotional, warm, or instinctual, and I will continue these conventional usages. That there is such a distinction between rational and non-rational knowledge we may take for granted as within the experience of everyone. It must be remembered, however, that the terms warm and cool are cultural judgments, and being such, follow cultural change. At times, warm knowledge has been disparaged (or worse). At other times, such as during the Romanticism of the nineteenth century, warm knowledge was privileged.

If the central question of the detective story concerns what knowledge is, then the business of the detective is the getting and deployment of it. The detective story is a quest, but getting possession of knowledge is only the first part of the tale. The rest of it concerns what to do with this knowledge, and so it is also a moral tale. The Detective is a shaman, a person who has acquired a valuable but dangerous stuff: knowledge, which may be used for good or evil. The Detective is an ambiguous figure, necessary to society but potentially destructive of it. He is a figure we cannot do with or do without. As with knowledge itself, the role the Detective is asked, or allowed, to play is a cultural decision. In this book I will be centrally concerned with how the detective story is bound up with our notions of what knowledge is and how it might or ought to be used.

At the end I will consider a related question: the possibility that knowledge is denied us, that we are not *knowing* beings. While this creates some technical difficulties for the detective story, it ought nevertheless be clear even by these rudimentary introductory remarks that this possibility is simply another one of the culturally driven fears that the detective story exists to confront and that, amazingly resilient as it is, it has confronted now for over two hundred years.

As I take up these matters my first task will be to work out how the genre, and the Detective, came into being. My analysis treats of this pre–Classic period as the coming together of the conditions necessary for there to be detectives and stories about them, and how these elements were assembled into what we now recognize as the detective story. I will find the beginnings of this process with Defoe and the very origin of the novel. Little by little, as powers and qualities come into being, authors work out how to tell an effective story with them. Poe, for example, showed how a story might be constructed using a purely ratiocinative investigation. Poe's Dupin is not a detective in the full sense, as we will see, but he was a lively demonstration of an aspect of one, and Poe's role in the creation of the detective story stands with others such as Dickens, Collins, Bulwer-Lytton, and Green.

All of this was finally combined into one character: Sherlock Holmes, to whom I will devote an entire chapter. With Holmes all of the elements that define the genre come together and we can now begin to talk of warm and cool knowledge; moral quests; logic and inference chains; insiders and outsiders; and the roles of thought, action, love and violence, which give the genre its enduring power.

The third chapter will take up the Classic tradition — or English Classic, commonly termed English from its first appearance in an English novel, Agatha Christie's *The Mysterious Affair at Styles*, in 1919. The English Classic was (as classics are) the culminating and hegemonic form of the detective novel, to which everything before, including Holmes, is pre–Classic. There were rules for the construction of a Classic story. These were informal and sporadically followed, not actually codified until later by the members of the Detection Club, but this looseness belies the distinct structure and identity of a Classic story form. It is a very well-defined formula that is still the standard of comparison and has been for every development since its time, which was 1919 to roughly 1940. A form of Classic tale that I analyze as the Neoclassic will be the subject of the penultimate chapter.

In my discussion of the English Classic I focus on Agatha Christie and her detective Hercule Poirot as proxies for the whole Classic tradition. Other authors were also at work, of course, developing story forms that would evolve into the successors of the Classic. One of these was Dashiell Hammett and his detective the Continental Op. Another was Freeman Wills Crofts and his invention of the police procedural.

The English Classic stands at the apogee of allegiance to cool knowledge. In succeeding chapters I will explore subsequent developments in the dialogue of warm and cool.

At one extreme is the police procedural. This formula tells of an unbroken causal chain marked by a trail of artifacts and circumstantial evidence, a trail that leads inexorably from the crime scene to the criminal for anyone who follows the procedure. Discovering the criminal is a matter of dogged persistence for which the police are distinctly suited. The pure procedural would now be thought a bit dull, but this variant of the detective story has proliferated nevertheless. Elements of it are now universal.

The opposite of the procedural involves the admission of warm knowledge as a legitimate way of discovering the truth. This was Hammett's contribution, but equally important was a French detective, Inspector Jules Maigret, the creation of Georges Simenon. The replacement of the hegemony of the Classic by that of noir and the hard-boiled story, roughly 1940–1980, is the concern of chapters 4 and 5.

Again and again we see that within a hegemony, new forms are being created that will become hegemonic in their turn. All through the period of the Second World War and its aftermath there were two variants of the detective story in play, both the legacy of the Classic. In one variant, the psycho-intuitive, cool knowledge dominated, with warm or intuitive knowledge informing it. In the other variant, warm knowledge dominated, ultimately in the form of violence: the hard-boiled tale. Some of these contain cool detective work in the Classic manner; some are constructed in different way.

The story-form in which cool knowledge dominates warm creates a sort of spy story of which the exemplar is John le Carré and his detective George Smiley, or a hard-boiled story-form such as that practiced by Robert B. Parker and his detective Spenser. The opposite valence of warm over cool grew into the hard-boiled stories of such detectives as Mike Hammer or Sara Paretsky's V.I. Warshawski, and into spy stories of the Len Deighton sort. The heritage of warm knowledge from Hammett through Simenon, Chandler, hardboiled, and spy-adventure stories culminated in the thriller. This progression is the material of Chapter 5. The opposite heritage of cool knowledge from Christie, again through Hammett and Chandler and variants of the hardboiled and spy story, culminated in the Neoclassic. This is the material of Chapter 6.

The change that noir made in the detective formula, a change that went hand-in-hand with the acceptance of warm knowledge, was to substitute, for the benign and only temporarily disrupted society of the Classic, a darker, incorrigibly and thoroughly corrupt society. In this world virtue is to be found in only a few persons, the detective being one of them. The consequences of this change for the figure of the Detective are profound. The entire genre, following the noir shift, is about working out the implications of the nexus between warm knowledge and moral decadence. The answers are various but everywhere tied to the importance granted to warm over cool.

It is essential to say now that I am not claiming that post–World War I society *was* benign and innocent, but that it was *portrayed* as such. That portrayal was a choice, made at a particular time and place, that will tell us a great deal about the mechanisms at work. It is also necessary to address two other matters.

The first is that I have consistently referred to the figure of the Detective as a man. That is because until recently, detectives *were* men. The exceptions— Miss Marple, Harriet Vane, P.D. James's Gray —confirm rather than break the gender separation, which is based on a deep-running conviction that women are not rational. Their field of influence is warm knowledge. And so it was that women did not have equal access to the status of Detective until the relative importance of warm knowledge to the detective story had decisively changed. I discuss this matter in two places: in connection with the noir shift and with the late hard-boiled tradition.

The second issue concerns my use of the word hegemony. At each point of change in the genre —from Classic to noir, from noir to hard-boiled — the situation resembles that of painting during the shift to Impressionism, or (also in France) the setting aside of the Classic drama of Corneille and Racine for the new Romantic plays of Victor Hugo. In the case of the detective novel there is no Academy to dictate the correct values. A genre is driven by public taste. It is the nature of a genre formula for readers to want more of the same. Changes in the formula are driven by the readers' changed values. During each period of stable values, the way in which detective stories are written is regarded as the right way. The best word for this domination of a literary form by a restricted set of demands is hegemony.

In this way the hard-boiled formula was replaced by the Neoclassic, just as noir superseded the original Classic formula, and we come full circle. But there is an enormous difference between the world of 1980 and that of 1920, and so, if my reasoning about the yoke that harnesses the detective genre to social conditions is correct, we should see that the Neoclassic and Classic formulas work in different ways and to different ends.

And that is so. In the same way in which economic depression and a new destructive war called an end to the increasingly desiccated procedures of the Classic formula, so the insecurities of our time have produced a reevaluation of two fundamental elements of the detective story. The Detective's moral quest has been put in doubt as a result of a degenerating consensus concerning right behavior, and the central task of the getting of knowledge has been made difficult by profound uncertainty over what it means to know something. How is it possible to write a detective story in which the detective knows nothing, nothing happens for certain, nobody knows how to find out, and everyone is in hopeless disagreement?

One response to this has been the essentially nostalgic Neoclassic. Is it possible that the detective story might find a way to assimilate these new fears as it has always done in the past? This speculative question informs the material of the last chapter. There I will explore the theoretical limits of stories about the Detective and whether a reinvented genre can yet again invigorate our means of understanding our place in the world.

1

The Pre-Classical Detective

The Detective is a phenomenon some three centuries old, nearly coextensive with the novel, and one that until recently was confined to Britain, where it originated, France, and America. There is a substantial literature on the reasons for this and for the social pressures behind the creation and success of the Detective. What are the sources of this success? How can it be explained? These are the questions that are the subject of this book.[1]

I might make some general remarks to set out the arguments that I will be making in more detail. First, the detective novel through most of its history has been a rationalist enterprise. Britain and France are rationalist cultures. Also, they are also secular cultures— France by revolution, Britain by evolution. The precedence given to rational solutions to problems implies, if one is consistent, a belief that the world (and the lives in it) serve a purpose. The Detective discovers a part of this purpose when he solves a crime, and by its solution restores the endangered precedence of rationality and purpose over their antagonists.

The same cannot be said of America, which is not a secular culture and so does not give the same precedence to rationality. America is a scientific and technological culture with a rationalist constitution, but American thought has always had a Chautauquan, transcendentalist element that was embedded in Puritan thinking and comes to the fore in the proliferation of testifying religions that are so characteristic of Americans. The pre–Classic Detective, originating for the most part in Europe, was systematized in Britain and exported in a relatively finished form to America, where several of its rationalist and secular characteristics were promptly stripped away. As we shall see, America played an important role in the evolution and the hollowing-out of the purely rational Detective into its present form.

Why did the Detective appear in the English seedbed particularly? What is necessary to understand first of all is what counts as a detective, and when there came to be a general agreement on that. To what extent, after a certain historical moment, can particular fictional characters be awarded the honorific of the Detective? And what, therefore, is a detective story and how does it differ from other sorts of story?

Present-day readers may think that to question what a detective is makes little sense. But the matter is not so obvious. It is easy to forget there was a time when there were no detectives. Rather, those things that came to define what we now think of as a detective then had no names and were thus unimaginable. The rule of law, for example, despite its importance to society, had nothing to do with detection until there *was* a detective, at which point it became clear that without a code of law that the members of a society wish to enforce, the detective, whose purpose is to do just that, could not exist.

Much of the creation of the figure of the Detective works in this way. The creation process resembles evolution, in that a feature that arises for one purpose becomes adapted for another when conditions change. The Detective was created bit by bit until in some tales *we* can now recognize the familiar character. At the time, writers and their readers only gradually came to realize that these bits constituted a brand-new role.

At this point the genre was born. When it becomes possible for an author to count on readers' expectations and to shape a commodity (stories) into a repeatable pattern, that pattern constitutes the rules of the genre. Such rules allow the reader to recognize what she[2] is reading *as a detective story*.

Let me briefly enumerate the elements of what will be the finished genre in order to better recognize them in nascent forms. But we must be clear that this is not a history of real detectives, whose work might be thought to form the basis of detective stories. If it were so, the origin of such stories would be conveniently and easily explained. Stories, however, do not attach themselves to everyday experience in that way. Rather it is the reverse, that by striking deep into our lives stories can be said to create everyday experience by giving it meaning and significance. As stories about wizards attest, or for example the robot-inhabited world of Stanislaw Lem, there is no requirement at all for things to be found in the everyday world in order to be valuable to us.

Here, then, is a brief inventory of the necessaries of the detective genre.[3] A detective story requires:[4]

   I. a crime;
  II. a criminal;
 III. a detective;
 IV. threatened innocent bystanders; and
  V. a chronicler: the tale is told by a character within it who has partial knowledge.[5]

The last is a rhetorical rather than a logical requirement. If the reader has perfect knowledge of the crime, which no one in the story has, including the detective at first, it is very difficult to keep up suspense. If the story is presented as a puzzle, then advance knowledge of the solution is fatal. That the story be a puzzle is important to the requirement that the crime be fully explainable by rational inquiry. To be explainable rationally is of major importance to the cultural purpose of the genre, which is to reassure the reader that, despite the existence of crimes and criminals, the world is in fact rational, intelligible, and controllable. Thus, to do away with the chronicler entails major changes in how the story is to be told and what satisfactions it can give.

These five elements have requirements in turn. Crimes, for example, have existed probably since there have been monkeys, but were not always thought of as *crimes*.[6] Even so, any old crime will not do. We must first have a stable society living under a code of law that is generally accepted by citizens who are willing to give up some of their rights and resources to see that the laws are enforced. When the means of enforcement come to be embodied in a separate institution (the police), we have met the minimal requirements.[7] But writers and readers are not interested in most crimes. Running a red light, for example, will not meet the purpose. It was Poe's discovery that the crimes most apt for genre use are murder and political intrigue. It is a technical challenge to authors to adapt crimes of other sorts. The effort has resulted in some curious tours de force, but unsustainable one-offs for the most part. Murder in particular threatens the social fabric in a local, personal way that gives it a special frisson and adds urgency to the demand that the detective put matters to right.

The requirement that there be a criminal can be understood in the same way. First, the importance attached to the local and personal threat to social stability requires that the criminal be a *person*, preferably *one* person, and not some faceless entity. The requirement that the crime be rationally explainable requires that the criminal be so also, with recognizable and preferably common human motivations, character, and habits of thought. Likewise, the collective force of these requirements suggests that the crime should be the result of the criminal's *intent* to commit it. Inadvertent crimes will not be acceptable to the genre until after the English Classic period, except as curiosities. During the developmental (pre–Classic) years there were experiments with criminals lacking the power of moral reasoning or even intelligent thought — animals, Andaman Islanders— but none of these devices were so effective at producing unease as the man next door.

The preferred local and personal context suggests that the best (that is, the most threatening) criminal be *one of us*, thus calling all of us into question and maximizing the need to repair the social fabric quickly, before it is shredded beyond help. Coupled with the hothouse of a closed society (such as a few people gathered for a country-house weekend) it is easy to see why the country house murder is one of the signature plots of the English Classic.[8]

The requirement that there be a detective may on its face be the most absurd of the five. Why else is it called a *detective* story? Nevertheless it is not hard to find stories in which the crime is solved in other ways than through the agency of a detective. This is the implicit technical challenge in Chesterton's Father Brown series, for example, or Ellis Peters's Cadfael, which are "testifying" stories openly accepting of miracles and thus liable to be resolved by divine intervention. Accidental discovery is another threat to the genre. And beginning with the hard-boiled period it has been increasingly common for crimes to be solved not by detection but by beating up all the suspects until one of them confesses.

The Detective is a specialized role. He[9] embodies the context of rationality as a spokesman for the power of thought and the intelligibility of the universe, which is possibly a more important function than solving the crime. Indeed, there are successful detectives who do *not* solve the crime (*Trent's Last Case*) and some unusually bumbling ones who perhaps will never solve anything (*Gosford Park*). The Detective's place as a defender of rationality positions him in the larger conflict between rationality and intuition (the life of the emotions) which is in its modern form a legacy of Romanticism.[10] Early on these two poles were constructed as cool and warm — slippery terms that are pejorative from one point of view and laudatory from the opposite — and assimilated to the supposed incompatibility of science and non-science,[11] non-science being the whole rest of human endeavor fatally tainted by irrationality. "What can be said at all can be said clearly; and whereof one cannot speak thereof one must be silent," as Wittgenstein famously said. (This, together with the physical requirements of the Detective's role, is the primary reason why women were thought to be incapable of detective work. We will encounter some early female detectives in later chapters.) It is a fascinating (but separate) question to trace the attitude of fictional detectives toward art and religion, from the famously cold Holmes's liking for the violin and opera to Jacques Futrelle's Augustus S.F.X. Van Dusen, Ph.D., LL.D., F.R.S., M.D., alias "The Thinking Machine."

The demand for rational intelligibility carries with it constraints imposed by the concept of evidence and the investigative procedure of testing hypotheses — the scientific method. This, together with the need for the crime to actually be solved somehow, whether or not through the agency of a detective, are among the factors that established the genre once it was discovered to be a particularly satisfying mode of story telling.

As with the criminal, the Detective ought to be a single person (partners will be introduced later, and still later groups like Ed McBain's 87th Precinct). Perhaps less obviously, just as the criminal ought to be within the immediate society, the Detective ought to be outside it — not outside society altogether as the noir detective is, but only not part of the threatened group. It is easy to see that when the detective is himself threatened his status as a magus or a wise man is also threatened. It was eventually worked out how to tell a story this way, but in the established formula of the English Classic this would not serve the purpose. A Classic story typically begins with the crime and the following consternation, which leads someone in the group to obtain the services of a detective. The problem posed by a detective who is "not one of us" is that the detective becomes himself a danger to a society that he has been asked to repair. The detective's compromising involvement with the crime — his taint — is existentially impermissible, downright upsetting. But it is necessary, in fact, that this be so if the detective is to be both intellectually powerful enough to solve the crime and spiritually powerful enough to overcome his taint. Thus, it is important also to the English Classic that the Detective be not himself physically threatened or liable to be murdered, as this would mar his status as the criminal's superior. This additional requirement both allows and explains uber-criminals like Holmes's nemesis, Professor Moriarty, who *are* able to pose such a threat. This dangerous innovation will eventually help to transform the detective story into a thriller, a related genre that will ultimately subsume the whole rational world of detection.

Finally there is the Chronicler — famously, Dr. Watson. This character serves several important needs. First, he is a locus of the reader's trust that whatever is reported, while perhaps not true, is not a lie — the Chronicler is as fallible as any ordinary character and as likely to be deluded into the transmission of others' lies, but does not himself tell lies. Characters may lie to each other, but the Chronicler may not lie to the reader. At the same time, the chronicler, acting as the reader's surrogate, cannot be allowed to know the whole story until the end. This would constitute a betrayal of trust. If, as is usually the case, the story is being told in retrospect, it ought to be told in story time[12] so as to preserve narrative transparency without sacrificing suspense. The sidekick whose stance is in the narrative present places his narrative at a time when he knows the outcome and can be accused of concealment and duplicity. Later narrative structures will make use of this for purposes foreign to the English Classic. Pre-Classical narratives, emerging from traditions in which it was common for authors to keep their cards closely held,[13] were able to utilize other strategies to achieve narrative fidelity such as the need to protect the reputation of another character until the resolution of the story made this unnecessary. Narrative transparency is one of the important indicators of the mature genre.

Given this list of necessities, let us see how they were met in the developing genre of detective fiction.

The Emergence of the Classic Form

Daniel Defoe's *Street-Robberies, Consider'd* (1728) may be the first English instance of crime writing as we now understand it.[14] The publication date puts it twenty-one years before the creation (by the novelist Henry Fielding in his function as a magistrate) of the Bow Street Runners. "Unlike the earlier thief-takers and the thief Jonathan Wild, who found ways of profiting through control of London criminals, the Bow Street Runners were an official agency, formally attached to the Bow Street Magistrate's office and the Magistrate, the novelist Henry Fielding. Unlike the Bobbies who succeeded them, they did not patrol or attempt to prevent crime, but acted as detectives to solve crimes."[15]

The date was also a century before the formation of the New Police by Robert Peel in 1829 (hence "Bobbies"), generally considered the first modern police force. Somewhat before this (1812) in Paris, Eugène Vidocq, a reformed French criminal, created under Napoleon Bonaparte the Sûreté Nationale. Vidocq is considered one of the first modern private investigators; he was the model for both Jean Valjean and Javert in Hugo's *Les Misérables*.

Vidocq's Sûreté was a different institution from Peel's New Police. Both had official standing, but Peel's were police: that is, uniformed men who patrolled the streets openly and were engaged first of all to keep the peace and *prevent* crime, whereas Vidocq's organization resembled (and still does) the FBI or MI6. Vidocq and his agents infiltrated suspect groups, used deception to entrap suspected persons and extract confessions, and, like Javert, or Porfiry Petrovich in *Crime and Punishment,* were implacable in pursuit, wearing down their victims by whatever means were available. Vidocq was, needless to say, much feared, whereas the Bobbie's reputation was quite the opposite. As we shall see in the English Classic novels, ambivalence concerning the two methods is embedded in the very heart of the Detective. He is at once a threatening, shamanic figure possessing exotic and dangerous knowledge acquired at an unknown price, and a benign avuncular figure dispensing reassurance and protection. The English Classic evokes this figure only with reluctance, as a last resort, and hustles him off the stage as quickly as is decent when matters have been returned to normal.

The "memoir" that Defoe includes in his pamphlet is of a career not unlike Vidocq's. Defoe also gives advice on prevention in the spirit of the New Police. Without standing, the New Police were unable to actually do anything to reduce street robberies, so if citizens were better informed they might be better able to help themselves. To this end Defoe includes a short dictionary of the "Canting Language"—Defoe was as canny in exploiting bourgeois curiosity and prurience as Eugène Sue was in 1843 with his immense panoramic *Mystères de Paris*. In Defoe and Sue we see the Detective prefigured, invoked by a new middle class uneasy in their relationship to the industrial revolution that had created them and the underclass from which many of them had emerged, and into which they would sink if they proved to be bad businessmen.

None of these — Defoe's "informed citizen," Vidocq, the Runners or the Bobbies, or Sue's undercover Baron Gerolstein — are detectives. But the developing nexus of law enforcement, crime, and a middle class in need of and able to afford protection opens the ground for a person who can take on all of these roles and relationships.

The other eighteenth-century contributor to crime writing is a contrast to Defoe's pragmatism: the Gothic novels of Horace Walpole (*The Castle of Otranto*, 1764), Ann Radcliffe (*The Mysteries of Udolpho*, 1794), and Matthew Gregory Lewis (*The Monk*, 1796) to mention the three best known. Walpole's is generally considered the first of the genre, preceding by a few years the German Romantic movement that was the engine of the Gothic. Gothic tales are the dark side of Defoe's bit of crime journalism — we have here not the light of knowledge but the stygian pit of fear and ignorance. England, especially after the revolution of 1688, may have increasingly lived under a rule of law, the people increasingly protected from arbitrary incursions by monarchs and aristocrats, but the Gothic genre makes clear how fragile this state was felt to be. The Gothic is a genre based on the same warping or tearing of the social fabric that will be used to invoke the Detective. The causes of the threat are different, but the cure is the same; the Gothic dream world evaporates upon waking into the rational one.

With the Gothic formula we first see the conflict between warm and cool knowledge that will prove central to the creation of the Detective. One of the children of the Gothic, Frankenstein's monster, is a creation of science placed in a cautionary tale concerning dangerous, unregulated knowledge — this product of science died in search of love. The golem, a simpler, pre-scientific ancestor of Frankenstein's monster, is also the product of esoteric knowledge, but only after 1847, when Wolf Pascheles brought the Prague Golem into print, did it acquire any patina of ambivalence. Before then the golem's nearest relative was a big brother who drives away playground bullies.

In what sense do these Gothic tales with their uncertain and ambivalent relationship to rationality contain detection? Four of the five elements of the detective story are present. The one missing is the Detective. Admittedly, the Chronicler is somewhat truncated, present only as a somewhat hysterical author looking over the reader's shoulder, speaking urgently in his ear. A crime, a criminal, and threatened bystanders are already well-developed elements because they are built into the definition of the Gothic genre. The most obvious new element in the Gothic is the precedence given to the crime, which is of interest in itself rather than being merely a plot-engine. This focus on the crime, plus the need for a positive resolution, opens a space for a character whose purpose is to rectify the situation. And there are, in these stories, characters with such aspirations, but they do not proceed by logic and reasoning because the Gothic rationale is hostile to cool knowledge.

During the first half of the nineteenth century, with some of the basic social apparatus now in play and a range of plot formulas available and adapted to the purpose, we begin to see the Detective come forward out of the mist as a distinct character, a role.

In 1799 the American novelist Charles Brockden Brown published *Edgar Huntly; or, Memoirs of a Sleep-Walker*. Brown wrote in the Gothic genre, replacing the ruined castles and other impedimenta of the European original with American counterparts: dark forests, abandoned houses, caves, and so on. As is apparent from the title, Brown's novel concerns a crime committed while sleep-walking, a plot device taken up by Wilkie Collins sixty years later in his *The Moonstone*. The differences between Brown and Collins are small.

In both cases some foreigners are suspected: East Indians in Collins and American Indians in Brown (whose book is certainly racist in its treatment of Native Americans). Huntly, as detective, suspects one Clithero, found to be a sleepwalker, but Clithero is exonerated when Huntly arranges a re-enactment; in *The Moonstone* this replication of the crime proves the sleep-walker's guilt in taking the Moonstone but exonerates him of the criminal intent, and the ominous Indians prove to be civilized men who regain their rightful property at enormous cost to themselves. In both books the solution is found when the detective concludes that the answer lies within the episode of sleepwalking. In *The Moonstone* the reenactment of this episode provides objective evidence to the observers, whereas Huntly reenacts the episode himself and discovers the truth in a dream, a distinctively Gothic and Romantic outcome rather than the more modern, rational one.

Edward Bulwer-Lytton, Pelham (1818)[16]

With this book we are not quite in the realm of the Detective, but we have advanced from Defoe's simple narrative of crime to a more expansive tale and begun to break the Gothic hold on stories of evil-doing and criminality. *Pelham* incorporated this Gothic content into a story about the doings of the fashionable world, intending the Gothic disruptive criticism of conventional society, but without the cumbersome Gothic trappings or the Gothic appeal to unreason. Pelham is the Gothic hero reconstructed as a detective, motivated by curiosity to solve a crime using observation and reasoning. A member of the nobility is murdered for his money. The gentleman Pelham, characterized as an "adventurer" in the subtitle, undertakes an investigation that leads him into the criminal underworld. In the use of a detective to track down the criminal, in its concentration on the crime and the criminal, in its use of crime for purposes of social criticism, Lytton provided a very early example of how this emerging genre might be put to work.

Thomas DeQuincey

A watershed in the development of attitudes necessary for the appreciation of crime fiction is Thomas DeQuincey's *On Murder Considered as One of the Fine Arts* (1827). This is a set of three whimsical essays originally published in *Blackwood's Magazine*, the most prestigious magazine of its age, both a cultural mirror and an opinion leader. DeQuincey was a major interpreter of Wordsworth and Coleridge, the first generation of English Romantics. These essays can be seen as an attempt to reinterpret the world in terms of emotion and a less formal standard of beauty (or more generally, of worth). The most interesting to a modern reader is the third, "Three Memorable Murders." As with detective fiction, the emphasis is on murder itself, not in the almost prurient manner of the Gothic but on the feelings and actions of those involved, and on the aftermath, without moralizing. DeQuincey is experimenting here with treating murder as an entertaining tale on its own, without the Gothic trappings. He marks the appearance of a new sensibility necessary to the detective story as we know it, and shows that, despite the later emphasis on rationality and science, detection rests on a layer of Romance, on stories of heroes and quests, solidarity with one's fellows, and an appreciation of beauty and fitness. The tension between the romantic sensibility and the intellectual abstraction is essential to understanding the form.

DeQuincey's identification of the aesthetic appeal of crime proved prescient. In his essay "The Decline of English Murder," George Orwell described the famous murderer Crippen as the exemplar of a "great period in murder," a golden age that lasted from about 1850 to the Great War. Domestic poisonings so fascinated the public that the details of these crimes were known to everyone, hashed and re-hashed in the newspapers, and made into novels as now such occurrences are made into films. This is part of the mythology of crime that includes *The Godfather*, *The Untouchables* and the Al Capone legend, *Bonnie and Clyde*, *Pulp Fiction*, and any number of other instances. Part of the appeal of *The Sopranos* derives from the collision of this melodramatic mythology of alien beings with the domestic tale or comedy of manners that comes to us from Jane Austen and others.

Nineteenth-century (and modern) attitudes toward crime also derive from the rise of a scientific or sociological approach to criminal acts that regards them not as evil deeds but as the result of heredity or defective social arrangements. In this, too, DeQuincey was prescient, and though he takes a mocking stance toward his "immoral" thesis as a protective coloration, the aesthetic analysis that he presents is seriously meant.

Cawelti writes, "Literary crime is an ambiguous mirror of social values, reflecting both our overt commitments to morality and order and our hidden resentments and animosity against these principles." It is the same "mixture of horror and fascination, of attraction and repulsion" that drives the horror genre and that persists regardless of whatever sort of crime is the flavor of the moment, from nineteenth century poisonings to twentieth century gangsters and urban violence to twenty-first century paranoid political conspiracies of global reach.[17]

Balzac, *La Fille aux yeux d'or* and *L'Histoire de Treize* (1833)

There are three novellas in the "13" series, which concerns a secret society of 13 anonymous men. There is little here for our interest other than an intimation of DeQuincey's ideas on crime writing. More overt is the other book, in which a decadent man falls in love with a golden-eyed beauty only to find she has another lover. He resolves to kill her, but when all is ready he finds her dead by the other man's hand. Frustrated in his *amour propre*, he remarks that women are only chattel anyway and insists that she died of consumption.

An impediment delaying the full development of the crime story was a difficulty that the Gothic did not solve: the absence of a language needed for straightforward talk about violence and death. In 1871 Théophile Gautier, trapped in Paris during the siege of the Commune, wrote a series of reports gathered as *Tableaux de Siège*. After a life in journalism he did his best to convey the atmosphere of privation and destruction, but the descriptive language he had at his disposal was that of art. To our ears, to hear the horrors of war continually reduced to a salon display of historical paintings of the Cimmerians and other ancient foes of Rome is ludicrous and totally inadequate. Balzac's novel is in the same position vis-à-vis murder. To our ears, Balzac is insensitive to the fact that a human life has been ended for the sake of a clever but trivial story. However, it must be said that the English Classic of the 1920s is only marginally better: the murder victim is nothing more than a pretext, a mere body in the library. It will be another half-century before a change in sensibility makes it necessary for the author to engage a reader's sympathy on behalf of the victim, the better to give a presence to the crime and to dispel the air of unreality that the older storytelling conventions had acquired. But Balzac nevertheless did take a step on the path that follows on DeQuincey's insight, that to shift the contemplation of crime from the prurience of a public hanging to the more distanced and thoughtful mode of aesthetics is to make possible the rational entertainment that is one of the necessities for the Detective's subsequent success.

The Emergence of the Detective

The Gothic tradition, of course, has continued into our own time. (Do genres, once born, ever truly die?) And elements of the Gothic will continue to be found in the detective genre, which evolved partly from it. But by the mid–19th century the two had separated, as the Detective with his nimbus of cooler rationality and scientific thought began to address some social needs inaccessible to the Gothic.

A book that stands at the crossroads is Eugène Sue's *Les mystères de Paris*, a tale whose enormous commercial success, intense appeal to all classes of reader, and significance in the history of publishing are hard to exaggerate. The story was published serially in the *Journal des Débats* and in book form in 1843. It was among the first to take full advantage of the new cheap newspapers' discovery of the *feuilleton*, which in this case refers to fiction published "below the fold" and which was in its time absolutely necessary to large sales. Sue made a fortune from this book and *Le Juif errant*. *Les mystères* was read all over Europe and Britain, repeatedly translated during its few years of frenzied popularity. Copies of each new installment were rushed to America by competing fast ships, translated overnight, and printed in American newspapers the following morning.

Sue was a writer of inferior swashbucklers in the spirit of Cooper, Scott, and Dumas until 1840, when he began to take up social issues. *The Mysteries of Paris* is set in the Paris underworld at a time before Haussmann cleared its filthy, narrow streets. The book is full of criminal slang and mores taken mostly from Vidocq's memoirs. It presented itself in the initial serial installments as a titillating guide to evildoings for the curious wealthy. This aspect was muted when it was republished as a book, by which time Sue's new social conscience had strengthened considerably.

The melodrama concerns the attempts of Baron Gerolstein, disguised as a Paris workingman named Rodolph but accompanied by a bodyguard, the fantastically strong Murphy, to discover the whereabouts of his daughter. Early on we suspect that she is Fleur-de-Marie, sold into prostitution to the Screech Owl and her cronies. One of the denizens of this place, Le Chourineur, befriends Rodolph, who brings out the escaped convict's essential goodness. After much intrigue the criminals are defeated, Le Chourineur finds salvation, and father and daughter are reunited.

We are now in a position to take stock. By 1843 the preconditions for the detective genre had been largely met and a detective of sorts had made his appearance on the stage. Under pressure from the rising middle class, attitudes toward crime were changing. The nature of violent crime, and the public imagination of it, is forcefully captured in Cezanne's 1870 painting *Meurtre*. This is the age-old art of murder. The sensibility here is not that of Gautier in the siege of Paris described earlier, or of an Agatha Christie novel. These are the thugs and harridans of *Les Mystères*, cutting a man's throat for a pittance. Imagine Cezanne's story as told by Captain Hastings, or about Lord Peter Wimsey. It is simply impossible. The elements of the genre are there, but they have not yet been transformed into a tale about the getting and deployment of knowledge. Only after it was worked out how to tell such a tale would it be possible to put back into it the warm knowledge of bloody murder that Sue displayed.

Let us glance back to De Quincey's *Fine Art of Murder* and the origins of this problem. Goya also drew images of murders that are no more civilized than Cezanne's. But there is a crazed look in the murderer's eyes, and the victim seems to be already unconscious. This is not Cezanne's murder. Cezanne's is passionate, Goya's is lunatic. The exposure of Cezanne's criminals is amenable to rational thought. There is nothing problematic about the *Meurtre*; catching the perpetrators (if anyone cares to) will be a matter of dogged police procedural. To discover Goya's murderers may be more difficult.

What the succession of DeQuincey, Balzac, Sue, and Gautier reveals is that the developing detective genre had not yet sorted out the matter of warm and cool knowledge. It inherited from the Gothic a taste for lurid violence that works counter to the need for a tale of murder treated as a rational problem.

The first writer to fully grasp this situation, to capture the genre at the moment of change, was a man of the Gothic, Edgar Allen Poe. In 1845 he published three tales, *The Murders in the Rue Morgue, The Mystery of Marie Rogêt,* and *The Purloined Letter,* in which a recognizably modern detective, C. Auguste Dupin — incidentally the first series detective as well — solves the crimes simply by thinking about them. There is some gathering of evidence, most of it by others and reported to Dupin, and a number of other characteristics familiar to us are truncated or not present. But Poe's most important discovery, that of the method of *ratiocination* and of how to apply it dramatically, has been laid out, available for subsequent development. That development will occupy the rest of the century.

The route from Dupin to Holmes passes first through Charles Dickens's *Bleak House* (1852) and Inspector Bucket, the creation of an author supremely sensitive to cultural winds. This complicated novel is mostly concerned with the law and its injustices and not primarily with crime as such. Bucket is the first well-known professional detective in literature. (There was, in an obscure novel in 1827, *Richmond*, of uncertain authorship, one earlier existence [Rzepka 67]). Despite his title of inspector, Bucket is a private investigator working for hire. His first client here is Mr. Tulkinghorn, a lawyer for Sir Leister Dedlock, who is concerned to protect the Dedlock family reputation against scandal. But when Tulkinghorn gets wind of something questionable, he too hires Bucket to investigate, which Bucket does by the usual means of surveillance, interview, and the suborning of evidence. The secret is traced to Lady Dedlock, who is found to have been previously married and to have abandoned her daughter. Tulkinghorn's efforts to suppress this by blackmailing Lady Dedlock have the opposite effect of inexorably bringing the secret to light and causing Tulkinghorn himself to be murdered. Sir Leister then hires Bucket to do the opposite of what he has been doing — to find Lady Dedlock and prevent her suicide. In this Bucket is not quick enough, and Lady Dedlock dies on her old lover's grave.

The character of Bucket is an interesting one. He is capable and intelligent, even witty, and makes his way through the clues by deduction and insinuation.[18] Although he is capable of empathy, he is also fundamentally amoral and treats what he does as simply a craft rather than something worth doing in its own right. He is, therefore, not quite optimal as a conduit for the iconic features of the mature Detective. And he does not drive events; he is driven by them. He is not in charge.

Wilkie Collins added to Bucket some important features, in two "sensational" novels of importance to literature far beyond their contributions to the detective genre — but nevertheless an importance entirely dependent on their *being just that*: detective novels. *The Moonstone* (1868) is the more familiar of the two (the other being *The Woman in White*, published in 1860). The plot concerns the disappearance during a country-house weekend of a valuable gem, the moonstone, originally stolen from India during an uprising there. It is assumed that some mysterious Indians in the area have recovered the again-missing gem by unknown means, but after all the main events and hardships suffered by the novel's characters are done it is discovered, a year later, that one of the guests took the gem under the influence of opium.

The detective in the case is Sgt. Cuff, based on a real person who was well known to the public as one of the first professional detectives of the London Police. The police differ from Peel's Bobbies in that their purpose is to solve rather than prevent crime, and Cuff differs from Bucket in that he has institutional standing. The police were created on the French model, and the counterpart to Cuff is portrayed by Gaboriau in the person of Lecoq. Cuff is an inscrutable person with that trick of the glance common in fictional detectives (Porfiry Petrovich, Gryce, Holmes, and many others) of seeming to see the hidden secrets of others. He is the first English detective to be deliberately mystifying both to his clients and to the reader — to cultivate a gnomic persona that will make his discoveries, when they are revealed, appear to be magical. He speaks and behaves enigmatically, letting us suppose he has found something out without letting us know what it is.[19]

But still the formula is not complete. It is notable that Cuff does not actually solve the case. That is done by a Mr. Bruff and an accomplice who restage the crime in order to prove the correctness of their conclusion as to how the diamond was filched. They have learned that it has since come into the hands of a broker who intends to sell it back to the Indians from whom it was originally stolen. What they don't know is that there is another party to the crime, one who was in the house at the time and actually saw the theft, took the jewel, and has attempted to profit from it since. Cuff does identify this man correctly in the end, solving what was a second, subsidiary and dependent crime.[20]

Recalling the elements of the Detective and the criminal outlined earlier, it is apparent that those elements are satisfied here. Or almost so. The original crime is not one of intent in the rational sense, but of subconscious feelings inaccessible to the interrogation of both the criminal and the detective himself (interrogation of the little gray cells, as Poirot puts it). The crime that Cuff does solve is of the Classic sort, and he does so by Classic methods, but that is not the crime that gives the book its resonance and dramatic power. But we do have here a culture of rationality and evidence, with a man of elevated powers who stands outside the group but not outside society. Cuff is a fair model for future characters of that sort.

But the example of Cuff was not taken up at once. We must wait a few years until Green's Mr. Gryce (1879) appears. The path from Dupin through Bucket and Cuff to Gryce and Holmes is anything but direct. In between are several novels out of the main line and of considerable interest for future developments.

Mary Braddon, a sensational[21] novelist contemporary with Collins, in *Lady Audley's Secret* (1862) took up instead the Mr. Bruff model for detection — the sympathetic amateur insider rather than the analytic professional outsider. By the 1870s the novel, now a standardized 3-volume product, was the dominant form of literature for the middle class. The sub-genre of the sensation novel grew out of the penny papers of the 1840s, such as those from which Eugène Sue made his fortune. These catered to the lower class. The sensation novel "combined elements from the domestic novel, which focused on courtship and social success, with stories of criminal behavior, emphasizing the potential of crime to occur anywhere."[22] Anyone, respectable or not, could turn out to be a criminal. This, coupled with distrust of popular, market-driven writing, thought to be stuff of low quality concerned with incident rather than character, produced some quite vituperative attacks by bourgeois *bien pensants*. The decorum of the publishing world and the segregation of the classes was threatened. And it was claimed that these novels were not true pictures of life.

Lady Audley is a beautiful blonde abandoned by her first husband and forced by poverty to desert her child and marry Lord Audley under a false identity. Her first husband returns, and during a squabble with Lady Audley she apparently kills him. A barrister friend of the dead man investigates and discovers the secret, to everyone's ruin. Lady Audley is a strong reminder of Lady Dedlock in Dickens's novel of ten years earlier, *Bleak House*, but that novel had many other concerns, and Lady Dedlock was no outright criminal. Braddon's hugely popular novel plays on anxieties about the home as a refuge, about violence and sex, and the urban anonymity that allows Lady Audley to change her identity so easily. Worst of all, Lady Audley gets away with it. The book remains popular. It has been filmed four times and made into a Broadway musical.

The detective in this case is Lady Audley's cousin, a lazy barrister who wants to know what has happened to his friend George Talboys and is drawn by a net of reasoning into suspicion of Lady Audley, and then to action. The transformation of Robert Audley into an amateur detective is emblematic of the change in modern life that the detective genre tracks— Audley reads people for information, attends to small details, and discovers that everything is potentially of significance. To Audley, the world is full of false information and careful reading is necessary to puzzle out the plot and to survive in the new world of information.

Audley is not a professional as Bucket and Cuff were but does engage in entirely authentic detection. The narrative method of the novel, however, relocates our interest in the process of detection to the cat-and-mouse game between the detective (Robert Audley) and the criminal (Lady Audley). This relocation occurs because we are privileged to the whole story from very early on, which undercuts any tale about the getting of knowledge.

Also published in 1862 was a novel with a plausible claim to being the first detective story: Charles Warren Adams's *The Notting Hill Mystery*. The book's origin in the conventions of the Gothic are plain. A sinister nobleman is suspected of murdering his wife. The world portrayed is filled with mesmerists, gypsies, poisoners. And yet, amidst this we have a detective, Ralph Henderson, an insurance agent, a resolutely rational man who refuses to accept the existence of the dark world of warm knowledge. The story is told by prosaic means, mostly depositions, reports, and other documents of the sort one might expect an insurance agent to accumulate in the course of an investigation. And matters are ultimately solved by the use of evidence and logical thought coupled with a persistence that reveals a man who never doubts the superiority of reason. Though embedded in the sensation novel of its time, *The Notting Hill Mystery* captures both the procedures of the future detective genre and some hints of its mythic belief in the power of cold knowledge to provide justice.

During these last few years of the century-long development of the detective genre, the years between the Adams's novel and the coming together of all the elements into both a novel and a genre, there are three more authors to consider: Dostoevsky, Gaboriau, and Trollope.

Fyodor Dostoevsky's *Crime and Punishment* (1866) was not available to English readers until Constance Garnett's cautious translation of 1914, but even then its one particularly important element was too early to make a mark on the detective genre. This novel, great in so many other respects, is notable for the person of Porfiry Petrovich, a judicial investigator. One Raskolnikov, a student, has murdered an old woman in order to rob her of a small amount of money. There is no evidence, but in looking into persons associated in some way with the crime, Porfiry Petrovich becomes convinced he knows who the murderer is. The rest of the novel turns on Raskolnikov's increasing need to confess, which he finally does under psychological pressure exerted by Porfiry Petrovich. This detective's method is entirely at odds with the rationalist trend of the genre and will not be developed at any length until the 1930s, when Georges Simenon builds Inspector Maigret's character around the deployment of intuitive knowledge. In this, the method of Dostoevsky's detective reflects the author's major themes of belief, expiation, and reconciliation through love, all of them counter-rational in nature. The influence of Dostoevsky had to wait until warm knowledge could be readmitted to the Detective's toolbox.

Recall that the setting of Poe's stories was French. France was a co-inventor of the genre, and an important strand in the development of the mature Detective runs through France from the early Vidocq. Emile Gaboriau's novel *File No. 113* (1867) is contemporaneous with Collins and Braddon and itself contributed some important features. Gaboriau's first novel had been published a year previously, introducing the series detective Monsieur Lecoq of the Sûreté, and at the same time popularizing the device of the series. At the time, Gaboriau had few models to draw on other than Vidoq. Gaboriau's innovation was to bring the detective to the fore *as a person*, concentrating on detection after the crime rather than treating the crime as the climax of sensational events. Poe had done this, but his Dupin was entirely cerebral. Gaboriau presented the detective as neither an incompetent official nor an authoritative one, neither a sinister agent nor a gifted amateur, but a somewhat neurotic and conflicted man given to jealousy and revenge, with a taste for self-dramatization. Gaboriau was also the first to introduce false trails into plots, and Lecoq is presented as a master of disguise (a characteristic of Holmes also) who builds both his skills and his character during the series.

File No. 113

File No. 113 concerns a safe in a locked room to which only two men have the key and from which a lot of money is stolen. The chief clerk is charged. After chases, a melodramatic confrontation in a lonely house during a thunderstorm, and a masked ball, an elaborate blackmail scheme is exposed. In a romantic finish, Lecoq sweeps away the mistress of the falsely accused clerk.

The organization of *File No. 113* will be unfamiliar to anyone expecting a display of post–Holmes practice. Unlike *Bleak House*, for example, the book is centered on and driven by a crime that the detective solves. This narrative arc, however, only occupies the first 200 pages, at which point M. Lecoq says he knows the answer (we are not told what it is) and that the remaining problem will be to smoke out and punish the thieves. This second story, somewhat anti-climactic and tedious to modern tastes, occupies the remaining 300 pages of the book[23] and is centered on Prosper (the falsely accused bank clerk of the first part), his relationships with the persons narratively attached to him, and his efforts to recover his reputation. At the end M. Lecoq reappears, the thieves are unmasked and punished, and there is a happy ending for Prosper. The book is in fact a romantic melodrama to which a detective novel has been attached. This same structure can be found in two of the Holmes novels, and some variants in several of the stories. With Conan Doyle, however, these are backstories. With Gaboriau the extra 300 pages constitute a huge digression that reveals the still-incomplete conception of how the genre ought to work.

The book has other oddities. There are two competing detectives, M. Lecoq (who is, outside the office, invariably in disguise — here, mostly as M. Verduret) and a subordinate, Fanferlot, known as the Squirrel, who is attempting to rise in the police by means of a *coup d'art*. Lecoq does not think much of this. Fanferlot's position corresponding to the Classic structure is that of the bumbling policeman shown up by the detective, not of the Detective proper. Lecoq himself does not appear as an active character until page 80, or almost halfway through the detective portion of the narrative, and even then he is usually presented as M. Verduret, who we understand to be Lecoq in disguise, though we are not told this explicitly until later. During most of the investigation the detective is in cahoots with the suspected criminal. This is not surprising in one hired as an expert consultant for the defense, but it is not a role ordinarily played by the police. In the course of the story there is gathering of evidence and genuine inquiry, clues are evaluated and conclusions are deduced, so in these respects the story conforms to what will become normative practice. But despite Gaboriau's oddities, Bucket, Cuff, and Gerolstein (also disguised throughout *The Mysteries of Paris*) are not so fully in the mode as is Lecoq.

Lecoq's alternate Verduret personality is much more fully realized than his own, though in no case do we find out much about the man other than what we can see in practice. This sort of mystification is necessary to all "Lone Ranger" characters as part of the aura that separates them and their legendary skills from ordinary life. This role of the legendary hero and its variants, the shaman and the wise old man of the mountains, more than anything else are what separates the Detective from the mere sleuth. All that is required for the now iconic Detective to be fully socialized without losing his aura is a chronicler to insulate him from our direct scrutiny.

Dickens made a second attempt on the Detective with his unfinished novel *The Mystery of Edwin Drood*, and Mark Twain did the same with Tom Sawyer and Pudd'nhead Wilson, the latter a dark book that had it been finished, might more readily have be seen as an example of the later noir solution to the first rehabilitation of the genre, which we will explore in chapter 4.[24]

Other authors essayed the increasingly popular detective story during the 1860s and '70s, before it became the property of specialized writers. Anthony Trollope (*The Eustace Diamonds,* 1871) was one such. This book is the third in his Palliser series, which concerns politics—which some might think a form of crime, and indeed Poe had shown it to be ripe material for the genre, so much so that a natural collateral line of development to the detective story[25] is the spy story and the action hero thriller. The interest here is how themes of secrecy and discovery, crime, and intrigue are integrated into work by a major novelist. The trajectory of crime to resolution controls the shape of the novel, though there is no attempt to mystify the reader, and the "detective," like Lecoq, is concerned more with how to bring about the desired conclusion — which he has known from the beginning — than with uncovering a truth.

The plot does not much concern the Pallisers. Rather, it is about Lizzie, a fortune-hunter who ensnares the sickly Sir Eustace, by whose quick death she becomes very wealthy. Lizzie (as was Lady Audley) is clever and beautiful but a pathological liar; hence the intrigue when she attempts to snag a family heirloom (a diamond necklace) to which she is not entitled. Through several romantic fantasies, exposures, and finally marriage to a disreputable clergyman who is discovered to be already married, Lizzie tries to put the Eustace family lawyer, Mr. Camperdown, off the trail of the diamonds. In this, of course, she does not succeed. Camperdown resembles Dickens's Tulkinghorn in many ways and the persistent interfering Robert Audley in others.

The Leavenworth Case

With this survey of pre–Classic authors in hand, we are in a position to examine the claim of Anna K. Green's *The Leavenworth Case* to be the first fully realized detective novel and its protagonist Gryce to be the first avatar of the Detective. (This honor is sometimes awarded to *The Notting Hill Mystery,* discussed earlier. The claim is considerable, but I would call it rather a precursor, for its author Charles Adams did not establish a tradition; his book belongs instead among the sensation novels and the tradition of Sue and Braddon. Moreover, Adams's Ralph Henderson appears in only one novel. Green was able to develop her achievement into a formula.) Conan Doyle and his creation Holmes are too well-known to need more than a tip of the hat — at the time, men did wear hats — and will be taken up in the next chapter. Anna

Green is the earlier. Her very popular *The Leavenworth Case* (1879) was published eight years before Holmes and Watson took rooms in Baker Street.

Green's detective, Mr. Gryce, a member of the police force, collects the qualities of his predecessors (Bucket, Cuff, Lecoq) in a human-scale character recognizably Holmesian. Gryce does not occupy Holmes's position in the story, however. There is a narrator on his behalf (Mr. Raymond, who reappears in other Gryce novels), but this narrator is not self-effacing. He attempts to solve the case himself, as did Gaboriau's Squirrel, and he is given plenty of opportunity to do that and to involve himself emotionally with the other characters and the facts of the case. *The Leavenworth Case* is a melodrama about false accusation, vulnerable femininity, and the dangers of love, with a strong element of class feeling. Gryce surfaces at important points to give Raymond an idea of what he has learned through independent investigation conducted almost entirely offstage, setting Raymond on new paths without entirely enlightening him (or us). Gryce's "legs" (one Q) does the work of gathering material evidence, while conducting the empirical tests that might validate his theories is left to Raymond. Gryce is not at the center of the story and his character and actions do not form the focus of our interest. The story is not about *him*; Gryce does not have the Detective's persona in the way that Holmes does—large, grand, attracting all narratives to himself.

Another important difference from what is to come after is that while Gryce, as an exemplar of the Detective, is appropriately infallible, on one point in particular he is not a Holmesian figure. He relies on confession rather than pure ratiocination and evidence to validate his claims. This is the French legal model rather than the British. At the end of the book he uses Raymond to set up a scene in which he pretends to be convinced of the guilt of the central woman in the case. This smokes out the true villain, a man who is in love with her and has fought off rivals and bursts out with the truth rather than see her continue to be falsely accused.

The Leavenworth Case was a best-seller. It was an important influence on authors of detective fiction to follow, but present-day readers might not find it obvious why this should be, as its surface qualities are riddled with class and gender attitudes that will seem to us a virtual parody of our own Victorian stereotypes.

Anna Green grew up in the well-off family of a prominent trial lawyer through whom she was much exposed to crime and the police. Well-educated, influenced by the novels of Gaboriau, she tried her hand at detective fiction despite discouragement from a family who preferred her to write poetry. All of her books were popular. Through most of her married life she supplied the family income. *The Leavenworth Case* is the first appearance of Detective Gryce, an unassuming, cerebral but human man, who "was not the thin wiry individual with a shrewd eye that seems to plunge into the core of your being and pounces at once upon its hidden secret, that you are doubtless expecting to see"—that is, not like Sgt. Cuff of *The Moonstone*. Gryce does, however, have Cuff's trick of not looking at whatever is the subject of interest. Gryce, Cuff, Bucket, and Lecoq all try to appear unassertive, though only Lecoq actually disguises himself. A "soft walk" is also characteristic. The character Columbo, created by Peter Falk, is one of Gryce's heirs. The Gryce cases are narrated by a series sidekick, Mr. Raymond, helping to make Watson, when he appears, a familiar device. The Classic practice of bringing the suspects together for a confrontation at which the guilty party is unmasked was also popularized here.

The *Leavenworth Case* concerns two cousins who are thought to have murdered their uncle for the inheritance. The two girls, in hoary tradition one fair and one dark, are threatened with a scandal that will destroy their society careers. Details of the crime scene are narrated forensically, with a ballistics report of the gun on which the case turns. Gryce later admits that he never suspected Mary (the dark-haired one) because no woman knows how to clean a gun. (Green was quite feminist for her time. We may take this remark as a sour social commentary, but it is Green's remark, not Gryce's.) The case is broken when a servant who knows too much is murdered, and the last connections are made through meticulous surveillance.

Consolidating the Genre

Before giving some time to developments between *The Leavenworth Case* and the roots of the English Classic—that is, the time bestrode by Sherlock Holmes—it is necessary to consider one question. I have already said that the figure of the Detective (and the genre he inhabits) is yoked to conditions in the surrounding society and culture in a stronger and more direct way than the linkage that is always a factor in the construction of any art form. So it must be asked: Why should the Detective make his appearance at just this time and place? I think the answer lies in the Industrial Revolution.

By itself, of course, that is too simple. The spread of literacy, cheaper books, the appearance of a new mass medium — the newspaper, and especially the illustrated newspaper, pioneered by Henry Vizetelly, the *Illustrated London News* (1842), and in America *Leslie's Illustrated Newspaper (1860)*—played a prominent role. These developments were closely bound up with the class-driven disdain of the educated for these new readers and what they read. The sensation novel was heaped with vituperative criticism, as any exploration of the reputation of Braddon will reveal. Braddon was also a woman, and the 1860s and '70s were a period of shift from a novel written and read mostly by women to a dominance of the field by men, by mechanisms explained by Gaye Tuchman in *Edging Women Out: Victorian Novelists, Publishers, and*

Social Change (1989) and accompanied by a denigration of "women's novels." The detective novel emerged from this culture of mass literacy, popular media, and class difference.

But the concerns associated with these origins were trivial. The Industrial Revolution was disruptive to every aspect of life, as innumerable sources from Dickens and Marx onward make clear. But this social uproar was accompanied by boons, at least for some. These improvements were associated with the culture and aesthetic of the machine. Machine culture seeks control. It seeks to minimize the risks of production and the risks to the capital that makes production possible. It also makes possible incremental progress toward a goal of perfection and reproducibility. This is markedly different from the handmade aesthetic that preceded it. The society of the machine is deeply bound up with rational thought: research and development, planning, engineering, quality control, and many other practices and habits of mind. This, again, is in marked contrast to the preceding numinous culture still present from pre–Renaissance times.

It was the culture of the machine, introduced and spread by the Industrial Revolution, that created the Detective out of the cauldron of necessary preconditions—preconditions that in many cases were also the product of rational management. And it was the fear of this revolution that gave the Detective his iconic and shamanic status. It is no accident that the detective genre appeared first in England, where the Industrial Revolution began, and where by Holmes's time the people had the most experience with its effects.

Green and Conan Doyle, then, produced the first fully realized detective stories. Inevitably, a new archetype such as this one will be tinkered with as authors seek to appropriate it for themselves. The maturity of the archetype comes with the appearance of parody. For the figure of the Detective we have a superb one, Fantômas. Significantly, Fantômas is French. Although France was slower than many countries to industrialize, they had the experience of the secularizing revolution of 1789. Satire appears when a literary form is strong and widespread enough to invite (and bear) the attack. The mere existence of Fantômas, then, is an indicator of what had developed out of the French origins of the genre, which we have already examined — Balzac, Sue, Gaboriau.

The Fantômas tales were written by Marcel Allain and Pierre Souvestre beginning in 1911. (Souvestre died in 1914. The series was carried on after that for another eleven volumes by Allain alone.) Fantômas comes from the long tradition of the picaresque, and his particular type would have been best known to the English as Raffles. But Fantômas is a more ambiguous and dangerous character than Raffles. He can be seen as a prototype of the early, dark Batman, the insouciant James Bond, and the modern-day serial killer. Cover illustrations portray him against a lurid Technicolor background typical of the 1950s pulps, in evening wear with cane and top hat and an ominous smile.

The official detective in the Fantômas tales is one Inspector Juve. Needless to say, he makes no headway, and his obsession with catching the arch-criminal draws suspicion onto himself as possibly insane, or even possibly the real Fantômas. Juve has a sidekick/partner (Jérôme Fandor, a reporter) and gets occasional indirect help from Fantômas's mistress Lady Beltham, and his daughter Hélène.[26]

The real, iconic Detective, is of course Fantômas himself, and one of the central and enduring interests of the tales is how he is able to play both roles, detecting his own crimes, working through surrogates like Juve to see that all the right people (excepting himself) are punished. The basic plot has roots in ancient theater and folklore, of course, and is the parent of, for example, the modern caper flick such as *The Thomas Crown Affair*.

Between Holmes and Fantômas a great many authors were at work tinkering, as I said — enlarging, exploiting, and modifying the figure of the Detective in interesting ways. We will look briefly at three of these to give an idea of the work being done up to about 1910, work lying on the path that crosses finally the border of the pre–Classic into the genre tradition we will examine in chapter 3. These three are Israel Zangwill, William Le Quex, and the master Joseph Conrad.

Israel Zangwill is noted for social realism. A Zionist and a socialist, Zangwill wrote novels about the London East End slums. His style in *The Big Bow Mystery* is more modern than typical of the genre in 1892 — strongly ironic, humorous, and mocking.

In Zangwill's tale Arthur Constant, a union agitator, has been murdered. (Compare Conrad's *Secret Agent*, where the attitude toward labor agitation and civic unrest is not so blithe.) No weapon was found inside the murdered man's locked room, eliminating suicide. Suspicion falls on a rival agitator, but this person was in Liverpool at the time. Two rival detectives attempt the case, the retired policeman who discovered the body, Grodman, and Inspector Edward Wimp[27] of Scotland Yard. Wimp ignores the facts and arrests the wrong man, who is convicted in a travesty of a trial. He is saved at the last minute from being hanged by the correct solution, provided by Grodman, who now confesses to being the murderer to save the convicted man.

This is usually considered the first locked-room mystery, and it is said that, although other novels had used this device, Zangwill's was the first to make the puzzle the principal element of the plot. A modern reader might think otherwise. While the locked room element is central to the plot it figures very little in the narrative, where it serves primarily — through being incomprehensible — to stave off a more summary and ill-considered conclusion about the circumstances of Constant's death. The attention of the narrative spends less time on the two detectives (we never see any detection, but mostly surveillance) than on the doings of the rest of the cast of characters. We have insufficient information about motive as well as method, and facts brought to light by Wimp are kept back according to the demands of storytelling.

It should be noted that the case *is never solved*. This is an important innovation. Outside the conventions of the genre it would be merely another plot twist. Within the genre it is a bid to enlarge the moral and epistemological territory. Wimp gets it wrong, and the other detective hardly needs to solve anything, since he proves to be the murderer. (His method will draw S.S. Van Dine's ire and be specifically forbidden in Van Dine's "Twenty Rules.")

William Le Quex was a prolific pulp author in the period leading up to World War I, specializing in stories about invasion (by subterfuge or infiltration) of England by the evil Kaiser. Le Quex was well prepared to write this sort of story, having reported the First Balkan War. The Kaiser's plans were always thwarted, of course, usually by ordinary citizens out birdwatching or something of the sort. Le Quex was possibly the first to create *truly* amateur detectives. More importantly, he discovered how the nascent spy genre could be reformulated as the detective tale, a shift to be taken up by John Buchan and Graham Greene and then, during the Cold War and following the demise of the noir solution, becoming a full transformation culminating in John Le Carré's character George Smiley.

Finally, there is Joseph Conrad, who wrote (in 1907 and 1911) two notable crime novels, *The Secret Agent* and *Under Western Eyes*. The first of these stands so close to the center of the genre, and presages so many subsequent developments, that particular attention to it is necessary.

Joseph Conrad, *The Secret Agent* (1907)

The story centers on the agent Verloc, who is summoned to "The Embassy" for an interview with Privy Councillor Wurmt concerning Verloc's dereliction of his duties as a spy. He is passed on to Mr. Vladimir for more browbeating. Vladimir threatens to cut off Verloc's funding, and thus his family's income, unless he commits an "outrage"—he is to bomb the Greenwich Observatory. Returning home, he receives a visit from his colleagues Michaelis, Yundt, and Ossipan. Verloc assesses his situation and finds himself without options. Ossipan brings into this group of terrorists "The Professor," a man who makes bombs using nitroglycerine, some of which he carries on his person for protection. Thus equipped, Verloc sets out, accompanied by a boy, his wife's brother.

Next morning Inspector Heat appears. A man has blown himself up in Greenwich Park. The dead bomber stumbled on a root and so set off the shock-sensitive bomb (meant to be "thrown"). Heat has found a bit of overcoat with a velvet collar. This scrap of overcoat had led Heat to Verloc, so his wife learns that Verloc has exploited and killed her mentally disabled brother Stevie, a boy who had to have his clothes labeled in case he strayed.

After Heat leaves, Verloc proposes that he and Winnie go into hiding abroad. He foolishly tries to make love to her, but she kills him. Then, intending also to kill herself, she goes out, where she is accosted by Ossipan, with whom she has been having an affair. Ossipan, too, tries to persuade Winnie to go abroad. Now she agrees, but Ossipan takes her money and abandons her. Winnie drowns herself. In the end, only the bomb-building Professor is left, still advocating what has in fact happened, the destruction of everything.

Here is virtually the whole past and future of the genre. We see a Bucket-like detective and a shadowy crime emerging from a sorry tale of poverty, powerlessness, expedient morals, frustrated desires, and impoverished ideologies. The crime and its solution take over the story against a backdrop of public fear — there actually was about this time a similar incident.[28] The threat to society is neutralized, an outcome not entirely obtained by cold reason, but nothing is achieved and everything of value is lost. The story ends in an atmosphere redolent of the ambiguities and ironies of the noir and espionage tales to come. The profound themes and literary language presage Graham Greene and the ambitions of Raymond Chandler to elevate the genre and imbue it with both a hard-won morality and a new fidelity to the life of the detective.

Conrad's comprehensiveness puts him outside the direct line of inheritance, which runs from Poe through Holmes to the English Classic. If development were limited to the Poe-Classic nexus, and had stopped there, we now would have inherited an impoverished tradition. We would have a substantial inventory of methods but a limited set of themes and a meager genre of small scope and simple speech, more like a bodice-ripper, incapable of taking on the large and complex issues that drive Conrad's novel — in a word, a genre inarticulate and ultimately powerless. Instead, in Conrad's tragedy we find what we are actually in possession of: a way of storytelling rich with options, with a cast of characters ranging from commedia del'arte to epic hero, detectives intellectual or quest-driven, villains large and small, a world of characters eccentric or quotidian, flawed, existential, perhaps mad. We may say that this is due to the influence of writers of Conrad's abilities, but it may also be that writers of ability were drawn to the genre because they saw, in the figure of the Detective, a trope or meme of wide significance that could anchor profound thoughts and deep-running fears.

2

Sherlock Holmes — Rationality and the Detective Artist

In my discussion of the pre-history of the English Classic formula I identified Anna K. Green's 1879 novel *The Leavenworth Case* as the first novel in the genre of the detective story. This was partly because it showed all the required characteristics. It was also because it was the first of several novels Green wrote using her detective Gryce, and it is this ability to repeat the performance, as much as the performance itself, that marks the fully realized genre. The essence of a genre formula is that it is a recipe for production, that it is able to supply readers with more of the same.

There was a forty-year gap between the opening of the new genre and its reduction in the 1920s to a common practice usually called the English Classic. At the end of the previous section I mentioned some authors at work during those forty years, but there is one who stands above them all, and now, nearly a century and a half after he first appeared in the pages of *Strand Magazine*, he is to many the Detective himself.

Sherlock Holmes is worth substantial scrutiny for that reason. But there are other reasons why we should do this. There is first of all his reputation as a cold man; Watson says it of him at the very beginning of "A Scandal in Bohemia," but this is the first story and Watson's claim has already been denied by the enthusiasm Holmes displays over his chemical research when we first hear of him in *A Study in Scarlet,* and many times afterwards, as for example in his French ancestry. The French are thought, by the cool and reserved English at least, to be warm and emotional. This association of temperature with rationality points to one of the central concerns of this book, the role of warm and cool knowledge in the detective story — as for example in this question: as a cold and rational man it is usually said that Holmes is a master of deduction, but is deduction actually what he practices, or is it some warmer logical method?

And then, because Holmes is so central a figure, he has been portrayed again and again in the movies, and his film reincarnations will enable us to take a first detailed look at my claims about the ways in which the detective genre responds to social change.

We first encountered Holmes in 1887, in Dr. Watson's account *A Study in Scarlet*.[1] In 1887 the situation was this: writers such as Dickens and Collins had given the crime novel an expressive power and range of character and incident that greatly enlarged its literary possibilities. Poe had suggested a set of principles around which a formula could coalesce, and Braddon and Trollope had demonstrated the narrative interest that might be attached to the victim equally as well as to the detective or the perpetrator. Green and Zangwill had pared the formula down to its essentials by tight plotting and a focus on the crime and its solution by emphasizing the dramatic tension between the puzzle and the infallible detective.

All this Conan Doyle inherited. What he did himself was to bring these elements together in a single character and a unified and fully extensible mythology.[2] This would be an accomplishment by itself, but Conan Doyle was also able to tap cultural ambivalences and antagonisms that he built into Holmes's character, giving him a depth and lifelikeness that is the source of his enduring attraction.[3]

We first encounter Holmes beating a corpse. This tells us everything we need to know about what is to ensue. His peculiar behavior is explained (he wishes to know how far injury can be sustained after death), but the explanation is hardly satisfying. We see Holmes engaged to an unusual degree with the empirical world of hypothesis and evidence, but at the same time it is obvious that this curiosity does not preclude, and may actually require, enthusiasm and pleasure. This mixture is part of Holmes's oddness, as we are given his oddness by Watson and Stamford at the beginning of *A Study in Scarlet*, and it remains a part of his uniqueness to the end. Holmes is not a Dupin or a Thinking Machine. We notice also the very name of the tale in which Holmes makes his appearance. The *study* is a term of art, and *scarlet* is an artist's color loaded with emotional significance and not to be confused with the layman's color red. Blood is red. Scarlet is something else. In this first incident we see the detective artist at work, and encounter the essential quality that is the making of Sherlock Holmes.

Let me return for a moment to the plot summary given in the discussion of the pre–Classical detective (a category within which Holmes must be included) of Conrad's *The Secret Agent*. The fear of "bomb-throwing anarchists" in Conrad's tale exposed the connection between what we most need, which is safety, and what we must acknowledge, the existence of the unseen, the primal, the arbitrary, the ineffable and *mysterious*. By situating his tale as he does Conrad exposes Verloc to an existential threat but enables us to stand away, unthreatened. The exploited Stevie has our sympathy, but we are not expected to participate in the story as we would in a cathartic Greek tragedy. This is why *The Secret Agent* is a crime novel but not in the detective genre. It lacks the frisson of the Holmes formula, which proceeds by first scaring us with the possibility that rationality is no defense, the possibility that there is no complete defense against an irruption of the unseen world. Holmes is able to reassure us that this is not so. It is he who confronts this fear on our behalf. Since the time of Rousseau it has been said that this particular ability to confront the unknown is a special property of the artist. There is nothing like this in *The Secret Agent* except perhaps the only survivor, the Professor, who considers himself an artist, though we would not say so except in a trivial way. Conan Doyle gives us that person in every story. It is Holmes himself.

Consider what Holmes actually does when he solves a case. The popular view, one supported by Holmes's own claims, is that he is proceeding by deduction. In fact, as C.S. Peirce shows, this process is actually *abduction*.[4] Abduction is a probabilistic method to be used when the facts to be reasoned with are uncertain.

Abduction

Broadly speaking, abduction is a method of reasoning under conditions of uncertainty. A syllogism is the simplest way to demonstrate this property. In the case of both deduction and induction both the major and minor terms are known absolutely. In the case of abduction one or both of these terms is only probably true. Since statistical (probabilistic) thinking is at the root of most of modern science and many other contemporary activities, abduction may now be considered the dominant mode of reasoning.

An exact grasp of the concept of abduction as a mode of reasoning used by fictional detectives requires first of all the understanding that detecting and finding out are not the same thing. One may find something out by any means; to detect indicates that what is sought has been discovered or revealed by thinking about it — that is, by rational means. Holmes's typical procedure is to observe and record data, which "facts" he then associates together or classifies. (Strictly speaking these data are not facts until they have been proved to be empirically true, but we may regard this as a quibble.) Holmes then advances a hypothesis that accounts for the facts in order to identify the possible causes for the observed state of affairs.

Deduction reasons from observations (postulated hypotheses) to their necessary consequences. Given the facts, what are the results? Thus: "Baldness is an absence of hair; you have no hair, therefore you are bald." Beginning with a definition and an observation, we conclude that the observable is (or is not) an instance of the general definition. This is the classificatory procedure of taxonomy.

Notice that this is not the same as: All men are bald; you are a man, therefore you are bald. The truth of this conclusion depends on the correctness of the initial generalization that all men are bald. This may be true or false. There is no amount of evidence that can prove it true, whereas one observation of a hairy man will prove it false. Karl Popper's contribution to our understanding of how science works is this concept of falsifiability. Science cannot prove anything to be true, only false. (This is the bone of contention in the cultural argument over evolution; that, being a theory, evolution is only *probably* true. To someone who accepts only absolute truth, probable things are *not* true.)

Induction reasons in the other direction, from the observed consequences to their necessary causes. Given these results, what are the facts? Given this state of affairs, what observable facts could have produced such a result? Notice that the facts we require must be observable. This is the problem with séances and divine intervention. Such things may be, but they are not observable, and so cannot be used in reasoning. The question of what is observable may be disputed by some believers in the divine; what is usually meant is that to observe a material object ought not require belief. (I will take this up again in chapter seven.) There is a dispute about observable, unless you regard an experience as also communicable; there is also now a dispute about the possibility of communication which is one of the legs on which postmodernism stands. Detectives are always debunking supernatural explanations. Agatha Christie's stories contain many séances and other occult things because these were such a popular fad at the time, but the occult is fatal to rational detection. G.K. Chesterton's Father Brown often invokes divine intervention, but it always has material means and consequences that can be reasoned about. The inductive reasoning process proceeds thus: "I have met a lot of bald persons; all of these were men, therefore baldness is probably a male attribute." Notice that this sort of statement is not falsifiable either by encountering a bald woman or a hairy man. The truth of its conclusion rests on an agreement about what frequency is required to constitute an attribute. Induction is only contingently true. Holmes reasons this way when he decides that ash of a certain appearance is from latakia tobacco because he has seen a great many cases where this was so and concludes that the probabilities are in his favor. Note that the more observed characteristics contribute to the conclusion, the greater its probability.

Or: "I have met a lot of bald persons; all of those were men, therefore all men are bald." In this case also the conclusion is probable rather than determined, but here the probability is introduced by the reasoning process itself. General laws are derived from observations in this way, before the proposed law undergoes falsification tests. But just because the proposed law is only probable does not invalidate its immediate usefulness. Such reasoning would not be accepted in court (in detective stories anyway), so wherever the guilty person must be induced to confess, this sort of reasoning is implicated. The outcome of many stories is stymied by the refusal of the criminal to confess. In these stories justice is usually dispensed in another way.[5]

Abduction, then, or reasoning when one or more terms of the argument is uncertain, is inherently probabilistic.

The second example above, correctly phrased as "*Some* men are bald, you are bald, therefore you *may* be a man," is one type of reasoning by abduction. The statement is true as phrased but requires additional evidence to rescue it from triviality. Abductive statements of this type then become one term in a new chain of reasoning. Holmes reasons this way when he identifies a certain ash as deriving from (say) latakia tobacco. (Notice the implied prior chain that made it probable that the ash was tobacco in the first place.) This initiates a new chain of reasoning as to the significance of latakia specifically, and so on until the criminal is identified. When he is caught and his guilt is conceded then the whole chain of reasoning from the ash to the confession is validated.

If we rephrase the case of the bald man to read, "I have met a lot of bald people; I suppose most of these people were men, therefore it is likely that baldness is a male attribute," it may be impossible to say whether a particular bald person is in fact a man. In this case we turn to statistics and argue (probabilistically) on the basis of such standards as "margin of error" and "degree of confidence" and "representative sample" and various tests of the data such as measures of correlation or frequency distribution. We all encounter such statistical arguments in everyday life, but some cannot be brought to count as true anything demonstrated only statistically. This is the basis for a major cultural division between Holmes's mode of thinking and common sense which, I think, accounts for the hint of magic in Holmes's method.

"Pure" abduction occurs when *both* of the terms are only probable. Action under conditions of uncertainty may be our greatest contemporary challenge, because we are uncertain about so much and the consequences of our uncertainty are so grave. The self-confidence Holmes has in his powers, and the courage he shows in acting on his conclusions, are important components of what makes Holmes fascinating, an adventurer, and a hero. He *guesses*. And what makes Holmes successful is not that he never guesses but that he guesses so well.

Abduction is the first step in scientific reasoning and a guess (a "prior," in Bayesian terms) is the first step in abduction. One wants to begin with the best hypothesis—that which is the simplest and most natural, the easiest and cheapest to test, and likely to contribute to our understanding of the widest range of facts. This hypothesis, then, is the most *probable*. It may not be correct. One obtains proof of its correctness by experiment—by seeing if it leads to the murderer. Holmes's advantage over Watson (and the police) is first of all that he is so much more imaginative — that he can see so many more options and combinations to pick from — whereas the police often fail not only because they are unimaginative (dumb, even) but because their priors do not account for all the facts, or because they begin with a prior and then look for the facts that would validate it (misplaced imagination). When Holmes praises a rival (seldom) it is always for careful observation or (even more seldom) for good reasoning. He never accepts anyone as his equal in imagination. For that he turns to music.

Holmes as the Rational Man

Holmes is the epitome in our minds of the Rational, and of the beneficial results of rational behavior. As we have already noted, Holmes when first encountered is engaged in beating a corpse, recalling the folk unwisdom of beating a dead horse — that is, a pointless and stupid, very *irrational* behavior. Yet it turns out that appearances have deceived Watson, and thus us. It is we who have not been rational in our thinking. We have made the mistake, in Holmes's famous remark, of hypothesizing in advance of the evidence. Could we have any clearer demonstration of what we are to expect?

And yet, as we shall see, Holmes is not, or not entirely, the rational man that we believe him to be, that shibboleth of penetrating observation and thought that we have made of him. Herein lies one aspect of his complexity, his influence, of the humanity that has helped him to endure.

We have, or sometimes have, the idea that thought and feeling are incompatible. Metaphorically the one is cold and the other warm; they are immiscible humors and people are one or the other, either coldly rational or warm, emotional, impulsive.

Where does this idea come from? I am not asking if it is true. Clearly it is not true. Still, how does it happen that (cold) thought, planning, and intelligence can be characterized as undesirable? Is that what we really think, when we're not thinking about it especially?

The notion resembles a prejudice that does not survive actual experience but somehow stubbornly continues to intrude. Even people who make their living by rational inquiry — scientists are the most visible — sometimes let this notion pass. And of course, some will find it agreeable and may even have chosen their life's work because of it, finding that warmth and emotional impulsiveness are not to their liking.

Rationality is, it is true, usually thought of as a good thing. This good is secured by objectivity, the main requirement. Science is objective, and hence rational, because it is supposed to yield knowledge that is disinterested, impersonal. But here the trouble starts, for *impersonal* has less happy connotations. The practice of science is usually said to require *rigor*, which has an ascetic note, or perhaps even *austere* rigor.[6] And so, ever tightening the screws of purity, we come to the plight of Sinclair Lewis's Martin Arrowsmith:

> Social life of every kind, even the social life inside the laboratory, is for Arrowsmith at worst a temptation to fudge his results, at best a distraction from the serious business of science. The novel leaves the hero in the woods of New England, withdrawn from all company, pursuing his laboratory research in splendid isolation. In this way he was protected from the temptations of power and reputation, dedicating his life to the relentless pursuit of stony truth and ignoring the social graces represented by soft and deceitful women.[7]

This is an excess of zeal, surely. A professional hazard, but avoidable. We are after a stronger claim, that rationality is in itself cold and will freeze anyone who dabbles with it. In this view, knowledge and truth are inimical to life. Those who traffic in knowledge (scientist, shaman, the scribe who manipulates the king when everyone else is illiterate) cut themselves off from humanity, human warmth and community. These people are not to be trusted, which our experience confirms. In G.K. Chesterton's *The Man Who Was Thursday*, the man who introduces Syme to the anarchist society in which he takes the role of Thursday gives as his reasoning that men are needed "whose fears for humanity [are] concerned rather with the aberrations of the scientific intellect than with the normal and excusable, though excessive, outbreaks of the human will."[8] Of course, Chesterton is speaking here as a partisan anxious to defend faith, Catholicism in particular. The defense is necessary because the industrial and scientific revolutions of the preceding generations had gathered all the benefits of rationality to forces hostile to faith, leaving religion with no mode (it was felt) other than to accept the irrational and oppose a culture of belief to an increasingly powerful culture of evidence. The confrontation is put more bluntly later in the book: "The tyrranic fear of the Professor had been the fear of the tyrranic accidents of nightmare, and ... the fear of the Doctor had been the fear of the airless vacuum of science. The first was the old fear that any miracle might happen, the second the more hopeless modern fear that no miracle can ever happen."[9] Today it is hard to credit that such claims were ever taken seriously by serious people. It seems cartoonish. Yet we have only to remember the division of the sexes between rational man and intuitive woman,[10] which is still a live idea with us, as seen in the many squashed efforts of female scientists, to appreciate the force of this prejudice and the fear that drives it.[11]

Marjorie Nicolson, in another foundational commentary, "The Professor and the Detective,"[12] attempts to pick apart the appeal of the detective story to educated readers who might have been expected to think it frivolous. Nicolson was the Professor of the piece (she was a dean at Smith College), one of the tribe of intellectual workers among whom the detective story is popular because of the visceral reliefs it offers. (A little too visceral. The university librarian, we learn, lays in a stock of detective novels kept sequestered from the students, who are yet too corruptible to be given a squint.) Chess players, bridge players and crossword puzzlers, physicists, astronomers and mathematicians — students of the new science all — stay up late to read them under the covers because the objectivity and impersonality of the form, its lack of sentimentality and love interests[13] all recommend it as relaxation. And it is these same rational qualities, she says, that lead the popular mind to associate detective literature with Mr. Einstein's destruction of the moral standard.[14] Rational and exotic at once, detachedly objective yet thrilling, a literature that deliberately forgoes nobility denigrated by its middlebrow readers (who do not play chess) as, well, being without nobility. What a muddle.

Having thus divided the darkness from the light, the beneficiaries and victims of hegemony strive to tar each other. Fifty years after Chesterton and twenty after Nicolson, Michael Gilbert's narrator speaks of one Mr. Hoffman, an accountant, as "a man who hunted down facts with the passionless pleasure of a butterfly collector and pinned them to his board with the same cold precision."[15] Modernism's great, impassioned butterfly collector, Vladimir Nabokov, would certainly have jibbed at that. But both slanders are easy tropes, trollops easy to pick up.

There are two routes to this position. One passes through the public need for experts who can stave off arbitrariness through rational formalism.[16] Public knowledge must be aloof from human agency to be reliable. Partisan subjectivity, which the existentialists more politely called engagement, creates a responsibility to that with which one has engaged. Politics and management are subjective. These people are moralists. One who would be an expert, or pose as one, accepts cold, impartial rationality as the consequence of public responsibility. The detective, an enforcer of truth, is one such expert.

The other route to a view of rationality as cold passes through Romanticism and the separation of mind and body. Descartes is an obvious source of this idea, but the trope is much older than that. Religions often privilege the mind, seeing our essence as being imprisoned in foul, fallible flesh. Flesh needs to be disciplined and subdued. Flesh is dangerous. Plato thought so. Gnostics think so. We are all a little gnostic — that's why it's a heresy.

It is easy to see that this dichotomy might be stood on its head to favor instead the body and the pleasures of the body, feeling and emotion. This too is an old idea, and human history appears to cycle through an ascendance of first one and then the other. The contemporary preference for the body over the mind is only the continuation of a complex of ideas that derive from the Romantic upheaval at the end of the eighteenth century.[17] Romanticism was more than the poetic sentiments of a few Germans or Britons, but a gradual reformation of Western thought throughout the nineteenth century in favor of the passionate, feeling, natural human being. To think in this way means to accept also the irrational and arbitrary, the horrors of the psyche for which Freud gave us a language and that made themselves known in a string of wars and atrocities. We are perhaps beginning to suspect that there is more to our experience of two hundred years than merely feeling run amok. Unreason has revealed itself everywhere, in the mindless and accidental processes of biological evolution, in the indissoluble bond between civilization and discontent, and in the inscrutability of Sartre's Being set off against our own nothingness, longing, and anxiety.

Into this stew comes the detective. Is it any wonder that this icon (or is it stooge?) should attract opposite fears, both extremes of the popular notions of what it means to traffic in knowledge and truth?

Of course, members of the educated elite can always put down or excuse these things as popular shibboleths, mere folk wisdom (or unwisdom in this case). All media that appeal to the indifferently educated or civilized, such as the movies, or the industrial products of genre factories such as the detective story, are vulnerable to being dismissed as kitsch. This position,[18] which may have been tenable in Leavis's time, had to be bootlegged into the argument by Susan Sontag (in her famous essay on kitsch) and is now thought to be without merit. The more typical modern reading identifies the detective story as a feel-good plot intended to reassure people that the truth is knowable, and attacks on the detective genre arise from the contention that there is no truth (or, a weaker position of epistemological agnosticism, that it is unknowable). The next move is to suggest, as Pierre Bayard does,[19] that the detective story is based on willful blindness, that we are unable or unwilling to see the truth because of some limitation, inability, or inhibition in ourselves, and that the detective exposes this. In postmodern terms, the truth is constructed by the reader, deconstructed by the detective, and then (falsely) reconstructed by the author. If this reconstruction is regarded as correct and final then (again in postmodern terms) the genre is hopelessly tainted with transcendental ideas.[20]

This face-off is built into the form, Todorov says. I am curious, then, what ordinary readers take detective stories to mean. What does the not-yet-deconstructed reader think knowledge is, what it is like to know things? A detective is a knowing person, an enhanced version of the ordinary reader. Perhaps (s)he knows.

A good way to satisfy this curiosity might be to study a resolutely popular art form such as the movies. Film imagery responds quickly and with subtlety to changes in popular thinking because that is what makes movies enjoyable and successful to the mass public. If we look at movies, not in themselves or to explicate the detective genre, but rather to winkle out how changes in genre conventions can expose changes in popular attitudes, what might we learn?

Do people really think that the mind is cold, that thought does not partake of feeling, that intellectuals are not to be trusted?

Who Was Conan Doyle's Holmes?

Before we turn to a study of Holmes in the movies we ought, if simply as a baseline, to try to establish what Conan Doyle, Holmes's creator, thought he was doing. To begin, let's examine a simple story, "The Naval Treaty."

The story is easily told. A young clerk leaves a sensitive draft treaty on his desk when he is working late, and upon returning finds that it has disappeared. Driven mad by his error and the destruction of his reputation and livelihood, he is brought home in a state of mental collapse and has to be confined to bed, where he languishes many weeks. Holmes is brought in. Attempting to work out why the valuable treaty has not surfaced in foreign hands, he concludes that it is sequestered in some place from where it cannot be retrieved, and settles on the invalid's room as a possibility. He arranges with the young man's fiancée to ostentatiously leave him alone and unguarded. Keeping his own watch, he nabs the would-be brother-in-law. It seems that this man had stopped by the office unannounced, saw the treaty lying there, and impulsively snatched it. Tucking it away in a safe place, he had found to his consternation that it was a little too safe. The treaty found, the young man recovers and the unwavering love of his betrothed is vindicated.

The initial situation is threatening, but the discovery that no one is attempting to profit by the theft of the treaty reduces the whereabouts of it to a worry. And we find in the end that the thief was an amateur, guided by the same impulsiveness that had also put him into financial ruin. He probably would not have known what to do with his booty if he had kept his hands on it. Yet Holmes keeps saying it's a "dark business." Our interest in the story is surely as much in the melodrama of the victim and his rescue, and in the contrast between Holmes and the thief — both mentally quick, both infinitely patient, and both masked. What then is it that marks Holmes out against the "darkness" of both criminal and victim? Surely it is that he alone is capable of the jest of returning the treaty by bringing it to the breakfast table hidden under one of the covers, disguised as it were as toast and stewed tomatoes. Only Holmes is immune to the weaknesses of both the intellect and the emotions, and indeed takes pleasure from the strength of both sides of his personality.

In this duality Conan Doyle was working against the Romantic tradition, which values the warm emotions. In William Godwin's *Caleb Williams* (1794) there is murder, detection, unrelenting pursuit of the murderer, and the crime story's distinctive construction from effect to cause, solution to problem.[21] Godwin showed how the detective could be used in serious literature. Nevertheless, some elements were missing. The story is tragic and anarchistic, and it condemns law and lawful punishment, features of Godwin's theories of politics and justice. These features are the essence of the story: if the inadequacies of law are what produce the tragedy, then the novel could never be redeemed for the detective genre as we understand it.[22] Law and punishment are bound, just as the motiveless crime of Raskolnikov requires the persecution of Porfiry Petrovich to expose it. (We will see Porfiry's like again in the person of Jules Maigret, and as Inspector Slimane in *Pépé le Moko*.)

Along with drawing attention to this earlier novel I might point to the Gothic conventions just at that time being assembled — a century before Holmes's time — or to the earlier criminal interests of Defoe. And during the century between there are Bucket in *Bleak House*, crime in Bulwer-Lytton, and above all Wilkie Collins's bestseller *The Moonstone*. By 1879, just a few years before the invention of Holmes (it is right that a detective should be not born but invented) Anna Green's *The Leavenworth Case* gave us Mr. Gryce.

Gryce, we are told, "was not the thin, wiry individual with a shrewd eye that seems to plunge into the core of your being and pounce at once upon the hidden secret, that you are doubtless expecting to see." Expecting? This suggests that Paget's iconic drawings of the newly imagined Holmes had their feet in existing popular imagery, a tradition going not so far back as 1852 (Mr. Bucket was "a stoutly built, steady-looking, sharp-eyed man in black") but perhaps to 1868 in Collins's Sgt. Cuff."

> A fly from the railway drove up and out got a grizzled, elderly man, so miserably lean ... dressed all in decent black, with a white cravat round his neck. His face was as sharp as a hatchet, and the skin as yellow and dry and withered as an autumn leaf. His eyes, of steely light gray, had a very disconcerting trick, when they encountered your eyes, of looking as if they expected something more from you than you were aware of yourself. His walk was soft; his voice was melancholy; his long lanky fingers were hooked like claws [chapter 12].

When your mother told you to stop reading so much and go outside and play, she probably had Sgt. Cuff in mind.

The inventor of detective Gryce clearly understands the metaphysical as well as narrative elements of the form down to small behaviors such as Gryce's habit of never resting his eye on *you* but on some insignificant object, projecting himself as unassuming, unforthcoming, self-deprecating, all so that we should underestimate him, be unguarded in deception. We see this gestural language again and again in the movies.

So then, as to the two sides of Holmes's personality: Sherlock Holmes is to us the epitome of rationality and deduction, and apparently he was intended by his creator to be so. Conan Doyle pronounced him to be "the most perfect reasoning and observing machine that the world has seen" (in "A Scandal in

Bohemia"). "Detection is, or ought to be," says Holmes, "an exact science, and should be treated in the same cold and unemotional manner." He upbraids Watson: "You have attempted to tinge it with romanticism, which produces much the same effect as if you worked a love-story or an elopement into the fifth proposition of Euclid" (*The Sign of Four*). "You are an automaton — a calculating machine," Watson complains a few pages later, after Holmes has made light of Miss Morstan's attractions. "There is something positively inhuman in you at times." These are the canonical statements, the ones we remember and that appear in the quotation books.

One of Holmes's immediate successors, Jacques Futrelle's Augustus SFX Van Dusen was shamelessly given the moniker "The Thinking Machine." Machines, of course, are metaphors of the link between rationality and objectivity that is essential to the detective's manifestation and social role. Machines are affectless and cold and lend these qualities to the man who imitates them. The detective is thin, meager both physically and emotionally, with a piercing and dispassionate vulture's eye, because that is what people are like who are driven, consumed by thought. The detective is perfect, infallible in the application of his mind. Holmes says he cares nothing for the world but devotes himself entirely to his art, but by the art of detection Holmes does not mean something intuitive or expressive like painting or music. He is an intellectual craftsman. His methods are scientific, or seemingly so. There is something unpleasant and a little creepy about him, which perhaps accounts for his having no sex life and no friends other than Watson.

Yet Holmes plays the violin. He keenly anticipates an opportunity to attend a concert and he has a painting relative in France. He himself might be a little French, inheriting both French sensibilities and something of the famous French police practice dating from (and popularized by) Vidocq in Napoleon's time. Holmes disdains French detectives out of jealousy. He is also loyal to Watson and has a strong sense of honor. There are many indicators of a deep emotional life. His gallantry, his treatment of Mrs. Hudson, superficially cavalier, and his admitted fascination with Irene Adler ("A Scandal in Bohemia") testify to his essential humanity toward women. With Holmes, both the warm and the cold are fused into the definition, the essence, of a detective. In him they are necessary to each other. They are found always together.

And yet the one side prevails. There is a hegemony of intellect. The detective genre exists for the purpose of defending truth and rationality against the forces of dissolution and its values are necessarily compromised on the warm side. It is inevitable that lesser men than Holmes should be either more emotional[23] or enslaved by the puzzle trope to the exclusion of anything else. This was given final form in S.S. Van Dine's rules.[24] A successful warm detective would have to await a new sensibility.

Both Agatha Christie and Dorothy Sayers were reaching for something like this in their creation of female detectives, Miss Marple and Harriet Vane. And of course as a genre ages, writers begin to muddle its attributes to keep from being tiresomely repetitive (which does not sell books). Early in the Classic tradition (1926) there was *The Murder of Roger Ackroyd*, combining the roles of murderer and detective.[25] More recently, there is the detective in Robert Altman's *Gosford Park*. Though Altman's imposter meets the minimum standards of craftsmanlike reasoning, he is terrible at it and the crime is actually solved by someone else. All formulas eventually become moribund, to be replaced by variations that in the detective universe will permit exploration of a more generous psychology.

If anyone says that Holmes is coldly rational, the texts themselves say otherwise. Using a rudimentary set of word-pairs that correspond to the opposite ends of the think-feel dichotomy, (think/feel, cold/warm, scientific/artistic, intelligent/imaginative, enlightened/enthusiastic) a count of the incidence of these, related words, and their roots (e.g., intelli-, art-) in five books[26] of the Holmes canon finds the two groups about evenly divided. Regarding the question of whether the Holmes texts present him as coldly rational, the answer is no. The incidence of words in the rational science group and in the warm emotions group, expressed as cases per thousand words of text, are found in table 1.

TABLE 1. COLD AND WARM WORD FREQUENCIES IN FIVE HOLMES TALES

Title	*Cold**	*Warm**
The Hound of the Baskervilles	2.19	1.94
The Adventures of Sherlock Holmes	2.07	2.37
The Sign of Four	2.06	1.54
The Return of Sherlock Holmes	1.74	3.13
A Study in Scarlet	1.32	1.01

*Number per thousand words of text.

This is no support here for the hypothesis that Holmes is a coldly rational man, nor for the opposite.[27] Perhaps the method is too crude. For example, no account is taken of these words as descriptors of *Holmes*; what we have measured, if anything, is the proclivities of *Conan Doyle*. If we require that the word "Holmes" appear in some proximity to one of these words, what do we find?[28] Again, the results are not entirely conclusive, but suspicion grows that Conan Doyle's Holmes displays the usual blend of opposite qualities characteristic of us all (except detectives), and that he is not an exclusively rational man with no pride in his work, no sense of humor or of the absurd, and no fellow feeling.

With Watson, our Chronicler, things are different. A reading of the first few pages of *A Study in Scarlet,* where Watson is first introduced to Holmes and to us, shows without a doubt that Watson is a man of feeling. Over the length of the canon this does color our perception of Holmes since we see him refracted through Watson's lens. And then, before we actually encounter him, Holmes is presented as "queer in his ideas" and an "enthusiast." He communicates only when the fancy seizes him. This sounds warm.[29] Eccentric. Passing through the outer parts of the hospital, familiar to Watson but referred to as dun and bleak, we enter the laboratory — spacious, charmingly cluttered, a haven from the colder outer world. Holmes springs up with a cry of pleasure, his features suffused with delight at the discovery he has just made and eager to talk about it. This first impression is decidedly one-sided, and it is not the side of coldness and unfeeling. Rationality is valued, but for its pleasure as much as for its effectiveness.

This is an inauspicious beginning for admirers of cold thought. The conventional wisdom about Holmes, it seems, is simply wrong. Conan Doyle did not portray him as cold and unfeeling and there is plenty of evidence for this in the canon.

Portrayals of Holmes
as an Index of Social Change

If we turn to the movies we can find an evolving Holmes, responsive to changing attitudes about rational knowledge rather different from the views of 1887. Many people probably read the Holmes stories early in life. This experience, the memory of which may have become dim without reinforcement, has probably been overlayed since by the impression of Holmes conveyed in the movies. Older people will remember Rathbone's Holmes, younger ones Brett's or the new embodiment by Benedict Cumberbatch. Is there anything in this range of portrayals that explains how the detective genre is pinned to its time?

Holmes has been portrayed on film often, possibly more often than any other detective. And how exactly are we to recognize a warm, emotional Holmes? The most frequently filmed of the Holmes tales is *The Hound of the Baskervilles*. If we focus on these films perhaps we can spot a shift in polarity of the think/feel axis. This in turn may reveal something of how Holmes became the epitome of the aloof, detached researcher in the laboratory of crime, so unlike such portrayals of contemporary scientists as the forensic wizards of *CSI* with their awful puns, cheerful obsessions, and love interests.

The Hound of the Baskervilles

This story is well-suited to a confrontation between science and art. It traffics (dishonestly, but that is another topic) with the occult and the inexplicable. There is the frightening and spectral hound itself, of course, and a haunting of the Baskerville clan as a consequence of past misdeeds, a spirit needing exorcism by hard-minded detection. There is fear of the man on the moor and his suspicious connection with the Baskerville servants, only two of them in this big, creaky and cold house. There is fear of the moor itself, which, significantly, will yield to study, but this science produces a somewhat eldritch knowledge acquired at risk. This and many other aspects of the story provide a preponderance of opportunities for Romance, which must be dispelled if the detective is to succeed by rational means. And finally, the cast contains a sympathetic woman (the typist L.L.) who starts the machinery of the plot by means of a love affair, a woman in peril, and an evil scientist who powers the action.

It was an original premise of the genre that the detective will prevail, will find the right path to the destination. There remains, of course, at least for dramatic reasons, always a possibility that there will be a wrong turning toward Romance. It would be a disaster if Holmes were to lose his way. Everything is predicated on him. If there are to be Romantic temptations (and in *The Hound* there certainly are), they must not ensnare Holmes. He must remain apart. It is not whether thought is privileged in these movies, which it is by the nature of the genre, but whether feeling (and thus activities such as art, which are assumed to have a special relationship to feeling) will be relegated as we wish it to be, or will break out like some supernatural hound and overwhelm us. This is the reason for the odd sequestration of Holmes during the middle of the story, so as to give full play to these dangerous elements without compromising Holmes.

The Hound of the Baskervilles has been filmed 16 times in sound, nine of these for television. Four of the five silent versions were German and one British; one of the German versions consisted of six parts made between 1914 and 1920 with different actors playing Holmes before and after the war. Of the talkies there are one each in Russian, Italian, German, and French; the rest are in English. Here is the tally (table 2).[30]

Four of these are readily available: the 1939 version starring Basil Rathbone, the 1959 version with Peter Cushing, and the 1988 and 2002 versions with, respectively, Jeremy Brett and Richard Roxburgh.

To begin, in the movies one can for the first time see a living Holmes. Can we tell if he is warm or cold just by looking at him? The gestural language of taking thought is probably not going to be of much help. The possibilities are too few: an inward stare, a finger to the lips, the contemplation of some object or the sudden breaking off of some activity are about all the actor has to work with.

Women, the carriers of emotion (or perhaps the Typhoid Marys) are kept well away from Holmes in the *Baskerville* films. One, referred to as L.L. (Laura Lyons), is expunged from three of the four versions here. Her original

TABLE 2. FILMS OF *THE HOUND OF THE BASKERVILLES*

Date	Made for TV	Title	Holmes Played By	Director	Running Time	Notes
2002	x	*The Hound of the Baskervilles*	Richard Roxburgh	David Atwood	100	
2000	x	*The Hound of the Baskervilles*	Matt Frewer	Rodney Gibbon	90	
		Le Chien des Baskerville				Canadian
1988	x	*The Hound of the Baskervilles*	Jeremy Brett	Brian Mills	105	
1983	x	*The Hound of the Baskervilles*	Ian Richardson	Douglas Hickox	101	
1983		*Sherlock Holmes and the Baskerville Curse*	Peter O'Toole	Eddy Graham	75	Animated, Australian
1982		*The Hound of the Baskervilles*	Tom Baker	Peter Duguid	120	4 episodes; British
1981	x	*Priklyucheniya Sherloka Kholmsa I doktora Vatsona: Sobaka Baskerviley*	Vash Livanov	Igor Maslenikov	154	Livanov reputes as the best Holmes
1978	x	*The Hound of the Baskervilles*	Peter Cook	Paul Morrissey	85	Comedy, USA
1974	x	*Au théâtre ce soir: Le chien des Baskerville*	Raymond Gérôme	Georges Folgoas	?	
1972	x	*The Hound of the Baskervilles*	Stewart Granger	Barry Crane	90	
1968		*Il Mastino dei Baskerville*	Nando Gazzolo	Guglielmo Morandi	?	
1959		*The Hound of the Baskervilles*	Peter Cushing	Terence Fisher	87	
1955	x	*Der Hund von Baskerville*	Wolf Ackva	Fritz Umgelter	80	
1939		*The Hound of the Baskervilles*	Basil Rathbone	Sidney Lanfield	80	
1936		*Der Hund von Baskerville*	Bruno Guttner	Karl Lamac	?	Nazi production, one of two found in Hitler's bunker
1932		*The Hound of the Baskervilles*	Robert Rendel	Gareth Gundrey	72	British
1929		*Der Hund von Baskerville*	Carlyle Blackwell	Richard Oswald	?	Silent, lost (see Michael Pointer)
1920		"Der Hund von Baskerville, teil 5"	Erich Kaiser-Titz?	Willy Zehn	?	Subtitle "Dr. Mac-donald's Sanatorium"
1920		"Der Hund von Baskerville, teil 6"	Willy Kaiser-Heyl	Willy Zehn	?	Subtitle "Das Haus ohne Fenster"
1920		*The Hound of the Baskervilles*	Eille Norwood	Maurice Elvey	?	British, silent
1915		*Das Dunkle Schloss*	Eugen Burg	Willy Zeyn	50	Silent
1915		"Der Hund von Baskerville, teil 3"	Alwin Neuss	Richard Oswald	?	Subtitle "Das unheimliche zimmer"
1915		"Der Hund von Baskerville, teil 4"	Alwin Neuss	Richard Oswald	?	
1915		*Der Baer von Baskerville*	unknown	Harry Piel	?	Silent
1914		"Der Hund von Baskerville, teil 1"	Alwin Neuss	Rudolf Meinert	?	Lacks Watson, silent
1914		"Der Hund von Baskerville, teil 2"	Alwin Neuss	Rudolf Meinert	?	Subtitle "Das einsame haus"

purpose was to serve as a red herring through the suggestion that she was the now-dead-Sir Charles's mistress. As such she threatened to divert the plot into sexual byways and away from the main line. In any case, this sexual diversion is better suited to the scientist Stapleton's ambiguous companion, variously wife, sister, or daughter. In Conan Doyle's version this woman is Stapleton's wife but presented by Stapleton as his sister, a duplicity explained and revealed by Stapleton's prior duplicity toward L.L. This presents the film-maker with a problem. To leave L.L in the story would constrain the use of Mrs. Stapleton as a lure to the young heir Sir Henry (as earlier, L.L. was herself presumed a lure to Sir Henry's uncle Charles). If Mrs. Stapleton seems to be a sister this frees Sir Henry from the onus of flirting with a married woman. Released by Stapleton's probable death in the Grimpen Mire, the two are free to consummate a happy ending. Rathbone follows this narrative, making it still more decorous by leaving out any suggestion of love affairs and L.L. altogether. Brett follows the original but counteracts the un-Romantic truth of the divorced and exploited penurious typist L.L. by includ-ing a thrilling rescue of Mrs. Stapleton from her husband's abuse. In the Roxburgh version Mrs. Stapleton hangs herself. This is necessary because, if Stapleton has gotten through the moor and escaped as claimed, he blocks with his inconvenient life any rapprochement by Sir Henry and Stapleton's wife. If Sir Henry's virtue is to be saved, the threat to it from Stapleton's wife must be gotten rid of. Finally, Cushing's version transforms the two Stapletons into a crofter and his daughter. The girl, who is complicit in the plot against Sir Henry, vamps him in the style of an Italian peasant from a Fellini movie and pays by dying in the Mire herself.

This is ridiculously complicated. The fact that it is so shows the lengths to which these films go to separate emotion from reason, distorting a quite straightforward plot.

Mrs. Barrymore, the third woman in the story, is a simpler case alto-gether. She tries to do the right thing, fails, weeps, feels sadness and regret, and finally soldiers on as the exemplar of wifely good sense, keeping female emotionality under control.

In the 1939 film (Rathbone), all this threatening femininity is simply waved away. In 1959 (Cushing) it is emphasized, but redirected as criminal. In 1988 (Brett) an uneasy bargain is made to pay for a sordid melodrama by acknowledging the exploited L.L. In 2002 (Roxburgh) the sordid melodrama comes free of charge (and given Roxburgh's cruel and cynical Holmes, we should not be surprised).

From this sequence we can read straight off a set of attitudes toward women and emotional knowledge, each belonging to its time.

There is also a contrast between science run amok in the person of Sta-pleton, a reproach to rationality and a caution to Holmes, and the good scientist in the person of Mortimer. In the Rathbone version Mortimer is an unexceptionable, mature man. The Brett version is more conflicted, more chiaroscuro, but his is the only version in which Stapleton is portrayed as a genuine scientist. Mortimer is allowed to be a young man as he was in the original text, but his science is to us tainted by an interest in phrenology. This would not have been a taint or a point of fun a century before (Conan Doyle included both this and a séance) [31] but in 1988 it served to heighten the contrast with the more serious, grave, and older Holmes. In 2002 that whole tension was simply ignored in the preference for a purer melodrama whereas in 1959, a significant period in the public perception of science, Stapleton was no scientist at all and Mortimer was turned into an elderly and irascible countryman.

The Stapleton/Mortimer nexus indexes rationality (cool knowledge) as the three women index emotionality (warm knowledge).

Rathbone is as accommodating to both thought and feeling as Conan Doyle was and not especially partisan, but it is not an active accommodation. It rather turns the whole conflict aside.

In 1959 and 2002 thoughtfulness is completely rejected as dangerous or boring and the character of Holmes degenerates accordingly. In the hysterical 1959 Cushing version Holmes is manipulative rather than clever and in the matter of the exposure of Sir Henry to the Hound he treats the man as a dupe to be bullied by some ugly remarks about unredeemable peasants. Cushing's Holmes really *is* cold, but in a way that disparages both the Neoclassical and Romantic ideals. Roxburgh's Holmes is supercilious and short-tempered. He may be clever — he is certainly not *ir*rational — but he is no representative of the mind calmed by reason.

Between 1959 and 2002 we have Brett's ambivalence. Intending to be faithful to the original, Brett's Holmes can be said to be actually conflicted. He is alert to the siege of the rational by the irrational and does not know whether the Next New Thing might be the haunting, spectral, jealous Hound. Conan Doyle too was, famously, drawn by the occult.

In the same period between 1959 and 2002 we also have Ian Richardson's version (1983). In the same year this actor made *The Sign of Four*, the aborted start of a television series. By contrast with that movie, Richardson's *Hound* is restrained, almost intellectual. A half-hearted attempt is made to create a foreboding atmosphere, but the village bustles and the whole place resembles a New England autumn for tourists. The plot is for the most part authentic, with one notable exception: the painter Lyons is left on the scene. This means that his obviously married and virtuous wife Laura cannot be duped into an affair by a supposedly bachelor Stapleton. This in turn hashes the charitable motive for Sir Charles's being out on the moor despite his fear of the hound. Laura and Stapleton are now in cahoots, and when Holmes gets close to the poor woman, who is in this version a crone with dangerous knowledge, she has to be done away with. Lyons himself is portrayed as a bearlike and cruel boor driven by the realization of his failure as an artist. Yet when his wife dies he breaks down and cries his heart out.

Why this melodrama, and at the expense of an economy of plot? (*The Sign of Four* is a good deal more so, approaching Roxburgh's *Hound* in gothicism.) If Lyons is the representative of warm, intemperate feeling then her evil counterpart is the Hound. Stapleton is positioned as cold, rational intellectuality, offsetting Holmes's worrisome dual aspect, warm and cold, muting the threat of each by contrast with the other. The 1959 film is seriously hostile to rationality. Evidently by 1983 audiences did not yet feel easy about the life of the mind and still needed some powerful balancing forces. Somewhere in the '80s there was a shift of sensibility that made Brett's authenticity possible, a tentatively redistributed tension between mind and heart. By 2002 our minds were made up: cold knowledge is necessary but corrupting to the personality. Ten years later, the Cumberbatch version rejects even this: cold knowledge is fun but not serious. Important truths are now to be found elsewhere, in tales of emotional struggle.

This sharply drawn progression, from dignified acceptance of rational thinking to a nearly complete separation of warm and cold with a preference for warm, will of course be muddied if we include more films. Matters are seldom as straightforward as that.

Richardson later (2000) played the part of Dr. Joseph Bell, the man on whom Holmes was modeled, in a film whose title—*Murder Rooms: The Dark Beginnings of Sherlock Holmes*—belies its stout defense of rationality. Indeed, thought and evidence are here a bastion and a salvation, the only source of a moral life. They are also, significantly, the right and the protection of women. This is very different from Roxburgh's contemporaneous *Hound*.

In 1985, *Young Sherlock Holmes* utilized the character in a Tom Brown public school romp and in 1988, in a seeming jab at Brett, Michael Caine played a slapstick Holmes in *Without a Clue*, a fake who is actually Watson's puppet. And then we have the 1976 *Seven-Percent Solution*, in which Holmes, disabled by his ungovernable cocaine habit, is returned to mental life by Alan Arkin's Freud and goes off at the end on a toot with the rescued heroine. And now in 2012 we have a version of the *Hound* with Holmes as a brash and witty young man and a totally scrambled plot. The hound is a product of government research. The laboratory is infiltrated, the geneticist Stapleton cracks the problem, and all ends in a thrilling confrontation. The science has been pushed back to the time of Frankenstein and both warm and cool knowledge have been sacrificed to thrills.

What trajectory is suggested by this sequence of Baskervilles and other portrayals of Holmes? In 1939, at the advent of the noir tradition, we have a

Holmes with gravitas, one who still assumes the wisdom of a preference for intellect which he takes with the new moral seriousness of noir, but which comes with a certain prudishness. At the height of the Cold War, this seriousness hardened into something rather desperate and cynical, and prudishness had become prurience. By the 1980s we were again ready to tolerate some commingling of warm and cold, but this proved fitful and unstable. The new century has abandoned any such balance and has given up completely any attempt to resolve the contrast of warm and cool and retreated into the gothic tale and the thriller.

If this trajectory tracks well enough the rudimentary social history we perceive lying behind it then we could go on to ask further questions. What, for example, can explain both the fear of sexuality and the rejection of rationality that we see in 1959 and then again in 2002 and 20012? If we could answer that question, then if I am correct, we ought to be able to find in the genre other cases of the same attitudes. Where society and culture go, there goes the Detective. This will be my contention in what follows: that changes in the genre formula can be explained by changes in the culture in which the genre is embedded. What does this simple conjunction tell us about the nature of detective stories?

3

The English Classic

Magic

A genre is a formula, a set of quasi-industrial procedures for producing texts sufficiently alike that the reader's expectations are not surprised and the demand for more of the same is satisfied. A genre is more than that, of course. However, the systematization of production is the feature that interests us now, for it is the dominant feature of the English Classic.

The rules for the English Classic detective novel were first formulated by Ronald Knox. I present them here as given by S.S. Van Dine[1] and reorganized logically. (Van Dine's list is jumbled.)

I. Fair play: the detective should have no advantage over the reader as regards inside knowledge and there shall be no tricks or deceptions other than those between the detective and the criminal. The detective himself cannot be the criminal; aside from this being a deception on the reader, it is an offense to logical deduction. The crime itself must be actual, not merely apparent, such as an accident or a suicide or an illusion.

II. Roles: there must be a detective, and only one detective, and this person must actively gather evidence (clues) and draw conclusions from them by logical *deduction*.[2] There must be a corpse — other forms of victimization are too trivial. There must be a culprit — and only one culprit — who must have a prominent part in the story and who must be a person of social standing (hence not a professional criminal).

III. Method: the culprit must be discovered only by rational means, i.e., "scientific" means. Rational truths are available to any reasoning person with the requisite knowledge, unlike imagination and fantasy. That is (to repeat), the detective shall have no advantage over the reader, and over the other characters except by his innate reasoning abilities. The story must concentrate exclusively on rational processes, without distracting love interests, literary description, irrelevant character development, and the like.

IV. Setting: all the murders must be personal, and committed for personal reasons. These motives, and the circumstances of the crime, must

55

conform to the quotidian expectations of the reader, neither exotic nor extraordinary.

Notice that the particular complaints that Van Dine makes in his rules on method are all derived from the Holmes stories, or from attempts (such as Hornung's Raffles or Bentley's Trent) to counter Holmes's dominance. Conan Doyle wanted first of all a dramatic story, and the *magic*[3] of Holmes's method was part of the drama. Exclusive emphasis on the puzzle over other storytelling devices such as adventure, quest, or simple human interest, despite such tinkering with the rules such as in Christie's Roger Ackroyd, is the characteristic modification of the English Classic.

What I am calling the English Classic begins with Agatha Christie and *The Mysterious Affair at Styles* (1919) and includes Dorothy Sayers, some authors of lesser note such as Marjorie Allingham and Ngaio Marsh, and then a great many others still worth reading. Some examples are Earl Derr Biggers, Arthur Upfield, R. Austin Freeman, Freeman Wills Crofts, Ernest Bramah, Anthony Berkeley, E.C. Bentley. The list could be much longer. Classic stories were enormously popular in the '20s and '30s and a great many people wrote them. What all these authors had in common was some allegiance to the Rules and a story that does more or less the genre work described in the first chapter, on origins. As the thirties wore on the fears and social needs addressed by the Classic faded. Stories in the Classic tradition continue to be written, of course, but the force had passed on to new genre variants. That passing on is a clear demonstration of the yoking of genre and the need to do social work and will be a large part of the next chapter.

Much has been written on the English Classic. Let me begin with what Brian Boyd has to say in his work on the evolutionary origins of storytelling.[4] "The mind is not inductive, as Shakespeare's contemporary Francis Bacon suggested it should be. We do not patiently wait for all available evidence.... Instead, we hastily construct inferences that ... hit home. Storytelling lies at the heart of literature, yet literary studies all too rarely explore our ability to construct a story on meager hints."

Our ability to construct a story from meager hints is at the heart of the Classic, for one of the things it attempts to do is to lead us to construct the *wrong story*. Rhetorically, this is what creates the Detective's superiority. He is not so easily fooled. This brings to the fore a problem with illusion and reality that is embedded in the story. Recall the magus Prospero in Shakespeare's *The Tempest*. Much of what he wants to achieve is furthered by his ability to create illusion. What is there in the play to convince the characters that what is revealed when the illusion is lifted is not just another illusion? One might say that the answer to the feeling of authenticity lies in the force of the feelings released: love, freedom, forgiveness. The Detective's power consists not only in rescuing reality from illusion but in convincing everyone that the newly uncovered state of affairs *is the truth*. The means used by the English Classic to achieve this is the resemblance of this new state of affairs to the one remembered from a time before the crime. The convincing force is the powerful desire for this to be so, just as the end of the war left so many with a longing for the way things used to be. It was no accident that the English Classic appeared in 1919. The Detective's power, then, arises out of our feelings and beliefs, and the use of evidence and rational deduction are in an important way *trappings*. The end of the hegemony of the Classic is, as we will see, bound up with our discovery that the supposed reality uncovered by the Detective is just that: supposed. Every successive change in the genre will be initiated so.

I conclude from this that the compulsively rational English Classic is an aspirational tale that hopes to show us how things could be if only we behaved accordingly. But storytelling does not work this way, as Boyd points out. It is always slipping back to its origins in the human ability to find stories everywhere, in our ability to construct a story out of what is really one thing after another. That given, we ought to find some remnants of an earlier story in the Classic tale of ratiocination. We are looking for magic.

Magical thinking is the interpretation of two closely occurring events as though one caused the other without any concern for a causal link.[5] Joan Didion describes this in *The Year of Magical Thinking* (Random House, 2005) as a personal language of secrets — interdictions, omens — the powers and forces that connect the world and the word. If we believe that the unspoken and the unseen will be released by their names and images, then refusing to name or depict them allows us some control over them.[6] Magical thinking corresponds (loosely) to what I call warm knowledge. To an extent that storytelling arises from, and obtains its resonance from, warm knowledge, there is a contradiction at the heart of the English Classic.

Glenn Adamson, in his book *Thinking Through Craft* (Oxford: Berg, 2007), articulates a description of Modernism that is relevant to the rational aspiration of the English Classic. Adamson's claim consists of two parts: the now familiar search for the pure form of the art, and denial of the craft by which the art is brought into being. Adamson gives as an example the Modernist challenge to the craft of the jeweler to construct a form that could simultaneously be identified as jewelry and as art without requiring the physical body it was originally invented to adorn. Adamson's schema thus reveals the English Classic as an instance of this Modernist agenda: the pure form of the rational detective story without the craft of storytelling — character development, allusion, rhetorical devices, humor, myth, and so forth.

Magic is the unacknowledged craft of the detective. But be he a magician, he is not a mere prestidigitator. He is a conduit to the spiritual world of correspondences to be interpreted as by a soothsayer, of interconnections to be disentangled, sign-posted as if by a spirit guide. Of course, the Classic Detective ultimately provides his rational explanation, but what gives that explanation much of its force is the dangerous and uncanny world with which we are threatened.

The Detective may be said to capture stories and bring them into the safe world of rules and expectations. We are entertained by this, but one who is capable of converse with the world of magic is a dangerous person possessing knowledge and skills forbidden to us who know only rules and habits.

Rules, of course, are invitations to impudence. Every one of Van Dine's strictures had at least one counter-example already by 1928. His codification's appearance in 1928, almost at the end of the high Classic, smacks of bolting the barn when the horse is gone.

Why so tardy? Consider this reminder concerning the nature of genre: Genres are not changeless structures ordained by natural law, destined to repeat themselves in every society, nor are they theoretical constructs. They serve a function in the overall cultural economy, an economy involving an industry, a social need for the production and consumption of messages, human subjects, technology, sets of signifying practices (social objects, possibly memes). Genres are not treasure chests of cultural values or rituals to exorcize cultural demons. They are a network of formulas that serve a regulatory role in delivering a certified product to the waiting customer. They ensure the production of meaning by regulating the customer's relation to the images and narratives constructed for the market in cultural goods, building and then satisfying desire. The values and rituals put to work by the genre will be whatever serves these purposes best at the time.[7]

These remarks should give some hint of the importance I attach to magic as an influence on the most ratiocinative collection of Detectives in the nearly two-hundred-year history of the genre. What I have said about demons, exorcism, rituals, and shamans bears on this, of course, but the Classic magic is in fact also entertainment: simple prestidigitation. The detective magician distracts our attention from what is actually going on, engages in some hocus pocus and produces some inexplicable surprise — raw eggs out of thin air, prescient playing cards, whole women sawn in two, amazing escapes— which often leaves us as mystified as were the witnesses to the crime who called in the detective in the first place. Sometimes, after the surprised audience has become receptive, a more or less full explanation is provided. Sometimes there are unexplained loose ends. We might learn nothing at all about how the trick was done, but this is of no moment. The genuine English Classic employs in more or less good faith this framework of theatrical magic. The magician tempts us into over-hasty deductions and then exposes our mistake. We are invited to inspect superficial appearances only to find them vanish, exposing the underlying reality. We are told what to expect and then encouraged to allow our expectations to mislead us.

But perhaps we are not fooled. In the best of the English Classics, behind this stage detective lurks the real one, the figure of the Detective, whose presence we might prefer to overlook.

Agatha Christie (Career 1920–1975)

Agatha Christie is the most published author of all time. Her detectives Hercule Poirot and Jane Marple cover the whole history of the English Classic, which Christie originated, along with some standard variants like the English Country House Murder. Miss Marple (and Dorothy Sayers's Harriet Vane) brought natural wisdom to supplement the cool knowledge of Poirot and Wimsey. No sooner was the English Classic established than she challenged the limits of her own Classic method in *The Murder of Roger Ackroyd*. Here the murderer is the narrator himself, and the virtuosity comes from not breaking the rules of transparent clues and fair play central to the Classic tradition. Christie also pioneered the courtroom drama, in *Witness for the Prosecution*, establishing a formula that was the mainstay of Earle Stanley Gardner's Perry Mason and that has continued into the present with any number of television shows featuring lawyers.

Christie's best storytelling achievement is her handling of Inspector Japp. This character is not presented to us as the usual bumbling policeman without a clue. He is given a personality and a history, we hear of his home life — and in more detail than just his feelings about his difficult wife — and he and Poirot become genuine friends. Hastings disappears early in the stories because he is a puppet. Not so Japp. He is not quite a fully realized character, but he is treated with sympathy and has been given more humanity than, for example, Campion's Lugg. We will not see anything better until 1936, when Sayers gave Harriet Vane the freedom of introspection in *Gaudy Night*.

Having found out a little about the uses of peripheral characters to create human interest and about how to work with the opportunities offered by her invention of Jane Marple, Christie was nevertheless unable to rescue Poirot. Her first detective is as famously wooden and comical as Holmes is cold. What do we know about Poirot besides his fussiness and his little gray cells?

Hercule Poirot

Poirot provides an interesting comparison with Sherlock Holmes. The Poirot canon is larger than Holmes's and we know more correspondingly a tiny bit more about him than we know about Holmes. Much of this knowledge we have independently, whereas what we know about Holmes is filtered through Watson's testimony. Both of them are flamboyant, eccentric and vain. Both are confirmed bachelors but neither is antisocial. Given these similarities, why is Holmes the echt Detective while Poirot occupies so much smaller a cultural space?

If Poirot is a marionette or a wind-up toy (which to some extent he is), this is usually attributed to Christie's inability to create rounded characters. The examples of Japp, Marple, Ackroyd, the ABC murderer, and others suggest otherwise. Poirot was wooden because he had to be.

First, the character of Holmes is open. He drives the plot, and the story is as much about him as about solving the crime. In comparison, Poirot is given the story rather than creating it. He does not drive the plot because he is so predictable and so much of the story is predetermined by the genre rules.[8]

Then, the English Classic is concerned exclusively with the puzzle. The characters are there only to embody the puzzle. They are, so to speak, the ground on which the puzzle walks. No modern story written in that way would succeed. Christie was able to work within these conditions through her own fecundity and propensity for small humanizing touches. The Neoclassic story, which we will examine later, treats its characters very differently not because we have a different idea of what people are like than Christie's and Conan Doyle's readers did, or because we have discovered anything new about storytelling, but because the Neoclassic stories are doing different cultural work. The disparity between what Christie says about Poirot and the way we see him shows this clearly. Christie's readers were concerned to defend a rational society according to their concept of what was civilized. Angst, cynicism, moral outrage, and epistemological niceties had nothing to do with that. We want characters of a different sort.

Who was Hercule Poirot? He made his first appearance in 1919, in Christie's first novel, *The Mysterious Affair at Styles*. Poirot is, as he will tell anyone who should make the mistake, not French but Belgian (and thus in this respect twice an outsider). He has had a successful career as a detective in the "Belgian police"—whether this is the national force or that of the capital, Brussels, is never specified. At the time of the Styles affair he is a refugee from the Great War who has been taken in, along with some others, and is living in the village of Styles, near the manor Styles Court. It is 1916. Captain Arthur Hastings, invalided out of the army, is telling the story. Hastings has been invited to Styles, where he runs into (literally) the man Poirot, whom he knew earlier in Belgium. We learn that the little policeman is five feet four inches tall and limps badly—an infirmity mostly ignored afterwards—has an egg-shaped head and a great moustache. This is about all we ever learn of him as a person.

I must say about Hastings that he is no Watson, and by his failure demonstrates the importance of the Chronicler to the Classic detective story. Hastings is if anything more wooden than Poirot. After the murder at Styles it is Hastings who calls in Poirot. He went on to narrate some of the early tales but contributed nothing. He was in fact a narrative liability, weighing it down rather than enlivening it as Watson had done, and also unlike Watson was no interpreter of his story's central character. He is presented as clueless naïf, not well-enough off to afford an automobile, for the workings of which he shows great but rather childish enthusiasm. He is finally married off and sent to Argentina, where he buys a cattle ranch and raises four children, returning now and then to England and his earlier persona as a hanger-on.

Altogether, Poirot appeared in nearly a hundred cases between 1920 and 1975; 28 of these were novels. (Holmes appeared in 56 stories and four novels.) Among the things we don't know about him is his age. A plausible estimate is, if we assume from his former career that he is in his mid-forties at the time of the Styles affair, then he would have been born about 1870. If Hastings is 30 in 1916 and the last of his four children was born in 1920 (the most hurried scenario we can imagine), then in 1945, the probable date of the final case, Poirot would have been 75, Hastings 60, and Hastings's daughter Judith, who is portrayed as of marriageable age, 25. We could easily be told this. In another sort of novel we would be.

We do also learn that after the Great War Poirot attempted to retire and devote himself to the cultivation of vegetable marrows (zucchini)— one thinks of Holmes retiring to raise bees— but professed himself, not surprisingly, bored (*The Murder of Roger Ackroyd*, 1926). Growing zucchini would not seem much of a challenge. He moved to London to set up as a consulting detective. Poirot was at the height of his career in the 1920s and early '30s. Professionally, Poirot's relations with the official police are good, not unexpectedly for one who was himself a policeman. Of course, the Classic tradition's rationale being the defense of social order, the guardian of order (Poirot) cannot be a rude, vulgar man. That role is allowed to a sympathetic Scotland Yard inspector, James Japp, who makes his appearance as soon as Poirot sets up in business. Japp is competent but lacks the imagination of his eccentric colleague Poirot. He is married in the conventional way that aims at contentment rather than happiness, and in marked contrast to Poirot, he prefers country food and beer and is completely without cultural pretensions.[9]

Despite Poirot's professionalism, he falls into the mold of the gentleman who engages in detection as a hobby, taking only cases that interest him. This aesthetic attitude toward detection is really a polite fiction. Roger Ackroyd was a personal friend. When Poirot is traveling (mostly to the Middle East, where Christie's own foreign experience was greatest) he is usually in the position of the doctor in the house who cannot refuse his services. And often enough — as when some young people living in his own building get into difficulties ("The Third Floor Flat")— he is sucked in by mere proximity. Poirot's true role is that of the village busybody who is always looking through the hedge in hopes of finding some strange goings-on. When Christie added Miss Jane Marple to her stable of characters it was to pursue this narrative strategy openly and engage with the human comedy.

Unusually in detective fiction, we do learn something of Poirot's final years. In *Curtain* we revisit the Styles case, with Hastings again narrating. Styles has become a country hotel. Poirot is well-off (rich, he says) but in declining health. He has become meager, dyes his hair, and is confined by arthritis to a wheelchair. All of this proves to be play-acting. Poirot, we find, has hijacked Hastings for a role in his plan to visit retribution on an unconvicted murderer, an Iago who does his work by goading others into violence. Poirot's endeavor succeeds, after which he hastens his own end by depriving himself of medicine needed to stave off heart failure. In this final tale, then, the roles are reversed: Poirot is the murderer and Hastings the detective. Hastings is a poor sleuth — he has to be told the truth in a testament Poirot has left to be read after his death. There might have been an opportunity in this story to learn more about Poirot, but as with all detectives in the Classic tradition, we are allowed to interest ourselves in him only insofar as he is wrapped in his function of the Detective. The touches of humanity for which I praised Christie earlier cannot extend to the Detective. And now, though his sleuthing is all done and his murderer's plot laid before the novel begins, he continues to play the role and this essential inscrutability is part of the disguise. What we learn in the end of his feelings and motives is no more than we have known all along.

A story in which Poirot is encountered only in passing, seen pottering in his garden perhaps while we are on our way to somewhere else, is unthinkable. In the later 1930s Dorothy Sayers experimented with her own second-string detective, Harriet Vane, as a fictional character in novels having less to do with crime than love, but this sort of crossover was in the heyday of the Classic an oddity. Christie tinkered widely with detectives of various sorts. In the end her first creation, Poirot the detective, was possibly her most popular.

An important feature of Poirot's working methods is the application of his "little gray cells." We are to take his meaning as being the operation of rational thought, but a closer scrutiny of his behavior suggests something more like subconscious speculation or mentally turning over the possibilities in search of one with particular appeal. The gray cells are an autonomous truth engine not under conscious control. Unlike Holmes, Poirot is rather often puzzled, and the mental impasse is not disassembled but exploded in a flash of insight and a rain of self-deprecating imprecations — the characteristic "Ah, mon ami! How could I have been so stupid!"

Poirot's method of work is different than Holmes's, and in a way revealing of why he is necessarily wooden in portrayal. Christie experimented now and then with the very central demand that detection should be rational, one example being the 1924 "The Adventure of the Egyptian Tomb," filmed in 1993 in the David Suchet series. None of these experiments were more than flirts. This was a time when séances and Ouija boards were fashionable. The problem is that between science and the occult there can be no fair fight. Except as mythopoesis, the two cannot exist together for, as in the Father Brown stories, the possibility of a solution arrived at with neither evidence nor reasoning makes the whole enterprise moot. There is a good dramatic reason why Conan Doyle kept Holmes out of the Baskerville story until it was time to act. Holmes cannot be portrayed as credulous on these matters, and would spoil the frisson generated by the hound.

Holmes says that he will not theorize in advance of the evidence, but he does expose his thinking to Watson at times. He can do this because he is actually guessing about some crucial matters, as we saw, and genuinely does not know. Poirot says that he is in doubt but never lays out a hypothesis for anyone — Hastings, Japp, or the reader. We can be given the inference chain without the clues, or the clues without the inference chain. If we have both, then we know the solution when the detective does. Such a story would have to turn on quite a different matter than the suspense of discovery. English Classic stories do not allow access to the detective's mind; a first person or third person indirect narration can't be used because then the author could not fairly hide the detective's developing conclusions from the reader. The alternate strategy of hiding the clues is a patent cheat. It resembles the film strategy of showing the criminal at work but only from the knees down. The consequence is that Classic detectives are, as fictional characters, wooden. We aren't permitted to know them as real, conflicted and fallible people, and at the same time the extreme focus on cool knowledge keeps the mythic qualities of the figure of the Detective under wraps. Touches of humanity had to be left to the more minor characters, and at this Christie was rather good, notably in the case of Japp. Given these severe limitations — the fragility of the rational veneer, limited narrative techniques, a limited choice of possible criminals and victims, the constraints of fairness — it is a little surprising, and a testimony to her powers of invention, that she managed to come up with so many interesting tales.

In this, Christie was helped by the invention of Jane Marple. The Classic story was necessarily intolerant of occult thinking. Anything extra-rational would spoil the story, deprive the solution of logic, and create an impression of arbitrariness. As extra-rational thinking was claimed to be a mode employed by women, Jane Marple threatens the genre premises by her mere presence. Christie was perfectly willing to use our (and the characters') wariness at the presence of a female sleuth as a dramatic device, and thereby created license for herself. Marple is as opaque as Poirot, but she gathers around her opportunities to speculate and to talk in a way the Poirot could not.

Hercule Poirot is mostly a collection of mannerisms. All English Classic detectives have this artificiality at their core as a consequence of the requirements of the tradition. This accounts in large part for the rarity of film realizations of these characters. Aside from Philo Vance, Charlie Chan, and Nick Charles, no sustained attention was given by the movies to the Classic tradition until the Neoclassic revival beginning about 1980. The immediacy and illusion of reality inherent in film made it very hard to embody any of the Classic detectives in their recognizable artificiality without threatening to turn the film into a comedy. (And in fact there is a very large comic element in the 1930s portrayals of Vance, Chan, and Charles.)

Hercule Poirot embodies this difficulty in the extreme. For Poirot, before David Suchet's portrayal there are only a 1935 movie of *Lord Edgware Dies* (a dismal failure and consequently now rare), Albert Finney's Poirot in the 1965 *Murder on the Orient Express,* and a handful of other performances. Finney's realization should be studied closely — his Poirot is a genuinely human eccentric whose neuroses and extreme oddity cover feelings of anger, pride, and empathy not to be found in the print original.

Dorothy Sayers (Career 1923–1937)

Sayers was an Oxford graduate whose education was as useful to her as Christie's Middle Eastern archaeological experiences. Sayers's first anthology (1929) used a very broad definition of "mystery" including occult, horror, and much else. However, it took her a while to put her education to work. Lord Peter Wimsey's foppish upper-crust manner was merely a convention that, it was thought, excused the privileged from the onus of meddling in other people's business. The opposite gesture, the vulgar assistant, contributed nothing. This person was an *assistant*— someone of interest but lesser importance, mirroring not mitigating the class structure. This is the pattern of Poirot/Hastings and Poirot/Japp, degenerating to the vaudeville of Campion/Lugg and H.C. Bailey's Reggie Fortune, reversed by P. G. Wodehouse's Jeeves and Wooster. The Neoclassicist Elizabeth George's team of the titled Inspector Thomas Lynley and Sergeant Barbara Havers, or the educated Inspector Morse and the uncultured Lewis, exactly follow this borrowed convention. In the U.S. it was copied by Philo Vance, with the district attorney and his sergeant becoming increasingly comic through the movies of 1930s just as the Allingham's Bailey became less and less serious, until the shock of 1939 brought an end.[10]

Sayers's solution to the problems of intellectual seriousness and human empathy ended with her invention of Harriet Vane — significantly a woman. Vane anticipates the way women have since been used to humanize police procedurals, cop stories, and all tales of cool (male) knowledge. It should not go unnoticed that, until recently, the role of a woman as the detective's love interest was not to the woman's advantage, but only a narrative tool.

Sayers's best Vane novel, *Gaudy Night,* was published in 1936, at a time when the admission of warm knowledge to the list of a detective's legitimate procedures was beginning. I will examine this shift in the next chapter. She is a considerable advance on Jane Marple in the development of the contemporary Detective from his Classic roots.

Harriet Vane begins as Wimsey's protégée, his equal in education and culture if not social standing. Wimsey is in love with her from the start, but this is a relationship that Vane controlled. After they marry and she became a lady, their relationship continues to be about such things as the conflict for women between love and work. Contrast the male detective, who inevitably sacrifices love and intimacy to work, who we are expected to congratulate on his moral courage. The detective traffics in cool (rational) knowledge, incompatible with love and parenting, both definitely warm and irrational. Also, Vane stands in distinct contrast to Poirot in the way she ages from novel to novel. The first of her children is born during the course of one story, "The Haunted Policeman." Along with the matter of warm knowledge, this is a step toward the realism that Chandler demanded in the later evolution of the noir formula, and that the closely related spy novel had been pursuing since Maugham's *Ashenden* in 1928, if not Conrad's earlier work.

The Police Procedural: Detection Without Magic

Between them, Christie and Sayers embodied all of the Classic forms except one: the police procedural.[11] Their female detectives, especially, began to push at the borders of cool knowledge. At the same time, the opposite reform was at work, which was the industrial, Fordist wish to perfect the process of detection for the maximum efficiency and the certainty of outcome. It is easy to see how this impulse too could do social work, could address itself to commonly held beliefs. Perfection and efficiency are moral as well as economic values, and as I suggested in the discussion of machine and hand-made cultures, they are aesthetic values as well. People who value perfection and efficiency for one reason are likely to value the others as well. One hypothesis for verification would be the rise in popularity of the police procedural accompanied by a decline in approval for behavior of the sort that the '20s are known for: drunkenness, crime, loose morals and loose women, bohemianism, cubism, and free verse.

The best examples of the police procedural are not so portentous and inflated as that. For the earliest exemplars we turn to R. Austin Freeman (career 1907–1940, series detective Dr. John Thorndyke) and Freeman Wills Crofts (career 1921–1951, series detective Inspector French). Thorndyke was the first detective to make direct use of medical knowledge and is thus also an ancestor of the forensic procedural.

Although not first in the field, Crofts (in *The Cask*) consolidated procedural elements that had been implicit in the English Classic and especially common in French writing because of the presumed thoroughness of French practice, inherited from Vidocq at the beginning of the nineteenth century. The nature of abduction, the dialectic of hypothesis and empirical validation, assures the importance of procedure. We will see in hard-boiled writing that when the method of detection changes to one that puts more value on warm knowledge, procedure falls away.

The procedural is an elaboration of the wish to exclude all elements from the story but the deductive through the exhaustive testing of inferences. The detective must be a member of the official police force in order to command the resources for this. The relentless, almost mindless quality of the procedural (Thorndyke is incredibly obsessive about detail) means that there will be rather few pure ones. Modern forensic dramas, which are inherently procedural, quickly find it necessary to introduce other elements such as love affairs and difficult personal histories to keep up interest. The diluted procedural is now the dominant form of the cop story. In the *Prime Suspect* series, for example, one rationale for the presence of Jane Tennison is to introduce humanizing elements (women, significantly) without sacrificing the procedural focus—Tennant can be relentless and intuitive at the same time. This tendency of rational detection to drift toward the procedural recapitulates the state of affairs in 1930, except that it is now usual to combine the contradictory elements of warm and cool in one person. The Swedish detective Kurt Wallander can be taken as example. This is a welcome development, as it shows how the malleable detective genre is able to renew itself, in this case by working out how to assimilate the ambiguities and contradictions long present in the mainstream novel without sacrificing the rationale of the detective genre.

The procedural drift has brought another change. Increasingly, since the hegemony of the Classic was broken, the unofficial detective has been harder to justify. Amateurs are now vigilantes, not generally tolerated or permitted access to the machinery of detection. In our time the home of the amateur is the historical drama and various adventure plots derived from spy stories and thrillers.[12] Cops and other people in the "detective professions"—chiefly lawyers and doctors (and accountants: remember that Ralph Henderson was an insurance investigator)—will dominate any story with a strong procedural element.

Freeman's detective, the medical Dr. John Thorndyke, first appeared in 1907. Freeman himself was a doctor, as were Conan Doyle and his creation, John Watson. Dr. Watson's practice, however, is kept largely off-stage and his expertise contributes little. Not so Thorndyke. Thorndyke's chroniclers narrate their stores in first person, giving the doctor's expertise full play, in the pure Classic tradition as developed from Holmes. Clues are presented transparently to all and the truth is made to give itself up by rational-empirical force alone. The detective is active throughout, never the beneficiary of opportunities happened upon. But the distanced affect of the English Classic taken to the extreme of the procedural cannot be sustained. In "A Mystery of the Sand-Hills" (1925) Thorndyke is at work with Anstey, then his Watson. The mystery begins with an encounter with a pile of clothes on the beach and gets bigger and bigger only because Thorndyke refuses to regard this or any other of his subsequent observations as ordinary occurrences. He does this because his chain of inductions cannot be closed. To the reader, however, Thorndyke's behavior will appear a little mysterious because we are given only partial access to his thinking. He talks to Anstey, or Anstey overhears him talking to himself. In this he resembles Holmes, and also in taking only his own counsel. (Compare the Holmes tale "The Blue Carbuncle" as a similar production of a large result from a trivial occurrence.)

Crofts's "The Mystery of the Sleeping Car Express" is a representative early procedural and typical of the Thorndyke stories as well. The omniscient narrator begins with a retrospective rehearsal of the facts. The overt emphasis is on "details, casually remarked at the time" with a distancing, anti-sensational affect. But the narrator Girard Jones cheats: "sinister little hole," "dreadful apparition" ring false as language that eschews overt emotion. The story shifts to free, indirect narration and the whole sequence of observations is then repeated as a conversation between two people in Scotland Yard. Finally, after a shift to first person, the story is repeated a third time, in the form of a dying confession. Nothing is solved. The solution is discovered literally by accident. When Girard Jones resumes in his own voice we find that he possesses the true answer only because he has had the fortune to come upon a bicycle accident in which a man who proves to be the criminal has had a fatal injury and wants to confess what he has done. This is a pure puzzle, three times narrated, derived from the device of the dying confession, which has been used since time immemorial to escape from a narrative cul-de-sac. The truth is that the pure procedural makes for poor storytelling. The end is foreordained, the method is stultifying. The only other option is failure.

Other innovators of the English Classic preferred to tinker with the form or explore its limits rather than seek the extreme of the procedural. Ernest Bramah, for instance, invented the blind detective Max Carrados for this purpose. In "The Coin of Dionysius," the first Carrados story, the bulk of the narrative is used to establish Carrados's credentials as a detective, to introduce Carlyle, the person who will become Carrados's sidekick, and (looking forward to Batman) also the butler Parkinson. Carlyle presages Rex Stout's Archie Goodwin, legs to the also disabled (by obesity) Nero Wolfe.

Bramah's narration is omniscient except when it is expedient to use Carlyle as the medium in order to excuse not telling the reader some fact or other (which is a violation of the fairness rule). The mystery itself is solved through special knowledge possessed by Carrados (also a violation). This is not expertise such as Holmes's knowledge of tobacco ash, though Carrados does possess such expertise in his knowledge of rare coins and other matters, but simply that Carrados happens to have had an experience that throws light on the case. This is a kind of knowledge, accidental in origin, available to Carrados alone, and is not the product of the empirical phase of abduction. When the narrative begins, this empirical phase is already over and we have only the Holmesian opening demonstration of virtuosity to form the whole story.

Anthony Berkeley (Francis Iles, career 1925–1939) was a founder of the Crime Club that institutionalized the Rules. His detective Roger Sheringham is in the mold of the upper-class amateur, but less foppish than Wimsey. "The Avenging Chance" is a condensed version of *The Poisoned Chocolates Case*, Berkeley's best tale. This story seems to be told to an unknown listener by one Moresby, but that is a feint. The method is omniscient. Compared with realist work written after Raymond Chandler's noir reformulation, such as Cornell Woolrich's "Rear Window," the plot is conventional and implausible.

The tinkerers are interesting but ineffective. Still, the English Classic could afford to be tolerant and inclusive. No other tradition or formula has dominated the field to the extent that the English Classic did in the 1920s. It is still the common tradition in England and Europe, where hard-boiled is regarded as "The American Style," and still interpenetrates its successors so thoroughly as to foil naïve periodization. Here, for example, from 1950 at the height of Mike Hammer's brutal reign, is a passage from Michael Gilbert's *Smallbone Deceased*: "Mr. Hoffman nodded. He was a qualified accountant attaché to the Fraud Squad. A man who hunted down facts with the passionless pleasure of a butterfly collector and pinned them to his board with the same cold precision."

Here truly is the cold man to set against Holmes.

The Classic on Film

Although it wasn't done until recently (with a few exceptions already mentioned), an English Classic is fairly easy to translate into film. The cast is limited and the characters are well differentiated, though the apparent differences may prove false. The action is straightforwardly presented and ought to be free of devices such as showing us the act of murder but hiding the actor's face. It is fairly easy to free the *mise-en-scène* from the kind of commentary that would draw our attention to particular clues, a practice common, almost necessary, in horror films and thrillers. These invariably attempt to ratchet up the suspense with appositely timed music and such devices. The main difficulty, given the omniscient narration common to (indeed, forced upon) all filmed Classics, is to keep the spectator from finding out what the detective knows until the time is ripe — that is, to preserve both the Rules and the suspense. Most contemporary films, which benefit as we shall see from both a relaxation of rules in general and from the introduction of subjectivity, get around this problem either by not allowing the detective to know more than we do or by dispensing with omniscience. This second option replicates the textual experience of a printed Classic. Narrative suspense in an English Classic depends less on the overt events than on solving the whodunit puzzle. There may be a little frisson in anticipation of the nearly inevitable second murder or of the consequences of the final revelation, but the atmosphere of an English Classic is calm in the face of the most bizarre and awful events. It is methodical, and above all gentlemanly. The detective is always a gentleman (or greater — *Lord* Peter Wimsey). Ungentlemanly characters come in for some subversive, class-bashing fun. The pervasive weakness of the tradition is that too much calm civilization too easily becomes comedy. This is a significant weakness, as comedy is one of the best means for disarming the threat posed by rationality, and with that threat gone the iconic heart of the genre evaporates, leaving nothing but the butterfly collector.

In the 1930s there was a surprising resistance to detection as a good thing — surprising in view of the massive popularity of the genre, not so surprising when we remember that the power of the detective to excise and reforge is not necessarily benign. The emotional grip of the genre, first explicated by practitioners of the Classic form and later elaborated by Chandler in his criticism of it, had this plot: an act of violence (murder) disturbs the sense of order and predictability necessary to middle-class comforts. The basis of these comforts are intelligent planning and rational thought, coupled with a materialist outlook and a standard of proof requiring physical evidence and an unbroken chain of causality. By this means the truth is recovered and our comfort and safety are assured. Entailed in this security is the belief that causality can be counted on and that rational decisions will effect suitable results. This program is highly vulnerable to existential doubt. Absent (or at least overtly absent) are the emotional imperatives driving this narrative. One did not ask, in the books and movies that put forward these ideals, why such a state of affairs was so ardently sought. That would have been self-evident. This is an Enlightenment program of scientific inquiry. The detective is a form of scientist and brings with him the cultural values and qualities associated with the scientist. Given the spiritual emergency that is built into the heart of the detective plot, we would expect the detective to be welcomed as a savior and regarded as a hero.

Such was not the case. The initial transference of the tropes of detection to the new medium of film revealed an uneasiness about intellect and the products of the mind. This ancient attitude, in our time expressed as a fear of science — weapons, threatening new technology, genetic mutation and monsters, meddling with life itself — was in an earlier time realized in the form of Frankenstein, Dr. Jekyll, the golem, and such German Expressionist films as *M*. These stories created a standard for representing the sources of power controlled by the *shamus* or shaman, a figure whose knowledge gives him authority over life and death. The Detective, among other things, is a sorcerer, a witch-doctor. His knowledge is forbidden. If it were necessary for the Detective to hold his dramatic own against Jekyll or M, then the English Classic movie simply could not be made. The Classic formula is too loaded with devices for hedging round the Detective. What would have had to be done was to provide the thrill of violence without actual danger to anyone except the nearly anonymous victim. In remakes of the Classic stories we now accept this as light entertainment. This was not the spirit in which these stories were forged.

The requirements of filmed storytelling trivialized the English Classic story, giving us Philo Vance and, unfortunately, Charlie Chan. In the 1930s when the English Classic was the hegemonic tradition in print, there were no rivals against which the English Classic could dispute the high ground. These stories were vulnerable. As movies they lacked drama and the genre was not taken seriously enough to protect its stories from being mangled or exploited.[13]

Basil Rathbone played Holmes with complete seriousness in his *Hound of the Baskervilles* of 1939; in 1930 he had played Philo Vance with the same gravity. But Rathbone brackets a decade in which Vance, like the genre itself, grew steadily more light-hearted and light-minded. The same drift can be found in the airy *Kennel Murder Case*, with Dick Powell playing Vance somewhat as he did Nick Charles four years later. All this came to an abrupt end in 1939. In *Calling Philo Vance* the comic aesthete is abruptly transformed into a muscular spy and an excuse for swashbuckling adventure. The filmed tradition came to an end here, in effect strangled with its own rules.

Marginalization

One of the features of the Classic we notice at once is the class bias in the exclusion from any significant role of servants, low-born persons (such as professional criminals always are), women (Rzepka 144–151, looking ahead to the psycho-intuitive tradition), and presumably anyone not white and Christian. Wilkie Collins's use of women and blacks (East Indians) was deliberate, a repudiation of exactly this feature of the then-nascent genre. One reason for this is rule three: The story must concentrate exclusively on rational processes, without distracting love interests, literary description, irrelevant character development, and the like. Given the pre-existing class bias, the intrusion of such characters would violate this rule.

Yet again we confront the problem of the female detective. In the woman we have a less threatening figure who does not command the power of cool knowledge and so could be filmed with less potential affront to moviegoers' expectations. There would be no complaints that she had not been given a power she never had.

Until 1935, women in detective movies were simply props serving a purpose similar to the maid who drops the breakfast tray on discovering the body. *The Casino Murder Case* introduces two new types, the Dame (a hard, cynical sort) and her foil the Lush, a more sympathetic character because softer, more emotional, more *womanly*. In the dame and the lush we recognize two of the stock characters of noir — one at the party and the other outside on the street, cadging a light for her cigarette.

The next step was to combine the Lush and the Dame into the pert female sidekick, an Audrey Hepburn type. Women are useful as sidekicks because their limitations (warm, emotional, physically weak) assure that they will not usurp too much of the detective's centrality and so they can afford to be portrayed as both brainy and intuitive. They can be as pert as necessary so long as they cry at the worst moments. Marple was of this sort. She solved the case, then deferred to the official male detective.

In 1930 Dashiell Hammett published a novel, *The Maltese Falcon*.[14] It is interesting to compare a sequence from *Dangerous Female* (1931, an early film version of Hammett's novel) with the 1941 film *The Maltese Falcon* and a film from the Falcon series (also 1941). The 1931 Sam Spade is a sleazy womanizer. Both the Falcon and the 1941 Spade are cosmopolitan (and womanizers), but the resemblance stops there. The Falcon is a wealthy dilettante with a pointless and completely superfluous "secret" identity. Bogart's version of Sam Spade is genuinely secretive, possibly dangerous, and streetwise. More important, Brigid O'Shaugnessey, the eponymous dangerous female, became in 1941 truly dangerous, sufficiently an opponent to Spade to be worthy of his long explanation at the end of why he is sending her over, a speech that defines the entire noir tradition for all time.

Perry Mason was another epicure and womanizing detective in his original film incarnation. Della Street is obviously his mistress, whereas the 1941 Spade would not have touched Della's counterpart, Spade's Girl Friday Precious. The commedia coroner from the Vance films makes a good reincarnation with Perry. Paul Drake is a thug but still a functionary, ceding his sidekick role to the Pert Dame, Della.[15]

The 1931 movie was conflicted in other respects. At the beginning Spade speaks Chinese, which Hammett's detective Spade does not. The use of Chinatown is only to heighten the drama with a spurious exotic intrigue. Spade's business partner Miles Archer is murdered in Chinatown. After that China has no further role. The 1941 film returns Archer's murder to where Hammett put it, at the intersection of Bush and Stockton, near but not within Chinatown. The sense of menace is still there, but it now emanates from the murder and from Spade himself.

The Classic Detective, with the exception of Poirot, has never been filmed with any respect or thoroughness. That this could be so is in part because of the dramatic obstacles the formula posed to the movies' need for spectacle. By the time the movies had become technically and aesthetically sophisticated enough, the power had moved on to a new formula, significantly one named for its portrayal in film: noir.

4

Psycho-Intuitive and Noir

Warm Knowledge

By the early 1930s the original aspirations of the detective genre had reached their apotheosis in the English Classic tradition. In the following years, as it aged, the Classic story began to seem more and more artificial; that is, unable to do the pressing social work needed. Post–war nostalgia for the old stability had abated.[1] Economic depression, post-war debts and the failure of the Versaillles Treaty, looming prospects of a new war, all made the genteel country-house mystery seem irrelevant and the police procedural inadequate. If the genre were to remain of interest fundamental changes were needed.

What followed were some years of mixed forms, until noir emerged in the late 1930s as the dominant formula. During those years a crucial shift in sensibility took place, which was the new importance given to warm knowledge. Sherlock Holmes, the first mature Detective, has a reputation as a strictly rational man, a cold person devoted entirely to the analytical path to knowledge. My remarks concerning Holmes were intended to reveal the falsity of this interpretation and to expose the artistic temperament mixed into Holmes's character, particularly his use of guessing to throw up testable hypotheses. Holmes was particularly good at guessing because his openness to others, the empathy that kept him alive to possibilities others discounted, simply gave him more material to work with. To make the contrast with analytical knowledge clear, I termed this alternative knowledge *warm*. This warm/cold terminology follows the common judgment that thought and feeling are different modes, valued differently. In the Classic formula the practice of detection is analytical, uncontaminated by feelings, which we regard as metaphorically warm. *Warmhearted*, we say. *Hot-blooded*, equating temperature with fervency, anger, passion — all those feelings that preclude or exclude rational, that is cold, thought.

The Rules that governed the Classic formula were not compatible with a felt life of moral complexity. In this there was a sharp contrast with the then-new entertainment of the movies. Film does not portray cerebration well. Its strengths are in storytelling, event, and physical detail. Film is warm.[2]

Stephen Kern, in his book *A Cultural History of Causality: Science, Murder Novels, and Systems of Thought* (Princeton, 2004), characterizes this shift from cool knowledge to warm as one from Victorian linear reasoning to contemporary systems thinking, a different distinction from the contrast I have been making between rational and emotional forms of knowledge. He makes the connection between the emotions and a system of reasoning thus: the shift "from a linear causal model of emotions as emerging from some inherent defect or sin to the ways they are generated in complex feedback networks" rather than by exterior forces such as destiny or God. This opens the way for the Detective to incorporate feelings and moods into a system of thought without losing what Heidegger called the sense of uncanniness and uncertainty characteristic of the emotions—the sense that formerly had disqualified the psycho-intuitive as a form of knowledge.

The inwardness that Freud brought to our attention changed our ideas about crime as well. The "crime of passion" could be seen as emerging from a failure of the will to control the emotions and opened the legal/moral question of whether a person could be held responsible for such a crime. Thus the insanity defense, a quandary still.[3] And we see the same process at work in the increasing tendency of novelists to align with characters' feelings and to tell a story inwardly, thereby opening doubts as to the existence of an objective truth and creating unresolvable questions about what happened. Narrative ambiguity and polysemy are inconsistent with cold knowledge.

Under pressure of a change in our understanding of the way the world works, from the time of Sherlock Holmes to our present condition, it was inevitable that the Classic formula should be discarded and replaced by a new sort of detective story. At the same time, nostalgia for the old certainties goes some way to explaining the persistence of Classic elements in the subsequent new genre forms, just as we will see that post–World War II nostalgia for unquestioned accountability explains something of the persistence of noir elements. Similarly, the newer traumas of Vietnam and 9–11, and vulnerabilities created by our mediated and networked connections to the external world, have helped to create a nostalgia for a time when what we took for causes had an obvious relation to effects and a constant probabilistic calculation of risk was not a feature of everyday life. By gradually stripping away certainty, accountability, and predictability it becomes difficult to understand how a detective story about the getting and deployment of knowledge could be constructed. The further work of this book will be driven by this conundrum.

If this is the tale we are to tell it is important to be clear now, when we are examining the first of these momentous shifts—that from the Classic to the noir — just what systems thinking is, even though the full consequences for the detective genre will not be seen for another sixty years.

Systems Theory, Fields, and Complexity

My remarks will be summary.[4] These ideas are broadly accessible in the work of the semiotician Umberto Eco; in structuralist, post-structuralist, and other postmodern writing; as well as in work in communications theory, linguistics, mathematics, anthropology, social theory, and other disciplines.

Cartesian and Systems Thinking

Cartesian co-ordinates were invented by the mathematician for whom they are named for the purpose of unambiguously locating a point in two- or three-dimensional space. Longitude and latitude are a familiar manifestation of Cartesian space. By extension, Cartesian thinking tries to locate objects in a system of classification. A dictionary is a good example of this. The Cartesian system is a closed one. This is not to say it is static or finite: the problem of continuous change, when two points get closer and closer but never converge, was mastered by calculus, by which we are able to say just where this imaginary convergence is to be found, which is at the junction of somewhere and infinity. Unfortunately, some things do not have a precise location. Wittgenstein pointed out that words are like this. This is why dictionary definitions are circular, and why the classificatory urge will never be satisfied except in the simplest of cases.

Systems thinking does not concern itself with objects, entities, or anything of the sort, but rather with the relationships between these things. The recipient of a message, for example, will need to decode it; that is to say, interpret the approximate meaning in terms intelligible to himself. It is sometimes possible to negotiate these decodings with the sender of the message and approach (but unlike calculus, not determine) an agreed-upon message content. Such negotiation is an example of systems thinking.

The Field

The field is a tensioned space resembling a chunk of the universe dynamically structured by interacting forces. A traversal of such a space by an object carrying forces of its own will be unpredictable. Here lies the work of chaos theory, where small differences create large effects. It is the realm of relationships and vectors replacing the earlier Cartesian one of objects and positions. It is the realm of continuous and incalculable transformation.

Simple and Complex, Open and Closed Systems

A complex system is one that cannot be completely described in its own terms. Mathematics is such a system, as Gödel demonstrated with his incom-

TABLE 3. OPEN AND CLOSED FORM

Element	Open Form
Design	Avoidance of teleology (design) and a preference for rhizomic, genealogical, path-dependent structures. The primary difficulty here is that an attack on design seems to endanger the values of humanism and the Enlightenment. Explore what can be salvaged, and look at threats to open form from the storytelling notions of "plot" and "evil."
Closure	Avoidance of closure. Parse the concept of "unfinished," ask whether something can be made unfinished on purpose or only left that way, explore the simulated openness of very large or intricate writings, propose that the desire people have to be done with things springs from a distaste for the messiness of life.
Totalizing	Seek local knowledge, avoid totalizing narratives. Encyclopedic aspirations are linked to the egotistic Romanticism which High Modernism was in reaction to, but which it accepted nevertheless. One difficulty here is that to attack individualism seems to deprivilege expertise.
Transcendental	Seek relativity. If all patterns are local (characterized as thick spots in the Tao), claims to objectivity are unwarranted. High Modernism followed two paths in the attempt to avoid the consequences of radical relativism. The heirs of James and Faulkner on the path of multiple truths ended by aestheticizing experience, while the minimalists (heirs of Hemingway and Beckett) simply abandoned ambitious speech for trivialities.
Certainty	Radical uncertainty, by introducing an arbitrariness fatal to patterning, undercuts drama and is thus fatal to storytelling. Is a locally patterned interconnected group of events anything but an arbitrary construction?

pleteness theorem. Or, as the Zen remark goes, mind cannot understand the mind. Complex systems are said to be open. They are dynamic, incompletely defined, fuzzy at the edges, always in flux. They are systems not of objects but of fields. One of the main tasks of our time, which is at the root of the culture wars that plague us, is to discover ways of working in conditions where everything is relative, when, as is said, it's semiotics all the way down.

Table 3 outlines the literary results of a confrontation with open form when the field to be traversed is cultural. From this it will be easy to see what the problem is for a detective story.

Features of Complex (Open) Systems

I. There are no invariant organizing principles, no fixed experience of oneself and the world. Hence there is a need to organize the unfamiliar and inevitably incomplete. Everything belongs everywhere, selection is always. This helps to explain the importance of affect (to be taken up soon) and the interplay between sameness and difference (Derrida).

II. The origin and deployment of knowledge: we can have only local knowledge (Claude Lévy-Strauss, most famously in *The Raw and the Cooked*, and later, Clifford Geertz). This requires the concept of the *frame*, which in social theory is a schema of interpretation that people rely on to understand and respond to experiences. In art, examples abound from 1915 in Dada, and there is the notorious exhibition of a toilet, signed R. Mutt, by Marcel Duchamp. As used in media studies, sociology, and psychology, framing refers to the social construction of a phenomenon (Erving Goffman). A frame defines the packaging of a rhetoric in such a way as to encourage or discourage certain interpretations. These factors ensure that explanations are genealogical (Heidegger) and meaning is not independent but a property of family resemblance (Wittgenstein). Duchamp's toilet carries, from its presence in an exhibition, a resemblance to the family of works of art.

III. Complexity. The mind cannot understand the mind (Kurt Gödel). Each element of the system is ignorant of the system as a whole, individual elements are solipsistic and embedded, and complexity is not a property of objects (in existentialism, of Being) but the product of the mind trying to understand itself (existential becoming).

IV. Recursion is non-linear, self-organizing, and must take into account the interaction between history, current state, and system environment.

V. Affect (experience): Modes of patterning of experience give rise to the actual, unique, emergent experience at hand. Unformatted perceptions give rise to the feeling of wholeness, or the Tao. The distinction between action and expectation gives rise to the feeling of freedom from intent and purpose (existential freedom).

Warm Detection

For the ordinary reader these features of an open system were not yet known, nor were they part of the everyday culture of 1940. Yet for someone versed in these ideas it will be easy to see how their spread might be driven by moral uncertainties, an increasing uneasiness over events inter-connected in such ways as to make common sense inadequate or even wrong, feelings of helplessness and horror from the experience of the Depression, memories of the last war and the dread of a new one. We were in need of a person who could confront these new realities and return with something to ameliorate them. This was something beyond the capacity of the purely rational detective.[5]

The admission of warm knowledge to the process of detection was, as it proved, the means by which the figure of the Detective could be revitalized. But of course, the transition could not be so simple as putting on a new shirt. The first practitioner of warm knowledge was the French inspector Jules Maigret, the creation of Georges Simenon, but the Maigret stories did not become popular in English until after World War II.[6] Warm knowledge had earlier been one of the working tools of Dashiell Hammett's Continental Op, an American, and it is as we have seen an important component of Sherlock Holmes's pragmatic use of abduction. When the hegemony of the Classic finally gave way it was not to the civilized policeman Maigret but to a different person, the ungentlemanly and morally ambiguous Private Investigator. An understanding of this complex transition is necessary to untangle future developments.

It is important also now to be clear about terminology. Maigret did not simply *intuit* the solution to a crime. This a form of what I have called "magic" or "black box" detection. The black box has a narrative advantage in excluding the reader from the detective's thoughts, but this can be done in other ways: by giving the narrative to a relatively clueless sidekick such as Holmes's Watson, for example, or Poirot's Hastings. When the omniscient author simply refuses to give readers the facts, or, more annoying (and destructive of the spirit of the Rules), when the detective narrates his own tale, either in first person or third-person indirect, and hides his results simply for suspense, this is narrative bad faith.

Maigret's way is not magic. He begins as Holmes did, by guessing. The difference is that Holmes obtained the material from which he formed his hypotheses from observation of physical details such as scuffed shoes, calluses, and cigar ash. Maigret's hypotheses derive from a cultivated empathy with his potential adversaries. This is a nonverbal, non-analytic process, but once the process has produced reasons to investigate further, that investigation is conducted in the usual way. I will call Maigret's method *psycho-intuitive.*

The Continental Op proceeds in an apparently similar way. Over time, however, the violence inherent in Hammett's millieux worked a change in his detectives' methods. Neither Sam Spade nor his contemporary, Chandler's Philip Marlowe, forgo inference chains and proof, but they make the job simpler by threatening to do so. As Spade says to Brigid O'Shaugnessy at the end of *The Maltese Falcon,* "Don't be too sure I'm as crooked as I'm supposed to be. That kind of reputation might be good business—bringing in high-priced jobs and making it easier to deal with the enemy."[7]

I will call this mode *noir*. Noir is of course a film term, used after World War II by French critics writing in the *Cahiers du Cinema* to describe a very specific atmosphere and outlook that they found in a particular, small set of American movies. By applying the word to fiction I mean to identify the sort of story that might become a noir movie: morally dark, streaked with emotion and violence, but that still proceeds by the methods of detection. By "noir" I also mean to distinguish such a story from what followed it, which is the hard-boiled tale. I will analyze the hard-boiled mode separately, but for now the essence of the distinction is that hard-boiled stories replaced the threat of violence with actual violence and used this in a crucial shift from evidence and proof to confession. Hard-boiled and noir are very often used interchangeably. This is quite wrong.

The Transition from Classic to Noir

Particularly in England, the Classic formula continued to be the dominant one throughout the '30s. However, looking back on that period with present knowledge, we would expect to find psycho-intuitive elements becoming more common in later stories. As it happened, rather than a gradual infusion we find a sudden paradigm shift of the sort that befell the Philo Vance movies. Throughout the '30s Vance, an American creation, continued to be portrayed as a foppish English aristocrat. After a dozen films beginning in 1929, this stereotype was abruptly broken in 1940 in *Calling Philo Vance*. Once thin and elegant, Vance suddenly becomes muscular and manly; once remote and cerebral, he becomes a spy who infiltrates a German ship's crew from which he makes a hair's-breadth escape. Initially played by William Powell as a lightweight Nick Charles, the 1940 Vance was played by James Stephenson, who the year before had appeared in a dozen movies with titles such as *Torchy Blane in Chinatown, Devil's Island, Wanted by Scotland Yard, and Confessions of a Nazi Spy.*

In considering the transition from Classic to noir, then, we are not to expect a gradual replacement of the one by the other, but rather an allegiance to the Classic suddenly broken about 1940. What we are looking for is, within the continuing presence of the Classic mode in the decade of the '30s, some growing but unacknowledged acceptance of warm knowledge.

C.P. Snow, *Death Under Sail* (1932)[8]

This novel is of interest for three reasons: because its early date makes it a possible benchmark; because of Snow's role in the later two-cultures controversy,[9] in which he argued for a balance between the cool and warm temperaments (the scientific and artistic cultures); and because of his other crime novel, the 1979 *A Coat of Varnish*. The 1979 book is psycho-intuitive through and through. The Chronicler is more interested in the victim (both a friendly and a romantic interest) than the criminal and the solution to the crime, pursued only desultorily, is never found. *Death Under Sail* is thus a likely place to look for a positive view of warm knowledge.

The narrative structure is a straightforward English country-house type, with a Chronicler (Ian Cartel) speaking in first person. There are two detectives: an incompetent official one and (the real detective) an amateur, Finbow, invoked in the usual way to set things right and to return a disturbed society to the *status quo ante*.

Ian, however, is more interested in the people of the story and their emotions than in the facts or the inference chains of detection. Birrell, the official detective, is an enthusiast with a mystical element to his otherwise rational methods. "It's the tempo of this crime which is the feature of it!" Birrell exclaims. "Murder's just like any other art. And what characterizes a work of art is its tempo. And the tempo of one artist is always different from the tempo of another. Find who thinks and works in the tempo of this murder and you've got the man!" (pp. 48–49). Birrell's immediate ancestors are Poirot's Inspector Japp and Holmes's Lestrade. These were grave and not incompetent men, but ordinary ones who lacked the Detective's extraordinary abilities. The descent from Lestrade to Birrell can be seen also in the series of Philo Vance movies, in which the district attorney becomes ever more comic and inconsequential, and at the same time in successive portrayals actually physically smaller.

Finbow is a close copy of Holmes ("Still it's absurd to guess until you've given me all the facts," he says at the outset [p. 49]), but he is nevertheless an observer of human behavior in the Maigret fashion. "People talk about material truth and psychological truth as though if you are interested in the one you can't be interested in the other," Finbow says (p. 67). In fact, the entire inference chain is based on an assessment of personality. Finbow admits (p. 192) a lack of material evidence. But more important to us is that the only fact, the one that validates the whole chain, is kept from us as from all the characters, and the final "proof" is accomplished by psychological pressure that causes the murderer to confess by killing himself. Throughout, a great deal of attention is paid to love and other irrational motives, and at the end Finbow remarks concerning the main suspect's innocence that she (the suspect) had given "an extremely convincing impersonation of a murderess. Not consciously, of course. She wouldn't have done it so well had it been conscious" (p. 219). The device of a suicide made to look like a murder is taken from the Holmes tale "The Problem of Thor Bridge" — a device at once proved to be fake — and there are many remarks on the pretense of stories based purely on deduction; the police procedural is treated with particular contempt.

This is what we predicted: that under the surface of the Classic story we would find more use of psycho-intuitive methods and warm knowledge, though perhaps not so early and thoroughly as this.

Freeman Wills Crofts

Crofts began as an engineer, so it is not surprising that his first novel, *The Cask*, published in 1920 at the beginning of the Classic period, should proceed by methodically collecting every bit of testimony and material evidence. The point of this is twofold: to trace the movements of a cask full of gold sovereigns and a dead body, and to use this information to break the alibi of the criminal. Supposition and inference are strictly blocked; the novel rejects both warm and cool knowledge for a mechanical discovery process. Obviously, as a narrative strategy this is limited, but elements of the procedural are present in most detective stories, for example the modern forensic tale, and the relative absence of these elements, as we have seen in the case of *Death Under Sail*, is an index for the opposite, psycho-intuitive strategy.

It is of no passing interest that the procedural eliminates the Detective, while the psycho-intuitive and its noir successor elevate this figure to a prominence that the Classic mode hedged on in trying to assuage its worries about invoking a dangerous shaman bound up with the need for a rational craftsman to repair matters. The rise of warm knowledge confronts this issue, because the exigencies of the times seem to require a shaman, while increasingly the craftsmanship of Poirot is seen as ineffectual. Paradoxically, the psycho-intuitive detective, Maigret being the exemplar, seems to be an ordinary working man, with a family and a home life and conventional values, quite unlike the bohemian, unpredictable Holmes. And this is true of Crofts's serial detective, Inspector French.

But is French at all psycho-intuitive? The earliest tales, *The Cask* and his much-anthologized first story "The Mystery of the Sleeping Car Express," are emphatically not. Crofts's two best Inspector French novels, *The Cheyne Mystery* (1926) and *Inspector French and the Starvel Tragedy* (1927), though they do not extend into the psycho-intuitive tradition, do ameliorate the rigidity of the earlier work. Crofts has worked hard to humanize him. French is lacking in flair — he might be called dull — but is proud of his craftsmanship without being vain. Nor is he overbearing — his manner of questioning suspects or witnesses is perceptive and sympathetic, though he is capable of applying psychological force. *The Starvel Tragedy* gives us a man who likes to be out and about (his superior chides him for looking for opportunities to travel) but has no intrepidity or taste for hardship. In contrast to the fictional detectives active in his time, French would have seemed strikingly ordinary. Most important for our present interests, he is capable of using empathy and observation of behavior to make inferences about motives. Unlike C.P. Snow's Finbow, however, French is unwilling to take more than one intuitive step without looking for some material evidence to validate it.

These qualities are those of Maigret, though less pronounced. It is *because* Maigret is an ordinary man that he is able to empathize as he does with the people he meets and to infer from this warm knowledge, as we all do, what they might be thinking and how they are likely to act. So we see again that the features of the psycho-intuitive mode have been present in the detective genre from the beginning, going back to the Gothic tale, the Sensation novel, the mainstream fiction of Bulwer-Lytton and Trollope, and Green and Conan Doyle, Father Brown and other detectives of the Edwardian period.

The oddity in this sequence is Poe, and it is likely that his credit is due to the fact that he *is* odd, that he draws attention to what he thought (and which is now a commonplace claim), which is that the necessary and sufficient first cause of the detective genre and the defining characteristic of the Detective: cold knowledge. With the rise of the psycho-intuitive procedure we see that Poe's, and the English Classic's, valorization of cold knowledge was historically contingent and temporary, and that Poe's claim to be the founder of the genre is false. As readers, without the trauma caused by the unprecedently irrational European War and that frightening confrontation with nature red in tooth and claw, we are not deeply interested in the intellectual puzzles given to the purely rational detective to work out.

The interesting thing about French, then, is his resistance to any irruption from his warm life into his cold work. In *The Cheyne Mystery* he does not appear until halfway through the book. After we have seen Cheyne thrashing about trying to protect himself by (unsuccessfully) finding out the truth about his adversaries, a sort of storytelling more like the thriller to come, French's cool competence is not only in marked contrast but implicitly critical of foolish Romanticism.[10] I will take up this matter again when I come to talk about noir — the uxorious Maigret is not *enough* of a shaman — and the Neoclassic revival.

Finally we ought to look at E.C. Bentley, whose early book *Trent's Last Case* (1912) is called by Barzun and Taylor the first send-up of the detective genre.[11] Twenty-four years later he co-authored *Trent's Own Case* (1936).[12] What has happened in that time to a detective who *began* psychointuitively?

Philip Trent, though he does work part-time as a genteel detective, is first an artist, and he is introduced in *Trent's Last Case* interrupted from painting, which he leaves reluctantly. Detecting is an attractive nuisance. And in the end, Trent falls in love with a suspect, makes wrong inferences, bungles the case, and quits the business. Perhaps Bentley intended to parody the emerging Classic, but what he has done is to belittle and reject the same warm knowledge that the Classic likewise rejects. Trent works psycho-intuitively, but Bentley considers that to be a failing and he expects his readers to agree. Trent is inept and naïve, and his preference for art and love was not thought at the time something a detective should have.

"The Genuine Tabard," a story from 1938 collected in *Trent Intervenes,* concerns a swindle. An American is sold a fake herald's tabard. Trent hears of it and proves it is false with an impressive disquisition on the history of the English arms, but otherwise he does little toward the solution. He is, however, in this story the soul of competence, and quite unlike his 1912 self.

What are we to make of this seemingly retrograde development? Simply that it is not so. It is only that the 1938 Trent has learned the business and Bentley is writing a straight story in the Classic mode, which he preferred right down to the end, when Maigret could be read in English and the noir shift put an end to hegemony of the English Classic.

Maigret

The Maigret tales actually sacrifice very little of the traditional formula. Aside from his moments of insight, Maigret reaches his conclusions in the ordinary way of reasoning. He operates within an institution created to protect the commonweal, he has the resources for gathering evidence and enforcing his conclusions given him as a policeman, and he has confidantes with whom he can speak freely if he wishes. The permission to be intuitive allows him to be emotive rather than merely quirky and makes it easier to humanize him. He can have a marriage and a family life, ordinary friends, and the story can dwell on and even utilize these things without dawdling or digression. He need not play the hero—indeed, one of his cases is solved by Madame Maigret. Most importantly for future development, Maigret can sympathize with criminals and victims in new ways without sacrificing his membership in the society he is required to protect. This leave to criticize gives him leave to obtain evidence by moral suasion or psychological pressure (a shift made even easier by the requirement of the French legal system for a confession). Compared to the Classic detectives, Maigret has an enormous affective range: disgust, anger, righteousness, uxorious domesticity, delight in simple pleasures and an enthusiasm for food and drink.

Genre and Social Pressures

We have reached the point of the first major transformation of a genre that had been created and perfected over a century and a half, which from this point and in half that time will undergo fission, four more transformations, and a decadence that threatens to end the genre altogether. In several places I have claimed that the detective genre responds to changes in the social milieu in which it lives, following its readers' hopes and fears into new ways of storytelling that nevertheless preserve the figure of the Detective on which the genre is based. Before taking a closer look at Maigret it might be well to review the connection between genre and social change.

The detective genre is a conservative medium, as are all literary formulas, constrained by the imperatives of mass taste and the profitability of a brand and so not inclined to defy expectations. With its origins in Victorian ideas of linear causality and Cartesian systems thinking, the Classic story consists of events arranged one after another around a dialectic of norm and transgression, expectation frustrated and restored. The detective formula is not comfortable with transgression and is constructed so as to suppress it as quickly as possible, whereas the literary novel relishes transgression as the generator of drama and prolongs it as long as possible. The misunderstandings and discreet silences that drive a Jane Austen novel would produce only longeurs in an Agatha Christie, or in the more consciously literary Dorothy Sayers's *The Nine Tailors,* a certain reluctance to detect anything. But if transgressions were to be simply shrugged off this would mean that crimes would go unsolved (or what is more irritating, be solved and found not to merit punishment and thus *not be crimes*). Outside the Classic tradition the unpunished crime is a social comment; in noir, a bitter one. Unpunished or no, the crime must be solved. Not to solve it is a radical statement about the impossibility of knowledge that, if accepted, would destroy the usefulness of the genre as an unguent for the injuries of social change. The Classic tale assuages any doubt that experience is solvable, that there is knowledge to be had that will alleviate the fears the detective is supposed to calm *by solving the crime.*

The detective genre, then, is caught in a relationship it can neither accept nor reject. Literary novels, less constrained, have flirted from the beginning with the possibilities of this condition. Most did not go so far as *Tristram Shandy* did to dramatize inaccessible knowledge in the form of unresolvable stories. A detective story sensitive to the complexities of life, accepting that most evidence is tainted and most knowledge is partial, concluding that most judgments are suspect — conditions ordinarily unsurprising — would be warm indeed. But there is one magisterial, magnificent example: *Crime and Punishment.* The great ancestor of Jules Maigret is Porfiry Petrovich. And it is because of Raskolnikov that Petrovich was invented.

Raskolnikov has killed an old woman for a bit of money, an existential crime much like Camus's Stranger. There is no evidence. Porfiry Petrovich is convinced of his guilt in the way that so many detectives since have come away from an interview muttering, "He's lying." If the matter is to be not *solved* but resolved, Raskolnikov must confess, and this Porfiry Petrovich cannot make him do. The will to confess is Raskolnikov's and is bound to his longing for salvation and expiation, which in Raskolnikov's case is not a longing for forgiveness, which will not be given, nor for admission to a realm of the saved, but to the realm of living people — still unsaved it is true, but a realm in which love and hope may be found. To join the living world, Raskolnikov must assent to be harrowed and for that he must confess. He wants to confess, but he cannot make the existential choice. All this Porfiry Petrovich knows, and so he knows that to resolve the crime he must be both patient and relentless. Through him, Raskolnikov, returned purged from the dead, will be able to minister to others.

This explicitly Christian reading of *Crime and Punishment* is, I believe, the standard one. What has not been noticed is that Porfiry Petrovich is a Detective of a specific sort. Like Maigret, his method is psycho-intuitive. The need for a confession is characteristic also of the post-war hard-boiled variant discussed in the next chapter, but the hard-boiled detective extracts his confession by force. What stands between Maigret and Mike Hammer is World War II and the Cold War bellicosity that followed. We became a society that had seen its orderly security and predictability slip away, and that moreover had been told, by Gödel, Shannon, Wittgenstein, Lévi-Strauss, Sartre, and the discovery of the quantum world, and in so many other ways, that the old society was an illusion and a sham. The noir ethic still believed that a rational accommodation was possible. The atomic bomb vaporized that hope. In the years since, the situation has gotten not better but worse. We now have neither Raskolnikov's way nor Holmes's, and the consequences for the figure of the Detective will be our exploration for the rest of this book.

None of this concerns Porfiry Petrovich. He understands the need for confession and sees that in Raskolnikov. Having seen it, he knows how to make use of it. His insight is psychological and religious and points to one of the origins of the genre in the quest, in the Detective's search for moral transformation that we hired him to find.

Georges Simenon

There are 75 Maigret novels in English,[13] plus two earlier ones in which Maigret appears as a secondary character.[14] The first English versions were published between 1932 and 1934, six out of the 17 written up to that point. Simenon took a break from Maigret until 1944. In the fifties and sixties first English publication was usually in *Argosy* or *Ellery Queen's Mystery Magazine*, with book publication as much as ten years later. Maigret's anglophone popularity thus dates primarily from the period of the hard-boiled to the Neo-classic transition discussed in chapter 6. Despite his being far from unknown in the half-century before that, the history of his popularity in English suggests that for us he is a nostalgic figure.

Simenon's writing methods have gotten much attention — Assouline devotes 65 pages, including a whole chapter, to them in his biography.[15] Maigret's creator was indeed a factory, writing a dozen Maigrets a year at times. He wrote in seclusion, taking a week plus three days for revision. Like Graham Greene, Simenon distinguished between his serious novels and the Maigrets. The serious ones were written in pencil and revised on a typewriter. Maigret novels were entirely typed. As many writers noticed on the advent of the word-processor, technology-aided writing can be less careful, and Simenon's practice reflects his judgment on the importance of the Maigrets, but again like Greene, this is not the critics' view.

Simenon was a tireless self-promoter, and his detective was deliberately nothing like those of his competition. His publisher at the beginning (1931) rejected the first ones, complaining, "They aren't detective stories. They aren't scientific.... The hero is a second-rate bureaucrat,[16] not strong, not handsome, not exceptional.... There are no riddles, and therefore no detective story."[17] But Maigret is the first fully imagined psycho-intuitive detective. He is the sort of man who, in the midst of an investigation, stops to think about catching snowflakes on his tongue as when he was a child. The plot device in the snowflake story, "Maigret's Christmas" ("Un Noël de Maigret"), had been used nine years earlier (1942) in *Félicie est là*. The earlier version is a short novel (all Maigrets are short) and Simenon used the extra space not to complicate the crime or the process of exposing it, as a Classic would have, but to expand Maigret's relationship with the former maid Félicie as he gently persuades her to admit her feelings. The genre possessed no one of Maigret's like until recently, in characters such as Donna Leon's Commissario Brunetti. It is routine to humanize a Neoclassic detective (again, see chapter 6), but the present practice is not so central to the story as this. We have quirks such as Morse's love of opera and absence of a first name; Dalgliesh is a poet; Lynley has marriage troubles—these things are referred to, but they are digressions. Not so Maigret. It is *because* he is an ordinary man that he is admired and sought out, that he agrees so readily to help, that he understands so well the feelings of the people he meets. Unlike so many of those who followed, Maigret is not on bad terms with anybody.

The Noir Shift

As we have seen, the English Classic proved unreceptive to the psycho-intuitive option but did incorporate some of the elements of warm knowledge. When the genre shifted abruptly to the noir formula in the late '30s it skipped over the Maigret-style Detective — who after all lay dormant during the war years even in his creator's workroom as a character incompatible with the times. It was the *Black Mask* authors of the pulps who perfected the noir shift. These authors came from a different milieu than the Classic authors, but they wrote during the Classic hegemony and their stories were Classic in form. Both Maigret and the noir detectives carried that heritage with them, but they made use of warm knowledge in a characteristically different way. Maigret came out of a genteel tradition of civil servants; the pulp detectives came out of a tradition of marginalized violence.

Noir had a short life of less than ten years; when it broke down the genre fissioned into several new forms: hard-boiled, spy stories, thrillers, and the Neoclassic. Each of these, with their dual heritage in noir and Classic, would have two variants depending on whether warm or cold knowledge dominated. This complex situation will require us to be careful in defining the genre variants that succeeded noir. I have already sketched the differences between the noir and hard-boiled forms. Now is the time to do so systematically.

Noir

The noir difference is this: Maigret worked within a humane and moral society and for a trustworthy institution, the police, as did his Classic predecessors. He was a *detective*, with the institutional rank of commissaire. Sam Spade, Philip Marlowe, the detectives created by Fearing, Ambler, Greene, and others work within a corrupt and immoral society policed by venal and sometimes evil guardians of the oligarchic hegemony. Marlowe, as he says, is not a detective but a *shamus.*

The meaning of this word *shamus* is unclear, and even how to pronounce it. It may have a Yiddish derivation from slang for a policeman. The word gains power by association with *shaman,* suggesting an incantatory or mythic role that needs to be taken into account in transforming a simple P.I. into a combination of gumshoe and oracle.[18] A secondary association to be found in dictionaries is with the Yiddish *shammes,* or the ninth candle from which the rest of the menorah is lit, from the Hebrew word meaning "attendant." In any case the word must include the fact that to be a shamus is an honorable calling[19] with a suggestion of supernatural authority and guardian of souls.

The shamus, then, is the heir of the Classic detective in his role as protector of society, but unlike the Classic version the shamus is an outcast, a *private* investigator, as Dickens's Bucket was. The shamus is a person of principle, who does the right thing because to do so makes possible the moral life that the shamus exemplifies and that stands in contrast to, and refutation of, the irrational and immoral lives around him. In such surroundings the continued commitment of the shamus to rational thought is heroic. The noir Detective's commitments ally him to Quixote, to the Grail knight, and to the mythic quest literature.[20] The noir tale is a moral quest as well as a search for knowledge — or rather, the getting and deployment of knowledge that is the basis of the genre acquires, with noir, a new conception of knowledge, and with that a new conception of how it ought to be used. Noir knowledge is less certain, powerful stuff with an imperfect provenance, dangerous to handle even by those with experience. The Classic detective was clever, astute, analytical. The noir detective is a holy man, a Man in the Mountain, a shamus. This is clear in the famous, long speech by Sam Spade to Brigid O'Shaughessey at the end of *The Maltese Falcon,* remarked on earlier.

The puzzle aspect of the Classic form was rejected by noir authors as unrealistic, but when the now-unrealistic rational society that made deduction possible is thrown over for an irrational one, Holmes's methods are no longer viable. Holmes reasoned by abduction under circumstances in which some but not all of the evidence is reliable. It is a mistake, he says, to proceed in absence of the facts — implying that there are such objectively knowable things as facts. In the irrational noir society (this being one of the main reasons why it *is* noir), when the truth of all the evidence is uncertain, then there is no leverage on which abduction can work. The noir detective must instead use the psycho-intuitive methods created for Maigret. And so, when it became clear to Chandler and others that the Classic formula was worn out and its assumptions about the nature of human knowledge were unacceptably narrow, the noir shift began, bringing warm knowledge into legitimacy. This had far-reaching consequences which mark it as the most significant event in the history of the genre.

To say this snares us in an anachronism of sorts. Maigret debuted in 1931, Spade in 1929. Anterior to both these were the pulp detectives such as Nick Carter,[21] the seedbed of the hard-boiled. Eventually, as the noir style evolved, the shamus grew out of the original proto-hardboiled operative into his hero's role as the man who, in Chandler's words, walks mean streets who is not himself mean. In an unjust world the shamus retains his commitment to justice. The Continental Op understood the bankruptcy of Classic rationality, but having no other resource with which to work, resorted to fists and guns. The Op plays to win, and not for himself or justice but for an employer, and while he prefers to outsmart his opponents he is willing to beat the truth out of them if necessary. The Op is clever and canny, a man of action whom we will encounter again as the engine of the thriller.[22] Both Maigret and Spade came into existence together as alternatives to the Classic. As we have seen it took the Classic a decade to wither away and expose the epistemologically and existentially driven social changes that had been at work underneath, and to bring noir briefly into the light.

The first proto-noir tales might be the Hannay trilogy of John Buchan (1919). These are significant for the spy and thriller types, so I will put off discussion of them until the next chapter to take up next the novels of Dashiell Hammett from 1923. Hammett clearly understood the noir principle before it became the controlling trope for the crime novel and the detective film. The 1941 film version of *The Maltese Falcon* is probably better known than the 1923 novel. There was an earlier version, in 1931—*A Dangerous Female*, ludicrous to our post-noir sensibilities even to its title, which exposes how little the noir sensibility was understood during the Classic hegemony. In this film Spade is a dandy in the mold of Peter Wimsey and Philo Vance. The murder of Miles Archer is moved from the vicinity of the Stockton tunnel into Chinatown itself, and Spade (for the nonce, anyway) is found to speak Chinese, all this resembling the Shanghai fantasy of the period, of the sort one can read in Milton Caniff's *Terry and the Pirates* and lampooned in the beginning of the second Indiana Jones movie. Joel Cairo has become an intellectual, as far from Peter Lorre's exquisite portrayal of a homosexual aesthete as can be imagined.

The year 1931 was simply too early. Hammett understood what he was doing at a time when other authors did not. The English Classic was still dominant, psycho-intuitive detection was unheard-of, and mean streets remained to be discovered. Hollywood had barely found out how to make a talkie and its storytelling resources lagged far behind fiction. The situation was exactly that of science fiction movies before the making of *Blade Runner.*

An illustrative pairing with *A Dangerous Female* would be a novel from 1952 during the transition from noir to hard-boiled, Mickey Spillane's *Kiss Me Deadly.* The famously hard-boiled Mike Hammer is in this story distinctly soft-boiled and displays sympathy and a sense of the right thing. As with the 1931 *Dangerous Female* it does contain (to us) laughable elements, most notably Spillane's misunderstanding of the nature of nuclear reactions. And as in 1931, elements of the previously dominant mode are still visible. Just as it took some time for noir to emerge, in 1952 the hard-boiled sensibility was still in the making. Mike Hammer is a crude, tough copy of the Continental Op with most of the detection stripped out. Noir is bracketed by these two.

Through the thirties and forties a double motion is at work in the written stories: the detective (the title of shamus was dropped in return to the P.I.) becomes more humanized and sensitive while the surrounding society becomes more sordid. Hammett's *Red Harvest* and *The Dain Curse* (1929) are fairly brutal and the criminals are self-aggrandizing and unscrupulous. After *The Maltese Falcon* we have *The Glass Key* and finally *The Thin Man*, ending Hammett's trajectory with a straightforward English Classic.

Earl Stanley Gardner's Perry Mason, who bears little resemblance to the sanitized TV version twenty years later, follows a similar trajectory. Mason is clearly sleeping with Della Street and Paul Drake's portrayal contains an element of the thug. Mason described himself in the first story, *The Case of the Velvet Claws* (1933), as "a lawyer who has specialized in trial work, and in a lot of criminal work.... If you look me up through some family lawyer or some corporation lawyer, he'll probably tell you that I'm a shyster. If you look me up through some chap in the District Attorney's office, he'll tell you that I'm a dangerous antagonist but he doesn't know very much about me." Spade had no qualms about sleeping with the women who came his way, including clients and his partner's wife. While Spade is opportunistic, Mason is calculating. When Spade is directly confronted by the police it is as a potential criminal enemy. Mason, a brilliant trial lawyer and a (raffish) member of respectable society, soon becomes only a nuisance. He never becomes quite noir, and as his character (and Gardner's portrayal of his society) matures he becomes less and less so.

With Dashiell Hammett, Raymond Chandler, Graham Greene, Kenneth Fearing, and a few others (including Nabokov's *Bend Sinister*), we are at last in the mythic territory of quest stories and moral fables, the home ground of noir. These are all bittersweet, Greene being the sourest, and pessimistic concerning the uprightness and authenticity of anyone but the detective himself. Traces of the questionable moral characters of Spade and Mason are gone. Greene's people are sleazy but the protagonists have at least the moral refuge of having been chivvied into their fates. With these authors we move out of genre limitations into mainstream literature. We have come a long way from the pulps to a style and outlook that, while it owes a great deal to noir, is ripe with new genre possibilities. One might look forward to such authors as Carlo Emilio Gadda, Leonardo Sciascia, and Alain Robbe-Grillet (*Les Gommes*) to find these possibilities realized.

Before we move on, however, there is an important caution. Raymond Chandler's famous manifesto for a new realism in the detective story was that "Hammett gave murder back to the kind of people that commit it for reasons, not just to provide a corpse; and with the means at hand, not with handwrought duelling pistols, curare, and tropical fish. He put these people down on paper as they are, and he made them talk and think in the language they customarily used for these purposes."[23] But as Cawelti points out[24] the plot of *The Maltese Falcon* "revolves around a mysterious age-old treasure, eccentric villains, and complex webs of intrigue" certainly not more realistic than a Dorothy Sayers novel of ordinary people and plausible motivations. We are not talking here of a realism that consists of grit, or of a resemblance to grim ordinary life such as Zola insisted on. That the story is about detectives and murder removes it from everyday concerns. The realism that Chandler sought was a *moral* realism, an honesty that the Classic was thought not to possess.

Here is a review of the systematic differences between the Classic and noir detectives (table 4).

TABLE 4. CLASSIC AND NOIR DETECTIVES

Classic Detective	Noir Detective
Defends society against attacks by individuals.	Defends individuals against attacks by corrupt society.
Clues assembled into a narrative through reasoning.	Clues assembled into a narrative through experience and wisdom.
Clues acquired by observation.	Clues acquired by testimony, sometimes forced, sometimes by guile.
The detective is never himself at risk.	The detective is the most endangered of all.
The second murder erases all hypotheses but one.	Subsequent murders only increase the violence and the urgency.
The detective's narrative construction is confirmed by the affirmation of the criminal when presented with irrefutable evidence.	The detective's narrative construction is confirmed only by confession, which is the only reliable access to truth.
The solution is always complete and the aftermath provides closure.	Solutions are generally local and partial and the aftermath provides only solace.

More on Movies

Earlier I suggested that, from perhaps the mid–'30s, movies are a good and sometimes better way to understand the popular attitude toward detectives, warm and cool knowledge, the rational and the intuitive, and the puzzle plot and its action replacement. So we might plausibly ask how film reflected the noir transition.

Noir introduced subjective narration through its exclusive focus on the detective and what the detective experiences. A written narration can simply refuse to tell the reader what the detective thinks. Film naturally gives away clues to this by facial expression, body language, and tone of voice. Not to do this would be to flatten the actor's performance, sacrifice immediacy, and forgo one of film's best dramatic resources, the ability of the viewers to see for themselves what is happening.

For material evidence to be hidden requires that we be not shown it, which violates the fairness rule, or that our attention be diverted as a prestidigitator would. But even if the discovery of a material clue is not crudely emphasized by portentous music or another device, the audience can guess the significance of a material clue merely because the film has chosen to let us see it. Because the noir tale sees what the detective sees, and only what he sees, it has no refuge from this problem. If the significance of some object or occurrence is to be hidden from the audience it must generally be hidden from the detective as well. This endangers our belief in the Detective as a seer, a wise man.

In written fiction the opposite prevails. Suspense has to be created against the natural proclivity of the medium, which is to talk. Movies happen; novels explain. Rules and puzzles and other linguistic devices are a problem to the movies, whereas behavior, as legible in film as in daily life, is a problem for novels. This accounts for the chess-like character of English Classic movies, with long periods of sparring punctuated by bursts of action. Noir films tend to the opposite: a series of action scenes punctuated by setups for the next spurt of action. Conversely, the noir film's emphasis on mood, affect, and nuances of behavior, with very little direct explanation of what is happening, is a problem to novels. It is easy to hide clues in a novel, simply by refusing to talk about them.

The Rules do not *require* transparency between detective and reader or viewer, only that there be no subterfuge. In the printed Classic narrative the detective, as Bordwell says, is a "closed mouth"[25] whose knowledge is given to us only when the author deems it to be the right moment. Film has difficulty maintaining this control and works with less friction when the viewer knows what the detective knows.[26] As a medium, then, noir is more natural to the movies. It will exacerbate the anxieties of the audience — those anxieties that brought on the noir shift to begin with — and enhance the relief when these dark matters are held at bay, if only temporarily.

As a genre ages and it becomes harder and harder to take seriously its central tropes, it tends to slide into self-parody. A weakness of the English Classic is that its surfeit of civilized calm facilitates comedy more than it does tragedy, whereas the noir style is inherently tragic. Unfortunately, the Classic style was fading just at the moment when the movies were discovering how to tell a Classic story, so the first Classic films were lighthearted, without frisson. Earlier we explored the threat posed by cold knowledge and the dangerous power wielded by the detective who possesses it. Comedy is a good way of disarming this situation, but due to circumstances the threat was never a real one until film noir was fully established.[27]

All of these factors — the puzzle mode, the closed mouth, and the susceptibility to comedy — worked to the advantage of noir once the noir sensibility began to take hold, and against the filmed Classic.

Let me recapitulate at this point some remarks I made in the previous chapter about filmed Detectives. There was in the 1930s a resistance to detection as a good thing — which is often so, as Cawelti (54, 58, 77, passim) pointed out. The emotional grip of the genre, first explicated by practitioners even in the pre–Classic period, and later elaborated by Chandler and the early critics,[28] had this plot: an act of violence (murder) disturbs the sense of order and predictability necessary to the ideology of polite society. Truth is obscured and its ontology called into question. The detective arrives to set matters straight. The detective's tools are intelligence and rationality, coupled with a materialist outlook and a standard of proof requiring physical evidence and an unbroken chain of causality. By this means the truth is recovered and our comfort and safety are assured. This is a tepid scenario, more suggestive of comedy than spiritual emergency. The Classic's uneasiness about intellect and the products of the mind,[29] is revealed in the speed with which the detective is hustled off the stage when his job is done so that marriages can be consummated, fortunes are safe, and ordinary life will resume. The *Detective* is a shaman whose knowledge gives him powers of life and death. The mere detective is none of that.

These compromises are completely absent from noir, and emphatically so in its filmed form. When the imperatives of noir were felt in their full force at the beginning of World War II, the natural power of film to portray these imperatives was unleashed.[30] Films of the thirties employed a number of strategies for hedging round the detective with plenty of fail-safes.[31] Not so noir.

Comedy is one means of neutralizing the threat posed by the Detective — Nick Charles, Philo Vance, and Charlie Chan are examples. Another solution is to industrialize scientific detection, to convert the process to something mechanical. This is a familiar strategy in all aspects of the Industrial Revolution, and indeed it can be said to have made that revolution possible.[32] In detective fiction this strategy becomes the police procedural, sometimes referred to as the *roman policier* in recognition of the older French tradition. A notable film procedural is *Secrets of the French Police* (1932). A notable feature of this film is the use made of the Paris pneumatic network. The Sûreté gets hourly reports from its agents in the field by this means and is able to maintain a Vidocq-like surveillance by industrial methods. There is a telling difference between this film and the 1937 film *Pépé le Moko*. Inspector Slimane works alone in the manner of Porfiry Petrovich.

A third strategy for neutralizing fear is to humanize the detective, to make him fallible and unheroic. Other than E.C. Bentley's *Trent's Last Case* already mentioned,[33] this was not a popular strategy until the Frenchman Maigret showed how a man of petit-bourgeois tastes could be spiritually satisfying as a detective. For that the grip of gritty realism (the noir and hard-boiled traditions) had to be relaxed, so that in film (English-language film) the first steps were not taken until the Neoclassic appeared around 1980.

The Charlie Chan films of the '30s contain a mixture of these qualities, as one would expect from a genre in transition. Chan is a respected, workaday detective.[34] While not a magician, his amusing "Confucian" remarks do mask his methods, which have a strong psycho-intuitive component; Chan walks about the scene, observing, touching, a shrewd man who gives little away. Chan's bumbling, hyperkinetic sidekick Number One Son is a comic element, cousin to the shrinking D.A. we see in the Philo Vance movies of this period, making Chan himself smaller and apologetic. His humanization, however, extends only as far as to be jolly, which he can afford to be as he is given nothing really menacing to work on — his villains are cardboard. We see Chan at home less often than we do Maigret, or relaxing with cronies, or enjoying himself. And Madame Chan does not solve mysteries by sage advice or even on her own as Madame Maigret did. A comparison of the films with the original written Chan tales of Earl Derr Biggers, which are straightforward Classics, underlines the mid-decade confusion regarding the figure of the Detective.

The film Chan is an outsider in the way that Poirot is, quarantined behind his foreign ways. He is the Chinaman in search of the Golden Mountain,[35] allowed to live among us for the services he can provide and then sent back Outside. The Detective will never be taken as an equal. Allingham's well-born Campion must use a false name so as not to embarrass his family. The poor middle-class inspector brought to Gosford Park can't even get the suspects to pay enough attention for him to introduce himself. The film Chan has been condemned as a Chinese Uncle Tom, but the shoe is actually on the other foot. Chan is the direct ancestor of Philip Marlowe.

A notable element in the noir transition concerns some tentative attempts to remodel a female character.[36] Until 1935 women in these movies were simply props serving a purpose similar to the maid who drops the breakfast tray on discovering the body. *The Casino Murder Case* introduces two new types, the Dame (a hard, cynical sort) and as a foil the Lush, who is more sympathetic because she is softer, more emotional, more *womanly*. The Dame is played so as to make her kinship with Mae West transparent. The Lush's antecedents are more complex, but like the Dame her narrative utility in focusing and polarizing a dangerous situation shows in her long cinematic career. We recognize here one of the stock characters of noir.

Because women are thought to be the carriers of warm knowledge, and also unfitted for detection in other ways, such as physical strength, either the lush or the dame will do well as a sidekick, able to contribute feelings or intelligence to the story without stealing the scene. The consolidated figure of the Pert Dame and the Detective was experimented with in 1939 in two movies, *Private Detective* and *Nick Carter, Master Detective*, and then was lost for three decades to the old view of womanhood, exemplified by the wiles of Beaver's mom.

In the first of these the Dame is the actual detective, a professional P.I. by the name of Jinks, and she gets some action sequences of her own — fur coat, high heels and all. Of course, in the end she marries the official detective, the man to whom she gives credit, and retires. That's a sop to convention. This is a vibrant, gutsy woman who gives nothing away to brains and is an admirable embodiment of warm and cool.

The second film, *Nick Carter*, is less straightforward. The woman in this case is definitely a sidekick. But she has the androgynous name of Lou, and Nick is an action hero in the mold of Indiana Jones. He solves crimes, but he needs Lou. In one memorable sequence she wins an automobile-vs.-airplane race that a male pilot lost in the first attempt, by taking the controls when he is incapacitated. Later on we find out she doesn't know how to fly! Lou swaggers like a man and gets caught like one, too.

In 2004 we find in *Sky Captain and the World of Tomorrow* both Jinks and Lou reproduced in a charming imitation of the late thirties pulp milieu. Lou is Polly Perkins, intrepid girl reporter, with a sideline in love with her superman Sky Captain, and Jinks is Frankie, the one-eyed, over-the-top leader of a mercenary air force. There's not much detecting here, but the anima of the two female types is fully displayed and strongly front lit. Here we have two versions of the dame together in one movie. One (Jinks/Frankie — their names tell all) is the hard woman with the soft heart,[37] and the other (Lou/Polly) the soft woman with the hard core. And here we have also the subtext of the female detective exposed. These are really adventure movies. There may be secrets to be revealed but there will be no metaphysical frisson in the revelation. The case of Jinks shows how hard it is to keep a detective movie with a woman in it focused on detection. At once, all the interest becomes an example of Samuel Johnson's famous remark about intelligent women — that it's not how well the thing is done but that it's done at all. Detached curiosity about secret knowledge evaporates in the excitement of the threat to a woman and the (very unlikely, in this genre) possibility that she will not escape. It is only since the 1980s that we have crawled out far enough from under this stereotype to have in a woman the detective affect that formerly could be had only in a man. The tradition of Maigret complicated this shift by giving new significance to the emotions; ultimately an enrichment but initially working to the disadvantage of the hard-boiled female — emotion and instinct that form the components of warm knowledge and the particular expertise of women, at the same time incapacitating the woman to be hard-boiled.

Noir at the Beginning of the Shift to the Hard-Boiled

The noir detective is an artist in both a modern and a Romantic sense. He is charged with channeling the contradictions of existence and casting them into an intelligible narrative, which he is able to do only by exposing himself to, immersing himself in experience. This requires guts, not brains. The detective's original rationality has been divided between two forces: a perverted form owing to the police and subject to politics and pragmatic cynicism and other definitely not objective forces, and a more respectable form owing to the private eye, an eye occluded by mud and desire and outrage. Under these conditions we would expect to find an embattled attitude toward rationality, the reverse of the English Classic. Rather than being dangerous and needing to be kept in check, now there is not enough rationality to be safe in the world, and it is the life of the body that threatens to overwhelm us.

This story may explain why so many excellent fictional detectives of the English Classic tradition were not filmed until after World War II, and mostly not until the '80s, when we began to need a respite from all this oppressive so-called realism. Noir had upped the standard of truth in reporting and closed off the merely puzzling sort of rationality of Poirot, Marple, Alleyn, Wimsey, Vane, Carr's locked-room formula, Nero Wolfe, Thorndyke, and the rest. Very few of these had any film presence until recently, when the Neoclassic revival and television made it worthwhile.

5

Hard-Boiled, Spies and Thrillers

Hard-Boiled

Earlier I offered a table showing the differences between the Classic and noir formulas. Here is the same comparison between noir and hard-boiled (table 5).

TABLE 5. CLASSIC, NOIR, AND HARD-BOILED DETECTIVES

Classic Detective	Noir Detective	Hard-Boiled Detective
Defends society against attacks by individuals.	Defends individuals against attacks by corrupt society.	Defends himself against self-interested individuals.
Clues assembled into a narrative through reasoning.	Clues assembled into a narrative by experience and wisdom.	Clues accumulate but are not assembled into a narrative.
Clues acquired by observation.	Clues acquired by testimony, sometimes forced, sometimes by guile.	Clues emerge through persistent, indiscriminant pressure.
The detective is never himself at risk.	The detective is the most endangered of all.	The detective's invulnerability is repeatedly tested.
The second murder erases all hypotheses but one.	Subsequent murders only increase the violence and the urgency.	Additional murders are part of the milieu and have little effect on resolution.
The detective's narrative construction is confirmed by the affirmation of the criminal when presented with irrefutable evidence.	The detective's narrative construction is confirmed only by confession, which is the only reliable access to truth.	The detective is presented with a narrative when the criminal is exposed and confesses.
The solution is always complete and the aftermath provides closure.	Solutions are generally local and partial and the aftermath provides only solace.	Solutions are personal, ameliorating nothing and providing only narrative closure.

The underlying difference between the Classic and noir, which affected all its manifestations, was a changed view of society and one's responsibilities to it. Classic society was upright, governed by convention, and one's duty was to preserve the status quo. Noir society was corrupt, governed by conscience, and one's duty was to a private morality. Hard-boiled society was anarchic, governed by personal advantage, and one's wisest behavior (not a duty) was to self-preservation.

The differences between the noir and hard-boiled formulas are more subtle than those between Classic and noir, and the coherence of the hard-boiled formula is less clear over its lifetime of about thirty years (1949 to the early 1980s). I intend to trace a line from noir through hard-boiled to the action thriller, that is, to trace the legacy of the introduction of warm knowledge, from which point we will be able to look back and see the progression more clearly.

In noir the two modes of Classic detection (cold knowledge) and psycho-intuitive methods (warm knowledge) coexisted. This double legacy was passed on to hard-boiled, and also to the spy novel, which we will take up presently. In every sort of story that followed, this legacy will be found, varying in its proportions — this story having a preponderance of the cold, that one of the warm — but never a complete separation. This is the main reason why it difficult to make a clean distinction between noir, hard-boiled, and their successors.

Nevertheless, differences are not hard to find. For instance, the hard-boiled detective has a reputation as a sexual predator. During the fifties "a standardized image of sensuality grew in importance. That image stressed the secondary sexual characteristics of both sexes. Mannerism seemed ever more significant: walk, gestures, voice, dress, size of tits and hips. External appearance was a woman's proof of her sensuality."[1] Noir detectives were more inward. They may have had an eye such as Sam Spade's, but they also had a code that went beyond these matters to the basics of right behavior toward everyone, including women.

The increasing use of violence to move the story forward; the demise of the chronicler, replaced by the practice of having the detective tell his own story; the changed relationship to women and the rise of the figures of the Dame and her counterpart the female detective; the replacement of observation by interrogation and of material evidence by testimony — these are indexes of the transition from noir to hard-boiled and will index the transition to come, from hard-boiled to the action thriller.

Rowland usefully summarizes Cawelti on this. "Cawelti," she writes, "acknowledges that myth is an element in what he calls the formulas of popular fiction. These formulas, both narrative and symbolic, are charged with feeling and work through social tensions."[2] Cawelti proposes four functions of the dialectic of culture and popular fiction. Resolving tensions is one; the others are to affirm existing attitudes, to explore the boundaries of the possible, and to help assimilate social changes.[3] These are the premises on which my arguments are built. Cawelti, however, was concerned with the Classic formula. We have now gone some way past that, and it is time to take stock. Are these premises still viable?

The first novel in the hard-boiled mode was Ross Macdonald's *The Moving Target* (1949). As with the time of the first Classic stories, society had recently emerged from a war of previously unknown madness and brutality. World War I was felt after the fact to have been senseless and brought about attitudes of revenge and resentment among the belligerents. The Classic recreation of pre-war conditions was a fantasy designed to distract attention from this. World War II, however, was felt to have been a moral war and brought about an attitude of goodwill for having been tested and not found wanting. The first three or four years after the war were not friendly either to noir or to hard-boiled, but natural to a realism now familiar to everyone, the sort of thing one sees in the crime-scene photographs of Weegee. The novels published were a noir-Classic blend of tough responses to outbreaks of crime. This "gritty hope" was destroyed by the Cold War, to which the response was the thoroughly disillusioned, hard-boiled detective.

As I said, the hard-boiled tale never dominated the genre the way the Classic did. It was more diverse, having inherited the noir fission into two modes, the one genteel and the other tough. Now the tough mode itself could be found in two forms, the hard-bitten fighter (who will evolve into the action hero) and the wily investigator, who will become the focus of the intellectual thriller. As the hard-boiled Detective aged, the difference became more pronounced. The tough Detective got tougher and the wily Detective more like his Classic ancestor.

The ascendancy of the hard-boiled Detective was in the '50s and early '60s. The first generation, Ross Macdonald from 1949, Mickey Spillane from 1950, and John D. Macdonald from 1953, ran close to the form. Their detectives (Lew Archer, Mike Hammer, Travis McGee) were hard men, hardened by their dangerous and uncompromising worlds. Of course, this is not always foregrounded. The hard-boiled detective, for example, carried forward noir's earnestness for the moral quest. MacDonald's Travis McGee, who is given to little sermons, says, "Anything you feel good after is moral. But that implies that the deed is unchanging and the doer is unchanging. What you feel good after one time you feel rotten after the next. And it is difficult to know in advance. And morality shouldn't be experimental, I don't think."[4] Love and warmth trump mere sex, and we are not entitled to take the latter at the expense of the former (113), but with the characteristic noir caveat that love is too painful to be possible. Archer's code of behavior obliges him to forego both.

"Hard" is a complex attribute. McGee and the others are physically hard. They take a lot of punishment and gives a lot back. Their fearlessness seems to attract violence. They are also morally hard, in several senses—inflexible where their code in concerned, cynically flexible where it is not, merciless toward others' infractions. And they are intellectually hard, openly critical and dismissive of the venal, exploitive, tasteless society in which they work and—regrettably—live. Then there is the iconic hard-boiled dialog—irreverent, hard-bitten, aggressive:

> There was a flurried rapping at the door. "Walter?" a woman cried. "Are you all right? Walter?"
> "Tell her to call the cops," I suggested. "We can all sit around and talk about how much pot you moved out of this place."
> "Walter?" she yelled.
> "Everything is fine, Edith," he called. "Go away!" He sat down again and said, "You broke my shoulder!"
> "It isn't broken. It will be OK again in a week."
> "But I can't move my arm. It's numb."
> "The feeling will come back, Wally."
> "Nobody ever calls me Wally."
> "Except me. I can call you Wally, can't I?" [125].

That was Travis McGee. Here is Mike Hammer:

> "I still have a couple of lives left, kid. I'll save one for you."[5]

Sam Spade talks this way. So does Marlowe:

> "Tall, aren't you?"
> "I didn't mean to be."[6]

Spade is hard. He has an exacting code, too. But he doesn't break anyone's shoulder. He humiliates Gutman's boy Wilmer, gives Joel Cairo a slap, nothing more.

The hard-boiled style is smartened-up, hollowed-out noir. But initially, still under the spell of Chandler's literary aspirations, it breaks several of Elmore Leonard's rules.[7] Here are the immediately relevant ones:

> I. Never open a book with weather.
> II. Avoid prologues.
> III. Never use a verb other than "said" to carry dialogue.
> IV. Never use an adverb to modify the verb "said" ... he admonished gravely.
> VIII. Avoid detailed descriptions of characters.
> IX. Don't go into great detail describing persons and things.
> XI. If it sounds like writing, I rewrite it.

The Detective affirms existing attitudes, Cawelti says. Where the noir detective's criticism of his society is implicit in his behavior, the hard-boiled detective is explicit, but his behavior often undercuts his indignation, which in any case is often perfunctory. Cawelti continues: the Detective resolves social tensions—in noir, mostly by talk and by siding with the little people. The hard-boiled detective invites us to join the winning side. Again: the Detective explores the boundaries of the permissible. Spade is barely legal, but takes advice from his lawyer about that. McGee accumulates such a list of violations that the operative Harry Max Scorf can use it as leverage to force McGee's cooperation. And finally, the Detective helps to assimilate social changes. Noir's concern is how to live with the changes; the hard-boiled way is to dominate them. All this has less to do with the dialectic of warm and cool knowledge, which drove the noir transition, than with the dialectic of reason and force driving the hard-boiled transformation. The first transition involves a change in the understanding of what knowledge is and how to get it, while the second involves a change in what to do with the knowledge so gotten. The noir detective gathers evidence; the hard-boiled detective gathers testimony, and such detection as he does is mostly for the purpose of working out who to interrogate and how to do it efficiently.

This outline of the characteristics of the hard-boiled formula and some of its differences from noir was derived from reading the novels of the period. Some of the more significant or representative of these will be discussed shortly. Given this outline, we can ask what connections there were between the social milieu of the time and the four purposes given by Cawelti: to resolve tensions, affirm existing attitudes, explore the boundaries of the possible, and assimilate social change.

Some connections suggest themselves at once. That the first hard-boiled novels should appear in 1949, in the same year the Cold War began, seems hardly a coincidence. The hard-boiled preference for domination over accommodation mirrors the early Cold War nuclear strategy.

The tensions associated with the nuclear standoff and the paranoia over infiltration by communists—exemplified in the United States by the McCarthy hearings and fueled in Britain by the traumatic defection of Kim Philby—were blocked by conflicting values. Some found the nuclear strategy unwise and the McCarthy trials deplorable, others felt oppositely. The hard-boiled dependence on confession and the corresponding use of suasion, psychological or physical, to obtain it, the uncertainty over clues—whether or not they could be knit together as a narrative that could be rationally analyzed for consistency, lacunae, and other suggestive features—and the concomitant belief in the superiority of expedient procedures over procedural ones reflect those few years between the disappointment at the frustration of the hopes that a good war fought well could rid the world of some evils—the Cold War put an end to that—and the prosperity and economic growth that followed, distracting people's attention. Those few years, roughly 1949–1954, are the cradle and crib of the hard-boiled formula.

Finally, the always unsatisfactory conclusion of a hard-boiled story (solutions are personal, ameliorating nothing and providing only narrative closure) reflects the belief that the war with communism was unresolvable and permanent. When that belief was shattered in 1990 by the dissolution of the Soviet Union, the fall of the Berlin Wall, and the reemergence of Eastern Europe, it was the coup de grâce to the hard-boiled detective.

We can look for confirmation of the relationship of events, above all the Cold War, with a middle-class, suburban zeitgeist of conservative, unchallenging values. The evident cognitive disjunct between these values and reality, just as it was in 1919 and again at the time of the noir shift, required the services of a certain sort of detective to repair. That detective was hard-boiled.

Tony Judt, speaking of transplanted Jews in 1930s England and their two ideals of universal values and international revolution, said, "The tragedy of our century lies in the discrediting of both these universals by the 1930s, with the implications and horrors of that unraveling rippling outwards for decades to come."[8] It is not hard to imagine why this might be true of others as well, and what effect such discrediting might have on a genre whose readers wanted to see a reflection of their own altered views and of a truer, albeit now grim, reality. The result would be a shift from the old Classic formula to something like noir.

After World War II there was a brief period of good feelings and a sense of accomplishment. Miller and Nowak, in their book *The Fifties; The Way We Really* Were,[9] point to such events as Mary McCarthy's essay "America the Beautiful" in *Commentary* (1947), which contrasts with the feeling only two years later, at the time of the Berlin airlift (1948–1949) and the opening of the Cold War, a time Miller and Nowak dub "The Age of Fear." After a long list of disruptive events, they write, "Such events shocked and frightened people, and the last years of Truman's presidency proved a trying time — a period of suspicions, accusations, loyalty oaths, loathings, extreme chauvinistic Americanism."[10] Again, it is not hard to see how this might be reflected in a new role for the Detective: aggressive, perhaps vindictive, self-righteous, willfully reductive — in short, hard-boiled. And most notably, wised up.

In addition to this post-war disillusionment, which the Classic and hard-boiled formulas had in common, there is another affinity rising from an observation made by Tzvetan Todorov concerning the importance of the second murder in the Classic formula.[11]

Todorov has noticed the complete separation of narrative time and story time at the beginning of a Classic tale.[12] The narrative begins at a point after the murder has occurred and continues through the invocation of the Detective and his first investigations. The reader's access to the story is remote, mediated by the narrative that stands between them. The second murder ends this state of affairs. It is the first event the reader experiences directly. At that point all three time frames — reader, narrative, and story — join. From this point the reader is in story time. As a plot element, the second murder provides the crucial validation of the detective's inference chain. As a rhetorical element, it raises the temperature of the story by changing the immediacy of events, as explained. As a theoretical element, it fuses the Detective of the early narration with the working investigator of the second half of the story, existentially grounding the reader's construct of the Detective. At this point the Detective ceases to be a static object and becomes another being, responsive and open to change: a figure both actual and mythic. (I am interpreting Todorov here.)

We see at once an important change wrought by the hard-boiled detective. There is no more narrative disjunct. The reader follows the action throughout because he is allowed access to the detective's experiences as they happen. The second murder means nothing. In fact, there is frequently more than one. The purpose of these murders is to expose a threat, to expose the Detective as vulnerable — that is, not the hero of myth but a simple working man.

Here lies the origin of the modern action thriller. From this point begins the hollowing out of the figure of the Detective, who becomes a mere statue to commemorate what he once was. From this point the development of the Detective will follow a different path more directly linked to the Classic tradition. From this point begins the withdrawal of belief in the efficacy of rational thought, the modern dilemma that I have already posed.

Some Examples

With regard to the early hard-boiled novels, those of the first generation of John D. MacDonald, Ross Macdonald, and Mickey Spillane, I have been describing the development of this form of the Detective as if it were a post-war phenomenon sprung out of the disappointments and tensions of the Cold War in 1949. This is true, but at the same time quite false; it is only that the *proliferation* of hard-boiled novels and the displacement of noir can be traced to the beginning of the Cold War. As with earlier transitions, we have not far to look to find predecessors among the earlier dominant forms. John Creasy is an example. This prolific author published his first crime novel in 1932 (*Seven Times Seven*) and continued to produce under several pseudonyms into the 1960s. His detectives are many and varied — the Toff, beginning in 1938, a hardened-up Classic amateur; a series of more than sixty spy novels starring Dr. Palfrey, which might be classified as action thrillers; and others.

Creasy's 1939 novel, *Death on Demand*, certainly qualifies as hard-boiled. The detective, Patrick Dawlish, is not invoked in the Classic way, though there is an unnamed client used as an excuse to have Dawlish beaten up at the very beginning. This is the hard-boiled invocation (or baptism) and it allows the detective to dispense with the client and work for himself, a rogue, frequently revenge-driven or simply left free to provoke whatever violence suits his fancy. Dawlish isn't an outsider and the society he is part of is not corrupt — he is even a member of a gentlemen's club, though we don't hear much about that. Like Spade, he does not put things right but only reestablishes the status quo ante, but unlike Spade, what he works to protect is not the integrity of a few but the Classic social fabric. Like Spade, he relies a great deal on testimony rather than material evidence; unlike Spade, he acquires that testimony not by suasion and threat but by actually beating the information out of the informant. Dawlish is not a cold man. He can be rattled. He can fall in love. But the bulk of the novel is a simple — and absurd and frequently ineffective — series of fights and chases. Creasy's 1961 novel, twenty-two years later, *The Scene of the Crime,* is no different, consisting largely of scenes of quotidian life overlaying psychopathic violence.

These are not detective stories. The "detective" does not actively discover anything. It is revealed *to* him when he presses in the right place. Events then determine what comes next. And unlike the thriller hero, Dawlish is only superficially immortal. If his enemies were better shots, or would simply get rid of him as competently and efficiently as they do everyone else, that would be an end to the story before it got started.

Compare this to the Op novella "The Girl with the Silver Eyes." Here the story ends with the same hard-boiled pyrotechnics, but the villains are seriously good at their work and the Op has deliberately created the confrontation by his relentless following up of clues. Hammett's Dame in this story is a copy of his later creation Brigid O'Shaugnessy, and the end of the Op's involvement with her invokes the same moral code and concept of justice. None of this is present in Creasey's novels.

What we have from Creasey in 1939 is what we would expect — a proto-hardboiled story incorporating unintegrated elements from several formulas. Creasy began writing at the time of a nexus of the waning Classic, the still unfamiliar psycho-intuitive, the rising prominence of noir, and elements of the hard-boiled and thriller modes that had been present all along. But he could not make this mass of influences coalesce into the mature form of the hard-boiled.

Some telling features of the hard-boiled mode can be found in a book coming late as Creasy came early. John D. MacDonald was of the first generation of hard-boiled authors. In *The Dreadful Lemon Sky* (1975), there is also not much detection. One important piece of information is imparted to McGee as a dream another character had. A dream is not evidence, of course, and this item is also hearsay. It was not sought for or set up. On the use of testimony we can say that the final confrontation between the criminal and Scorf is based completely on supposition — baseless accusations that, if they hit the mark and the detective is fortunate, might produce a confession. The criminal is not caught for the crimes he has been sought for but, conveniently for the resolution of the story, for murdering Scorf. There is a plethora of murders and, it turns out, four murderers against whom nothing is ever proved. With all these murders, where are the police? (Scorf has some uncertain official status.) Amid all these deaths, McGee has a free field, free to explore the boundaries of the possible, as Cawelti says.

The situation in 1975 is little different from what it was in 1939. Creasy and Macdonald are both conventionally regarded as authors of detective novels. I have demurred, but it seems now that the final judgment ought to take account of the demise of the Rules. In the two tables listing the functions and procedures of Classic, noir, and hard-boiled detectives (tables 4 and 5) this progression is apparent. We still have the Classic roles of criminal, victim, detective, threatened bystanders, and chronicler, but the way these roles are performed has completely changed. What has happened is that we now have an excess of warm knowledge just as the Classic had an excess of cool. The balanced personalities and methods of Holmes and the noir detectives are gone.

Among the first generation of hard-boiled novelists the formula was a little too hard-boiled. For some, it did not remain so. Ross Macdonald, in his 1959 novel *The Galton Case,* tackles the matter of the getting of knowledge head-on, in a conversation between Archer and one of the criminals:

"The facts?" I said sharply.

"The apparent facts, if you like. I'm not a philosopher. We lawyers don't deal in ultimate realities. Who knows what they are? We deal in appearances. There was very little manipulation of the facts in this case, no actual falsification of documents. True, the boy had to tell one or two little lies about his childhood and his parents. What did a few little lies matter? They made Mrs. Galton just as happy as if he was her real grandson" [173].

It is difficult to imagine many authors who would give a character, and certainly one who was not a criminal, such a speech. Questioning not only the accessibility of the truth but the point of seeking it strikes at the heart of the genre. The whole story has been about false identity and delusion, not just simple untruth. Even the supposed criminal is deluded — about *himself:*

"How was he involved?"

How wasn't he? I thought. His life ran through the case like a dirty piece of cord. He had marked Anthony Galton for the axe and Anthony Galton's murderer for the knife. He had helped a half-sane woman to lose her money, then sold her husband a half-sane dream of wealth. Which brought him to the ironic day when his half-realities came together in a final reality, and Gordon Sable killed him to preserve a lie [184].

"Recursive delusion" is not hard-boiled speech and it is not a hard-boiled idea. Throughout this last scene there are references to obscurity and clarity: working one's way out of the darkness, looking up at the sun, light and darkened windows, a night-time confession and a dawn departure.

Leslie Fiedler says of this time that he was troubled by "the question of *why* my manifold sponsors have been willing to pay up, what they are paying me *for*," and goes on to say, "Like other entertainers I have been paid to allay boredom — in my case, by making our country and our culture seem more interesting and amusing than most academic accounts would lead us to believe."[13]

Yet coexistent with this lethargy, present throughout the dominance of the hard-boiled formula (to about 1980) we see an embattled people defending themselves with repressive rules and displays of outrage. These were the times of the Comics Code Authority and the Senate Subcommittee on Juvenile Delinquency (1954), which emasculated a vibrant popular artform, and a similar desire to pasteurize rock and roll after the scandal of Elvis Presley, in the period between Buddy Holly and Chuck Berry and the appearance of the Rolling Stones, Janis Joplin, and so much other transgressive music. These were the times of *Catcher in the Rye* and attempts to ban it, of the Beatniks, of Grace Metalious.[14]

By 1960, "the American propensity for critical self-evaluation had become obsessive." write Miller and Nowak.[15] But matters ran deeper: "Guilt was not the only silencer. Intellectuals were also quieted by grave doubts about human nature." The authors go on to describe how the liberal belief in the possibility of human improvement came to seem dubious, liberal thinking declined, and finally "to talk positively of human nature in the fifties was to risk contemptuous dismissal as a utopian."[16]

Here we have a crisis of confidence, a search for authenticity, something no hard-boiled detective could be accused of.

Ross Macdonald's first novel, *The Moving Target* (1949), was closely bound into the traditions of noir. His detective, Lew Archer, was named after Miles Archer, Sam Spade's partner — who was dumb enough to get himself killed by Brigid O'Shaughnessy and whose wife was two-timing him with Spade. Macdonald acknowledged the literary influence of Chandler also. The later hard-boiled author Sue Grafton acknowledged Macdonald. She located her detective Kinsey Milhone in Santa Barbara, Ross Macdonald's Santa Teresa.

Archer gets himself beaten up, though not with the regularity of Mike Hammer. Already at the beginning of Mickey Spillane's first book, *One Lonely Night* (1950), there has been a murder and Hammer has been lectured for it by a frustrated judge explicitly linking Hammer's behavior to the violence of the war. Now he is standing in the middle of a bridge in the middle of the night looking at the distant city, thinking of his coming death and hanging onto "the last shreds of reality." Not many pages later Hammer gets beaten up, and there are more murders to come. The contrast with the relatively peaceable Archer and McGee is marked. Yet these books belong together, and they are as a group different from what went before.

If we move on to the second generation of hard-boiled novelists, from Ed McBain beginning in 1956 to Robert B. Parker in 1974,[17] here we see the mellowing and maturation of the formula in the hands of a group of novelists working along the same lines.

Ed McBain pioneered the use of a detective team, the 87th Precinct, men who are also ordinary policemen. And ordinary they are. We see their vulnerabilities, emotional and physical. We see friendships, pride in their competence. We also see the seedy and corrupt milieu in which they work and see the emotional and moral hardness that can create in them. Some of them are simply no good. In a late book, *The Last Dance* (New York: Simon and Schuster, 2000), a pair of cops get illegally into the jail cell where a hit man is being held (his white partner has been let out, another injustice) and smash all the teeth out of his mouth out of frustration with not being able to prove what they know.

The blond detective Kling and the black medical officer Sharyn make a couple:

> Watching the show in bed, eating Chinese food with Sharyn Cooke, Kling wondered aloud if Lieutenant Byrnes had done the right thing.
> "Because you know, Shar," he said, "Pete had no idea Blaine would suddenly open up, no idea at all. He just threw her to the lions, was what he did. After she gave us her trust."
> ...
> He thought it miraculous, and so did she, that in the face of overwhelming odds, they were actually making a go of it. Just think of it. A little colored girl from Diamondback grows up to be a deputy police chief, and a white boy on a bicycle he won , grows up to be a police detective, and in this hurried hating city, they find each other [168–169].

This does not seem very hard-boiled. These cops are hard and clear-eyed but almost mellow at times. They work for an institution, the police, which is charged with protecting society, and they take that charge seriously. And yet this is not so different from the novels of ten years before. These cops are not P.I.s, but they work primarily for themselves against individual criminals—there is mention of a drug cartel in *The Last Dance* but predatory organizations are kept off stage. The cops accumulate clues by interrogation, not as indiscriminate as it will be in later authors, and information emerges sometimes by accident, not forming a narrative used to narrow the focus of continued investigation but simply to keep it going. The milieu is violent, hard, and amoral; the cops themselves are not for the most part amoral, and they are rather hard-bitten than hard, inured to violence and not averse to it if required. They know their way around. They are a little cynical. They fit in.

The long career of the 87th Precinct novels—49 years, from 1956 to 2005—shows how an evolving genre formula is clouded by the persistence of older styles among the newer. Sixteen years after Ed McBain began publishing his 87th Precinct novels, Robert B. Parker published his first Spenser novel, *The Godwulf Manuscript* (New York: Delacorte, 1974). In the intervening years there had been long war that polarized the country, a war revolting to some, including some of those who fought it, with a peace revolting to others; a war that produced psychotic returning veterans who got no thanks, and a number of hard men with specialized training in subversion and killing who wanted to continue in business. The country had not seen this number of entrepreneurial mercenaries since the aftermath of the Civil War. The ground was prepared for Spenser, and with Spenser we now encounter the echt hard-boiled P.I., completing the vision of Mike Hammer.

Spenser is brutal. He cracks wise even through his own narration. An ex-policeman fired for insubordination (a pattern now to be common), he works as what is in effect the enforcement arm of the official police, gathering testimony by methods unavailable to them. Toward the end of *The Godwulf Manuscript* he goes to interrogate a previously unwilling source of information. He bursts into the room.

> [Tabor] tripped over the bed as he staggered backward and fell on it. I shut the door hard behind me for effect. I wanted him scared.
> "Hey, man, what the hell," he said.
> "The hell is this, stupid," I said. "If you don't answer what I ask I'm going to pound you into an omelet."
> "Who the Christ are you, man?"
> "My name's Spenser. I was here before, and you proved too tough for me to break. I'm back for another try, boy, and this time I'll try harder."
> ...
> I was on his side of the bed now and close to him. He tried to jump onto the bed and away from me. I grabbed him by the shirtfront and slammed him back up against the wall.
> "Before you tell me about Hayden, I want to speak to you about the manner in which you address me."
> I had my face up very close to his and was holding his very tight up against the wall. "I want you to address me as Mr. Spenser. I do not want you to address me as 'man.' Do you understand that?"
> "Aw, man..." he began. I slapped him in the face [153–154].

This is, so far, quite mild. Needless to say, Spenser gets what he wants. A little farther on he kills two mobsters, taking a bullet in the side, and the next day, with a wound that would have immobilized anyone else, he jumps a man the size of a tree carrying a gun to match and strangles him to death.

Future hard-boiled detectives would have to match this. And they do. V.I. Warshawski (Sara Paretsky's hard-boiled woman) gets herself into a notorious women's prison to interrogate some very hard people and takes the same punishment herself (*Hard Time* [New York: Delacorte, 1999]. And in a late Sharon McCone novel (Marcia Muller's 26th), the increasingly hard McCone gets shot in the head (*Locked In* [New York: Grand Central, 2009]) but keeps *Coming Back* (New York: Grand Central, 2010).

With the advent of Spenser all of the characteristics of the hard-boiled formula are fully present. Spenser defends himself against corrupt people motivated by their own greed or fear and considerations of society do not intrude in this deadly struggle. Clues (of a sort; there is very little in the way of deduction) are extracted by threatening everyone (a macabre but unsystematic police procedural). Spenser is invulnerable and never at risk; the Classic detective was not at risk either, but his mortality was never tested as the hard-boiled detective's is. There are plenty of more or less inconsequential murders. The criminal is found, finally, and induced to confess, but much or nearly all of the information leading to his discovery is suppositious, with some scraps of evidence to make the constructed narrative plausible. And finally, the main effects of the solution are that Spenser and a few others are no longer under threat and an insubordinate police detective is returned to grace.

This is as far from the structure and purposes of the Holmes tales and the English Classic as it is possible to go. Significantly, Parker and other such authors are said in their publicity to be crime writers, not authors of detective stories.

From this point there are two possible paths. What is left of the detective genre can be hollowed out by substituting for the Detective the figure of the Hero and for the discovery plot the action adventure story. The second option is to retreat, either to a less hard-boiled formula or to some other variant of the Detective.

Both of these options were taken. The third generation of hard-boiled novelists contains some who carry on the Spenser style. Others, breaking away from the purified formula of the second generation, just as the first broke away from the older noir formula, show a greater diversity. This is the generation of the 1980s and '90s, distinguished by a lighter touch, a wittier humor replacing wisecracks, the writing sometimes slyly self-conscious (Ellroy, Mosely). A darker, noirish or foreboding atmosphere replaced the narrative purpose of pervasive violence (Rankin, Lehane). Classic features reemerged —faint, with some small measure of gentility (Grafton).[18] And James Ellroy has made a name for himself as writerly, with a distinctive style concisely explicated by his ten (actually eleven) rules, which I referred to earlier. This has not been seen since Raymond Chandler aspired to the same authority.

Early in this chapter I also referred to some observations made by John Cawelti concerning the social purposes served by the detective novel: the element of myth that charges the story with feeling — I would say gives it resonance — and grounds it in moral and social concerns: the resolution of social tensions, the affirmation of existing attitudes within an exploration of boundaries, and the assimilation of social change. The hard-boiled myth is strong, but it is that of the Hero, not the shaman or the quest, and as such it appeals more to a fantasy of power than to moral or social concerns. Hard-boiled stories resolved social tensions and assimilated change by removing the source of problem, and the boundaries explored are transgressive, particularly the freedom to kill with impunity. With the retreat of some in the third generation of hard-boiled writers we should (and will) look for signs of the return of the original values of the Detective.

At the start of this exploration of the hard-boiled formula, I acknowledged the difficulty of separating it from its noir predecessor but claimed there was a family resemblance among the hard-boiled tales that would form them into a distinct group. I have already explicated some of these distinguishing characteristics in the course of my narrative of changes in the hard-boiled formula in the forty years after Ross Macdonald's appearance. There are some other commonalities.

One is the almost universal use of first-person narration: the detective speaks in his own voice. The demise of the Chronicler had several consequences. Most important, it eliminated the distance at which the reader stood from the action. In the Classic story of detection both the drama and the purposes of the story were best served if the reader was encouraged to be judicious and thoughtful. This served to focus the suspense on the detective's reasoning and enhanced the surprise of the solution. Any emotional response to the events of the story could be assigned to the Chronicler, one of whose roles was to channel this important dramatic element. A first-person story could not follow this plan. The reader was required to participate as the story unfolded and encouraged to respond to the story's events with strong feelings, rather than treating it as a puzzle. The suspense of the story shifted from detached curiosity to a more engaged set of hopes and fears for the narrator and those close to him, and so the intellectual suspense of detection could be downplayed in favor of the physical suspense of action. The nature of first-person narration abetted the dramatic purposes of the hard-boiled formula, which were to make the atmosphere, the violence, and the dangers strong enough to support the events of the story. One cannot imagine Watson reporting Spenser's threat to pound some witness into an omelet.

When the narrator is also the detective, there is another important consequence, which is that the author cannot legitimately withhold information from the reader on the grounds that the Chronicler did not know or understand the situation. When the detective is the narrator, if the drama depends on the reader not having certain information, then the detective cannot have it either except by lying to the reader or hiding information; neither is acceptable in a story without meta-fictional procedures. Given this, it is easier for the author to shift the process of detection toward testimony to slow the rate at which clues are acquired. If we have full access to the detective's reasoning, then if he is like Holmes we will know the solution almost from the start. If he is not like Holmes then we will have to trundle along through a series of wrong conclusions, second thoughts, and dead ends in order for the author to delay the solution to the end. A clever author, of course, can find narrative strategies or plot structures to circumvent a problem that is all to the benefit of the hard-boiled style.

Another commonality is the remodeling of the female character. I have already spoken of some attempts at creating a female detective, usually subordinate to the official male. I also spoke of the creation of a pair of female types I called the Pert Dame and the Lush. The Dame is smart in tongue and mind, savvy, sexually aware, in charge of herself. The Lush (usually literally alcoholic in the films of the period) is the opposite: slow, passive-aggressive, unresistant to circumstance, exploitable sexually and in other ways. Both of these characters existed in hard-boiled fiction, but the Pert Dame became increasingly common during the life of the formula in response to the changing role of women in society. Even Spenser was cautious and loving toward the women who came his way, many of them scared and vulnerable. We have noticed this about Travis McGee and, surprisingly, it was true of Mike Hammer also. The avatars of the Pert Dame were of course the self-sufficient female detectives such as Millhone, McCone, and Warshawski, who debuted in 1982. Stieg Larssen's Lisbeth Salander, part Detective and part Hero, is a new version. *The Girl with the Dragon Tattoo* is an impressive specimen of the type, with some of the characteristics of Spenser, particularly the use of detection only to locate informants and an unusual brutality. The subsequent novels shift the detection to the male character and leave Salander to the deadly battles with villains more usual in the action thriller.

One family resemblance in particular requires notice: the hard-boiled formula shifted the problems posed by noir in the direction of expediency. Earlier detectives' concerns included the deployment of knowledge, because it was through the use of knowledge that the relationship to society was created and maintained. The noir detective's outsider status did not interfere with this. The hard-boiled detectives' understanding of this relationship was clear but limited to the little sermons of social criticism that they all liked to give, and the relationships they were interested in were with sidekicks and the women who came their way. In the degenerate action thriller to come, the Hero's concerns have little to do with knowledge and nothing with a relationship to society. Society is simply the enemy threatening the Hero's well-being.

To reduce, then, the character of the hard-boiled variation on the Detective formula to its simplest form, on the two matters of the exploration and improvement of a social world fractured by a crime,[19] the first of these, incorporating cold knowledge and detection, degenerates from a nearly exclusive focus on knowledge acquired by reasoning and material evidence in Holmes and the Classic to a mixture of evidence and testimony in noir to a preference for testimony elicited by threat or actual violence. The second concern translates, as we have seen, into knowledge used to return the social world to its status quo, to the prevention of further decline in order and morality, to the hard-boiled concern for the survival of the detective and a small circle of people important to him. (To clarify this second concern, it may help to realize that the successively narrowed goals—from restoration to triage to survival—are not cynically solipsistic *in the context of the formula*. It is the reduced aspirations and the resistance to change of the *society* that limit the Detective's options.)

The hard-boiled Detective's dominance has waned. Novels will of course continue to be written in this formula, but the pure form of Spenser is no longer viable. We want detectives of psychological complexity, with human failings, a little more mellow, witty rather than cracking wise. Kurt Wallander (the Swedish creation of Henning Mankell) is an instance. Wallander is a close relative of that other, older Swedish detective, Martin Beck. The crimes Wallander investigates are closer to the thriller formula, with hair's-breadth escapes, chases, and gun battles. Wallander is wounded several times. He also has close (if difficult) relations with the women in his life and has the friendship and loyalty of his subordinates. He does not hide his feelings or his inference chains from the reader nor his associates; there is no magic detection here.

Wallander, like many inheritors of the hard-boiled tradition, is halfway between the detective thriller and the Neoclassic, two modern forms I will be looking at shortly. On the one side is a propensity to extralegal methods and a talent for getting into confrontations; on the other hand is some genuine detective work along with a more complex psychology and a sensitivity to social and moral issues and the feelings of others.

The hard-boiled ascendancy lasted about thirty years, and it was strong if not dominant for another decade after that. Old genre forms, like old technology, never disappear entirely. At each turn — we have several turns yet — the detective genre expands like a language, adding new words and dialects, assimilating new speakers and influences. Its assimilation of the spy story is a good example.

Spies

Spy stories are not old, because spying is not an old profession. There have always been spies—there are spies in the Bible—but not professional spies, people in the employ of governments who do nothing else for a living but spy. Detectives do a lot of spying. Undercover work, disguise and infiltration, data mining, wire-tapping, and so on have been part of the Detective's options since the beginning, but though spies may be detectives of a sort, detectives are not spies. Policemen and private investigators have a domestic mandate only. Insofar as an industry has the size and weight of a government we allow ourselves to speak of industrial spies, it is true. Influential international organizations—a multi-national bank, for example—can be major players in government policy and international diplomacy. But their range is limited. They are part of the commonweal. The spy works for the commonweal.

Until recently spying was an amateur activity. Adventurous or intelligent people did it using largely their own resources. Before 1940 the infrastructure of a large, established institution, with the training, support, and technology to sustain it, and with a regular voice and role in foreign policy, was not in place.[20] In the introduction to his book *Intelligence and War* John Keegan remarks on the influence of spy novels on the public perception of spying, and points out, "It is notable that very few of even the most celebrated spy stories actually establish a connection between the spy's activities and the purpose for which he presumably risks his life in the field."[21] It is as I said, that only recently have we had spy stories that are actually about spying, and this is connected to the professionalization of the field.

The first masterpiece in the spy genre is surely *Kim* (1901). Early in the nineteenth century James Fenimore Cooper wrote two spy novels: *The Spy* (1821) and *The Bravo* (1831). Rising German imperialism and the Potemkin Uprising in Russia in 1905 provoked a spate of "invasion literature"—*The Riddle of the Sands* (1903) by Robert Erskine Childers, with more books to follow from William Le Queux, E. Phillips Oppenheim, and others. None of these has much literary merit, and their plots show no sign of what we now think of as respectable spycraft. Sherlock Holmes was involved by his brother in government, Mycroft, in some incidents of nominal spying. In the best of these, "The Adventure of the Bruce-Partington Plans," Holmes entraps a professional agent, but the man has acquired the plans on his own, as a speculation, hoping to peddle them to another government. He is not a spy.

Conrad's *The Secret Agent* of 1905, which we examined at the outset, is not properly a spy novel, either, though like the others it has implications for spying. The first novel to portray what we would now recognize as a spy, and the first novel to treat espionage as a job of work, is Somerset Maugham's *Ashenden* (1928), partially filmed by Alfred Hitchcock as *Secret Agent* (1936). Maugham's inauguration of the modern spy novel grew out of his own experience of the workaday nature of spying, which he built into the flat voice he used to convey this sense of the mundane. Maugham muted or moved offstage sporadically sensational events that had formerly been the whole point of the spy novel. The neutral morality of the writing created a different sort of suspense by opening up possibilities in a story with no good guys and bad guys to predetermine the outcome.

All these features of the book were ignored in the film. Hitchcock's movie is a throwback to the older sort of spy. It is a melodrama, full of spurious romance, anxiety, and hand-wringing. The story as filmed was shifted from distinctly cool to warm. Ashenden's control of daily events is nill, his knowledge of circumstances meager or simply wrong, and his ability to go about the business he was hired to do is hampered by the naiveté of his conventional morals. He is, in fact, an out-and-out amateur (a suborned novelist, in fact), a version of Erskine Childers's busybody yachtsmen of 1903. Moreover, he is quite ignorant of the professionalism of *Kim* (1901) and the *Great Game*,[22] the far more serious moral conundrum of Conrad's *Secret Agent* (1907), or the pervasive menace of John Buchan's Hannay triology, beginning with *The 39 Steps* in 1915. In fiction, by 1936 the essentials of the modern spy had been in place for a generation. In the movies these matters were not yet understood. But they would be.

The noir aesthetic could not survive post-war social changes and by 1955 was dead. A new fear had replaced the earlier one that lay behind the origin of the Detective. The original task of the Detective had been to remove or at least patch over the eruption into settled society of irrational violence. Now, after World War II, the threat was global destruction, irrational violence threatening not merely the comfortable conventions of the gentle people of Styles but society and civilization altogether, perhaps life itself. This could hardly be contained or patched over. A new strategy was needed, a new manifestation of the Detective. One of these, we saw, was the hard-boiled detective. The other was the spy.

The post-war spy was a version of the noir detective, but more compromised, darker and more ambiguous, capable only of ever smaller victories—in the end, as small as mere survival (to be a major rationale of the developing thriller)—while the spy story became less and less a Romance in the mold of Lancelot or Roland or a domestic comedy such as Ashenden's. The moral ambiguities of the spy's work had been laid out half a century earlier by Joseph

Conrad and now, in the uncertain and ambiguous world of the Cold War, Conrad's lesson was there to be learned. The terrorist and quondam spy Verloc was a poor fool manipulated by a still more corrupt power. Verloc was a spy whose mere survival seemed unlikely. In the end, only the solipsistic and amoral Professor survives, still with his insurance against capture, the pocket full of nitro. Inspector Heat does a modicum of detecting but is co-opted by his aggrandizing superior to do nothing more than frighten Verloc into self-accusation. Heat is a pale and thin heir to Dostoevsky's Porfiry Petrovich. In Conrad's *ne moin ultra* story, detectives and criminals are equally compromised and the only thing accomplished is the death of the good, dull-witted Stevie. Mediated by John le Carré, this is our current understanding of how the spy story goes, and this is what is expected of the spy: martyrdom and anonymity. The spy's only recourses are the acuteness of his mind and the resources of his body. The spy whose survival depends on his wits and what knowledge he can acquire about his opponents is the heir of the detective and one progenitor of the thriller.

If the modern spy does share some important features with the detective, it is important to remember that the spy story is a distinct genre with its own history and rationale. In comparing the spy to the detective, for example, it is worth noting what has happened to the word *intelligence.* This used to be an attribute and a working tool of the detective in solving crimes. For the spy it means information and is a property of the external world. The detective embodies intelligence. The spy seeks what he has not: intelligence.

The nexus of spy and detective created a venue where the detection and cold knowledge of the Classic, increasingly displaced by noir and then hard-boiled, could flourish naturally. Through the spy story we inherited detection in its Classic form. The spy, like the Classic detective, is concerned with the getting and deployment of knowledge. Much of this work has to be done by deduction — anyone who might be able to testify is either not accessible or too risky to approach. The psycho-intuitive modification of the Classic that helped to set up noir provided a model for the ominous and paranoid atmosphere needed —facts lie, and feelings are a truer guide; factual knowledge may not save you and in the end might even make the defeat more bitter. Le Carré's 1963 novel *The Spy Who Came In from the Cold* brings all this together.

Le Carré's vision was bleak, and it was inevitable that it would be modified or ameliorated. Buried within the spy story is the same bifurcation that lay in noir, and one originating in the same way: through the introduction of warm knowledge into a cool script. So it was natural that the subsequent history of the spy story followed two paths. When warm knowledge dominated the tendency was for the story to become an adventure. This is the path of the hard-boiled and the action thriller such as those Len Deighton wrote about Harry Palmer. When cool knowledge dominated, the tendency of the story was in the direction of the Classic story of rational detection, which in the context of the modern spy story evolved naturally into the Classic-inflected thriller alternative to the action hero.

From the hard-boiled P.I. tradition come spy stories such as *The Ipcress File* (1965). More complicated than *The 39 Steps* and not so lugubrious as *Confidential Agent,* it is nevertheless a story of the same sort. Every man's hand is turned against Harry Palmer. He is an amateur snatched up by circumstance. His survival depends on his detective abilities, but also on his brashness and fortitude. The story is resolved by a thrilling escape from doom. Palmer is a closed mouth to his associates, as the Classic detective was, but now not to heighten the drama but to keep from being betrayed. We know what Greene's confidential agent Denard knows because he tells people — everyone, in fact — but we are denied Palmer's knowledge. Spy stories and Classic-inflected thrillers thrive in an atmosphere of magic detection; transparency is antithetical to the spy.

All of these options — spies, thrillers, bitter noir and hard-boiled — served to domesticate the cultural anxieties of the fifties and sixties. If culture is what prescribes the boundaries of the ordinary, stories domesticate anxieties by reformulating them so as to fit within these boundaries. Thus cultural coherence is maintained.[23] Domesticated narratives legitimize certain transgressions as interpretable, adding them to the acceptable unexpected and making the unacceptable invisible. What remains (the domestic, the interpretable) comforts us with the assurance that there is nothing so very new in the world. A genre formula is a narrative of this sort. The worse the perceived danger of cultural disintegration, the more heroic the efforts required to hold things together. A detective of the type of Holmes or Poirot cannot be turned into a Hero. Philo Vance had to be reincarnated as a different person under threat of war, as we saw. The Cold War figure of the Detective drifted inexorably toward the Hero. The difference between warm and cool versions of the formula that appeared in noir became wider. Hard-boiled stories inherited the warm aspect of noir — knowledge acquired by discovery and confession and deployed for protection from a corrupt world — and moved slowly over forty years toward the Heroic action thriller. Spy stories inherited the noir bifurcation and split apart under pressure from the Cold War into a Heroic version of espionage and adventure and a cool version that preserved in some form the features of the Classic. Cool spy stories were built around a core of rational deduction. Heroic spies are of the James Bond type, though not usually so flamboyant. A more realistic example would be John le Carré's *The Spy Who Came In from the Cold* (1963). Cool spies are of the George Smiley type, also a Le Carré invention, as in *Tinker, Tailor, Soldier, Spy* (1974) and its two successors.

Le Carré's career has followed this trajectory. In 1962 he published a novel of cool detection (*A Murder of Quality*). His also relatively cool first spy novel (*A Call for the Dead*, 1961) featured the prototypes of Smiley, his sidekick Peter Guillam, and Mundt, an early version of Smiley's nemesis Karla. The sequel which followed in 1963, with Alex Leamas (*The Spy Who Came In from the Cold*), was distinctly warm. The end of the Cold War destroyed much of the rationale and infrastructure of the cool spy, and Le Carré's novels since have drifted out to the edges of the spy genre, concerned more with his personal obsession.

At the same time as these changes in the way knowledge was acquired (shifting from detection and evidence to interrogation and confession), beginning with noir there was also a change in the way acquired knowledge was deployed. The Classic Detective worked on behalf of society as represented by its proxies, the "innocent bystanders" in Cawelti's theorization of the genre. The noir Detective worked on behalf of a group of persons representing a segment of society threatened by the corruption of the wider world. The hardboiled Detective worked more for his own protection and a small circle of friends. The next step in the chain is for the Detective to employ his skills not for society, some friends, or himself, but the tribe. The Classic Detective worked for society. The hero of the thriller works against it. The Hero helps to erect a pale against incursion. The relationship is now antagonistic.

Spy stories, however, remained hospitable to all aspects of the Detective. John Buchan's Hannay trilogy, published during World War I, are early thrillers of both the action and detection types, a familiar mode — one thinks of *North by Northwest* — with a dash of noir. Graham Greene's tales published during World War II are much more strongly noir but still with the same blend. Eric Ambler's novel *A Coffin for Dimitrios* (1939, retitled for the 1944 movie as *The Mask of Dimitrios*) is a nearly equal blend of all three. The detective is again an amateur, as with Ashenden actually a novelist, a writer of detective stories, who intrudes himself into the business of one Dimitrios Makropolous out of curiosity. Makropoulos is a smuggler who engages in espionage and other international rackets for whoever will pay, and the novelist's reward for playing detective spy in his turn is to endangering himself and to receive a lesson in the sleazy truth.

Jean-Luc Godard's film *Alphaville* (1965) mixes the two genre traditions of detective and spy differently. It opens in decent noir — the criticism of cold by warm — but with new, un-noirish gestures of self-awareness, genre referentiality, irony and parody. We do not immediately discover that Lemmy Caution is a spy, and when we do his detective affect becomes confused. Lemmy knows some things we don't about his mission and its importance, but apparently as little as we do about Alphaville itself. The first half of the movie, up to the death of Lemmy's predecessor Henry Dickson (an earlier infiltrator from Outside who had gone native), is a mélange of cultural matèriel, silently critical of scientific rationality as malign, a criticism that is carried into the often mystifying narrative procedure.

Halfway through the film the science fiction elements begin to bubble to the surface and the story becomes a straightforward, inside-out plot of the escape-from-dystopia type. The noir atmosphere disappears and is replaced by the sleek industrial style of Monsieur Hulot's *Mon Oncle*, a movie made about the same time and to the same critical end but with a very opposite affect. There are in fact many parallels between the two. In both, the quest to understand is voiced as a social problem — re-voiced in the case of Lemmy, who has worked out the solution and now wants mostly for the woman of the piece to run off with him. To agree to this she has to step outside the illusion of Alphaville, which imprisons her in a loveless condition. The explicit existential standpoint is of warm blaming cold rationality for the loss of the good things of life, art and love. This just the situation of *Mon Oncle*. Alpha, the creator of the world, is a computer, the icon of scientific rationality, the twin to Hal in the movie *2001*, whose failed coup will come a few years later. The cold contrast with Hulot is nearly the same, a habit-ridden marriage in obsessive pursuit of a status-driven life of plastic and steel modernism. The division with which we began this, from the detective artist Holmes and the hegemony of cold knowledge, could not be more stark.

Godard's work here (and the French New Wave generally) is ancestral to the metaphysical puzzler variant of the detective genre, which I will look into later. There are a number of features of interest, but the most immediately relevant is a new relationship between the detective and the spectator. Godard has limited our knowledge of circumstances in noir fashion — Lemmy knows more than we do and can interpret the significance of events when we cannot, with magic results. But set aside the fact that we don't know even what the crime is, only that an investigation of some sort is going on. For us as spectators it is the movie itself that is the crime; that is, in other words, that is the subject of investigation. The method of inquiry forced on us is the psycho-intuitive. We are pulled along by events, relying on intuition and guesswork to keep our footing, filling our pockets with bits of things— uninterpretable observations, disconnected facts— waiting for a quiet moment when we will be able to sort it out. Our detachment has been radically reduced and our pretense to objectivity disabled and we experience the condition of not knowing in a new, more cathartic way. The opposite procedure to circumvent an epistemological black hole would be *Last Year at Marienbad,* made four years earlier. Godard's goal is the same as Brecht's. But whereas Brecht wished to increase distance by breaking the dramatic frame, Godard pulls us within it. Both procedures are ideological in intent, but Brecht's ideal of self-criticism is rational while Godard's is not. All of this shows the range of the detective formula, from Poe and Dickens to Godard, *The Purloined Letter* to *Alphaville,* which is coming under our analytic control.

When we look for features of the spy novel that lie on the direct line of inheritance from the Classic, one especially stands out. The recruitment of the spy has the same importance to the story as the invocation of the Detective in a Classic novel. Spies are natural outsiders to the society they have engaged to protect, though part of their skill is to make us believe otherwise. But spies, as we read about them in novels, are rarely as humdrum as Ashenden. The crisis that sends the spy into action is one for which ordinary spies are inadequate. Thus the importance of the recruitment scene.

In *Ashenden; or The British Agent* (1928) the novelist Brody, reincarnated by Intelligence as Ashenden, is a little annoyed at having been impressed but as a soldier he can't object. In any case, the unnamed spymaster R appeals to his patriotism and he gets immediately to business. Ashenden must be recruited in this way because he is an amateur and as such, will respond better to coercion than argument. In this he is the opposite of the amateur Classic Detective, who meddles willingly out of curiosity.

Harry Palmer in *The Ipcress File* (1965) is also a military man and cannot (officially) object to his assignment, for which he is fitted not so much by patriotic feelings as by his criminal tendencies (so called, but which are in fact only insolence). Like Ashenden, he is reluctant. Unlike Ashenden, his is a pragmatic reluctance. Also unlike Ashenden, he doesn't take orders or accept the modus offered. Palmer seeks truth out of self-interest and only enough truth to neutralize the threat to himself. This is the basic thriller plot.

George Smiley was recruited twice in the diptych *Tinker Tailor Soldier Spy* (1974) and *Smiley's People* (1980): Smiley was already a spy, but retired. Recruiting him is a matter of overcoming his reluctance to take on a distasteful task; he is overcome not by coercion or by the appeal of setting wrongs right but by the fastidious desire to correct mistakes. He is also a competitive man. Appeals to his conscience are brushed off. Appeals to his self-interest (his vanity as the venerable master) are ignored. Smiley is not a forthcoming man, strongly like the closed-mouth Classic Detective. He is content to let Lacan come to his own conclusions. He has taken the measure of everyone and allows a bit of contempt to show around the edges for their willfulness with facts, except the rookie Mostyn, who shows that he might come to know his business. With Palmer, attitudes and feelings are needed for survival. With Smiley they are an impediment, dangerous in themselves. With Ashenden in his workaday world they are irrelevant. Both Palmer and Smiley are gourmets. They cultivate their sensibilities. Palmer is a hedonist; Smiley is an epicure. The two are as hot and cold. Palmer is the reduction of Marlowe; Smiley is the reduction of Holmes. Ashenden so far as we can determine has no tastes at all. Charles Latimer in *A Coffin for Dimitrios* might be called a gourmet of knowledge. Thus, in a progression of recruitment scenes— Verloc, Ashenden, Latimer, Graham Greene's D (in *The Confidential Agent*), Palmer, Smiley — we see the progression from crude terrorist to modern spy recapitulating the progression of the Detective from his prehistory to the Neoclassic, passing through working amateur, Classic, noir, and hard-boiled.

Chandler's Phillip Marlowe was a moralist. Ashenden was merely a patriot. For Ashenden it's only a job. For Palmer, spying is life and death. Palmer is a pragmatist; Smiley is a fatalist.

There is one more thing of importance concerning the spy formula. In the 80 years from Verloc to Smiley we see a progression from warm knowledge to cool that is retrograde from that of the detective story. In terms of rational knowledge the spy Smiley looks backward to the premises of the Classic tradition rather than forward to some new formulation of the figure of the Detective. Why?

That is probably not the right question. Elements of warm and cool are always present. First one seems the more important, then the other. But against the pronounced disinterest of the hard-boiled formula in rational investigation and the even more pronounced disinterest for the thriller to come, the ideal of cool knowledge is unusually sharply segregated. I suggest that it stems from the controlling metaphors of the spy story, the battle against communism and the Cold War, cast as the final struggle, which could have no ambiguous outcome. The spies and the heroes simply differ as to method.

Thrillers

"I don't know what is to be done — this isn't war," bemoaned Lord Kichener — so Robert L. O'Connell begins a description of the effect of World War I on those who lived through it.[24] "Armaments did not simply dominate, they made a mockery of the warrior ethic. Strength, swiftness, skill, cunning, and bravery were rendered largely irrelevant. Combatants were gassed, torpedoed, mined, bombarded by unseen artillery or mowed down by machine guns more or less randomly; there was hardly a valiant death to be had." The conflict would render heroism, O'Connell goes on to say, a thing of the past.

Here we have, coincident with the appearance of the English Classic, the origins of a formula that, when it came into its own at the end of the twentieth century, was the complete antithesis of its sibling. Both were born of the distress and incomprehension of that war. One drew on the figure of the Detective to repair things. The other drew forth a much older figure, a myth of great power heard in the ancient literature of Achilles and Gilgamesh: the Hero.

The Hero is the ground and center of the thriller as the Detective is of

the mystery. I have already said that the thriller, the heir of the Detective lin-
eage through the hard-boiled tale and the spy, is the endpoint of that development. The Hero is a different figure and serves different purposes. At least
one of those mentioned by O'Connell, however, is familiar. In the face of
meaningless, unpredictable violence one longs at least for an explanation —
which cannot be forthcoming. One longs for rationality. But one longs also
to strike out, destroy. This, not the getting and deployment of knowledge, is
the business of the thriller.

There are two forms of the spy story, detection and intrigue; both are
concerned with identity and with uncovering allegiances — with outing the
truth.[25] It is a recognizable and familiar truth, though turned inside out: spies
threaten the local and conventional ideology and it is the job of the counterspy
(Smiley) to restore the balance and reestablish the hegemony of the proper.[26]
This is also the work of the Classic Detective. That figure, however, looked
back to a recent state of society, which he is hired to restore. The spy story is
not retrospective and is not concerned with restoration, but with altering the
present and the relations of power. Any detection done is in service to that
goal. The spy operates with partial knowledge, with which he constructs and
tests hypotheses intended to explicate events. The spy may explicate the truth,
but his real goal is to understand events only sufficiently to obtain the powers
needed. We know (or rather, there is nothing in the fictional premises to resist
the suspicion) that sometimes the spy does not succeed in this, whereas the
premise of a detective plot is that there will be a solution and the truth will
be found. In a detective plot the detective knows what we do not, and tells
us so. In an intrigue plot the situation is (or can be) reversed — often we know
what the spy does not, and we can only bite our fingers in the hope that the
truth will be discovered in time. The Detective, even when under cover, is
never himself a participant in the misdirection and uncertainty characteristic
of spying, nor is he (as a consequence) personally threatened. He is not
embedded in events as the spy is.

Herein lie the seeds of the post–Cold War problem. The spy formula
became ineffective. Of course we still have spies in plenty, but their purposes
and methods have become too ambiguous and uncertain to assuage our fears.
In fact, the contemporary spy of ambiguous motives and questionable morality, working in the service of an imperialism that threatens social cohesion
and may be repugnant if it fails and disgusting if it succeeds only partly, as it
must do in the present world, operating out of a secrecy threatening not as
much to the criminal as to us bystanders, exacerbates contemporary fears
rather than assuaging them. The action thriller is one solution. The other,
more hopeful that the mind has as much to contribute as the body toward
survival, is of a different sort. Recognizing its affinity with detection, I will
call this the classic thriller.

The Action Thriller

The thriller world is radically uncertain despite its hard, clinging embrace of science. From the Classic of the 1920s to the spy novel of mid-century, the scale of the ever-growing threat with the advent of the thriller was orders of magnitude greater and the consequences of failure were immeasurable: Armageddon. This is why we call them thrillers. What we wanted to know, what we feared, was, if we crank up the magnitude of the terror and the intensity of the struggle, whether it would still be possible to prevail? Thrillers, however, are not limited to Cold War spy stories or contemporary terrorist dramas. Any piece of derring-do is a candidate for a thriller, as the television show *Mission Impossible* demonstrated. Here is a table laying out the differences between the hard-boiled formula and the two varieties of thriller: action and Classic-inflected (table 6).

The action thriller radically alters the already tenuous connection with

TABLE 6. THE HARD-BOILED FORMULA AND THE TWO TYPES OF THRILLER

Hard-Boiled	*Action Thriller*	*Classic Thriller*
The detective defends himself against individual criminals.	The hero defends himself from a faceless corporate opponent.	As in the action thriller.
Clues accumulate but are not assembled into a narrative.	As in the hard-boiled story.	The hero constructs a narrative of the threat from information sought.
Clues emerge through persistent, indiscriminant pressure.	As in the hard-boiled story.	Information is acquired from people found by luck or located by deduction.
The detective's invulnerability is repeatedly tested.	As in the hard-boiled story.	The detective's invulnerability is tested but is always in doubt.
Additional murders are part of the milieu and have little effect on the resolution.	As in the hard-boiled story.	Additional murders provide clues or suggest new informants.
The detective is presented with a narrative when the criminal is exposed and confesses.	Exposure of the hidden threat is the objective rather than a narrative that reconstructed a crime.	As in the action thriller.
The solution is personal, ameliorating nothing and providing only narrative closure.	An agent of the corporate opponent is neutralized or killed but the true opponent is unharmed.	As in the action thriller.

detection found in the hard-boiled story. First, there may or may not have been a crime; more often a plot — the threat of a crime — is uncovered. What is threatened may not be a crime in the ordinary sense of a murder or a robbery; it is usually on a large scale and involves destruction, massive fraud, strategic assassination, and similar threats not to individual victims but to the entire society, or the world. The face of the threat may be that of powerful individuals — politically, financially, physically powerful — but the actual antagonist is a hidden corporate entity such as a government or some other powerful institution, or a group within it. In the Sherlock Holmes stories, Moriarity himself, or Colonel Moran, is the face of the shadowy criminal organization, the malign presence that is never touched or harmed by Holmes's feeble opposition.

In the action thriller the Detective is replaced by the Hero, a figure entirely concerned with locating and neutralizing the threat posed by the antagonist, usually as fast as possible. The innocent bystanders in an action thriller are everyone — anyone who is not directly involved in the struggle, possibly the entire world population. There is no Chronicler; the story appears not told at all, but simply happens. An actual crime is not required, and the victim likewise is only potential.

There is an important distinction to be made, however, within the thriller formula. In its broad social function the action thriller does resemble a detective story enlarged and intensified. Thriller stories are mythic by nature, recalling the tales of great battles, sagas of the heroes of war — Roland, Achilles, Hector, Beowulf. War is the controlling trope of the action thriller, as fought by those who wield the sword while the warmongers control the puppet strings. Achilles is such a tool, a Goliath hired by the architects of the Trojan War to fight in the battles they arranged for. The modern version of the legends of war changes the moral valence of the heroic originals but leaves the underlying structure untouched. *The Apocalypse* and *The Iliad* are related in this way. The typical plot begins with the discovery of a conspiracy, very big and very dark, fomented by a foreign power or a faction within the hero's own government, or some other comparable entity. Intrigue is essential to this sort of thriller, inherited from its roots in the detective story. Uncovering a hidden conspiracy is not the same as discovering a murder, nor is neutralizing the threat the same as solving a puzzle, but the shadowed figure of the Detective is nevertheless a presence that separates this story from one of natural disasters, runaway buses, or invading aliens — unless there is, perhaps, a conspiracy to suppress knowledge of the alien threat, to use it to get power or wealth, or some other hidden story of intrigue for which the aliens and disasters are only enablers or catalysts. Indeed, the aliens may eventually be welcomed as allies in the fight against the real enemy.

This is the action thriller. As with the detective story, the thriller works through social tensions to create a story out of our anxieties. The story works to resolve these tensions by its affirmation of existing ideas about such matters as the sources of evil and the right and necessary response to the discovery of that evil. The discovery of the conspiracy puts the improbably little person who has stumbled on it at mortal risk, a risk from which he (or better, she) can neither run nor hide. The one way she can save herself is to reforge the broken sword and plunge it into Fafnir's heart, and this she will do, at greater or lesser cost. As inevitably as the crime once had to be solved, so must the threat to survival be averted.

This is as far as the similarity extends. The action thriller's use of deduction and causal reasoning are superficial. Detection in a thriller is secondary to the action. The battle of wits common in the discovery phase of the thriller plot is only the entrée, the necessary preliminary to the battle of muscle — the true task is to destroy or be destroyed, and any trail of clues serves only to bring the two antagonists together. Reason as a means to fight this battle is replaced by technology.

The thriller world is a lawless, Hobbesian one. The thriller is concerned neither with true and false nor with right and wrong: it is about the just and the unjust. This is, as Richard Bulliet points out, a distinction Westerners are not accustomed to make. It is plainer in the sharia.[27] Traditional Islamic political thought had a horror of *fitna*, a word signifying upheaval and disorder and embracing everything from riot to civil war. We recognize the affinity with the detective peripeteia at once. Government (the detective) was to be a check on this anarchy. Rulers tend to the opposite evil, which is tyranny. The guarantor of moderation is law: the sharia, which in a Muslim society is administered and kept pure by the clergy. Sharia is a balancing power to that of the government. Westerners have become accustomed to think of good and bad in terms of tyranny and liberty. In traditional Muslim society the converse of tyranny is justice, not goodness, freedom, or happiness. The just ruler rules by right (he is not a usurper), according to law and (hopefully) moral principle. Being just, his deeds are right and true. This is the pure form of the thriller, and we see by this analogy why it does not give primacy to evidence as the detective story does. Evidence and proof are simply irrelevant.

It is the breakdown of justice rather than morality that generates the thriller. The actions of those in power may be wrongheaded, overbearing, arrogant, and ignorant, but so long as they threaten neither law nor order they are just, and thus acceptable. That which creates the thriller also justifies it.

A detective who behaved this way in a noir or a Classic plot — seeking justice at the expense of (or at least concern with) truth and right — would be repugnant. He would be part of the problem. The armature of the thriller is vigilante justice and its affinity is with the Western, that other story of what is going on at the Hobbesian frontier.

Given this concern for justice and the causes of its breakdown, reason is not the best tool for redressing the situation. Tyranny and anarchy are more nakedly about power and are resistant to anything but power and a calculus of self-interest. The tools best suited to enable the Hero of the thriller in his quest for justice come from technology. In the Western these were the gun, the horse, barbed wire, the railroad. In the thriller they are the same: bigger guns, faster transport, better infiltration. Knowledge serves mostly to obtain these tools, a connection famously parodied in the Bond films. Much of the story is heavily dependent on toys. Listening devices, remote sensors, clever boobytraps, magic wands and secret passages are all means to an end that was once mediated by thought alone — by little gray cells.

The thriller also shows how we have refocused our anxieties. In the English Classic it was the actions of individuals that disturbed the social order. In noir the social order was disturbed (corrupted) from the beginning, though perhaps not hopelessly, and the detective showed that if we are tough and unblinking we can navigate through the narrow channels of honor. But we began to doubt that these channels remained open. Guile and wile were better suited to keep us safe, and the spy story came into prominence. The detective spy engages in a battle of wits — which he may lose, and sometimes does — with a superior adversary, a battle in which warm knowledge (empathy and intuition) are important weapons. The action thriller hollows this out, removing the detection, substituting reflexes for wit and muscle for empathy. Being about justice and the right use of power, the action Hero has no need for the apparatus of wit, honor, guile, analytic thought, or knowledge either warm or cold. The Hero's commitments are to survival and to the defense of a cause. The justification of this cause is usually thought to be obvious and is seldom given an explanation or defense — for instance, attack by adherents of a foreign ideology, subversive elements within, coups and assassinations.

Here at last we confront something that has been lurking within the idea of intuitive knowledge since the beginning, which is the relationship between intuition and religion. Having worked through noir and hard-boiled we now have a deeper understanding of the way warm knowledge functions in the detective genre and are in a better position to see the relationship between religion and the thriller that is central to three elements of the thriller plot. First, religious conversion recalls the discovery of the conspiracy that will force the Hero's participation. This is the reverse of the invocation of the Detective as the rational man, protector of society from the forces unleashed upon it, forces the thriller unleashes not on society but on the Hero himself. Second, the acquisition of religious knowledge is a psycho-intuitive process similar to what I earlier called magic detection. Finally, there is the oceanic experience, the wholeness that is the prize of religious ecstasy. In noir this desired state is never achieved, and this fallen condition is part of the distinctive noir affect. In an action thriller this experience is embedded in the final scene of physical transcendence achieved by the Hero through the destruction of his adversary.

William James allows for a type of conversion by logic or rational thought, but from within the framework of his scientific or phenomenal psychology the much more puzzling case is the irrational one. "Now there are two forms of mental occurrence in human beings," he writes, "which lead to a striking difference in the conversion process." Citing the well-known experience of trying consciously to remember a name, he notes that sometimes the memory is jammed. But "give up the effort entirely; think of something altogether different, and in half an hour the lost name comes sauntering into your mind, as Emerson says, as carelessly as if it had never been invited. Some hidden process was started in you by this effort, which went on after the effort ceased, and made the result come as if it came spontaneously."[28] What brings such changes about is the way in which the emotional excitement alters. Things hot and vital to us to-day are cold tomorrow. It is as if seen from the hot parts of the field that the other parts appear to us, and from these hot parts personal desire and volition make their sallies. They are in short the centers of our dynamic energy, whereas the cold parts leave us indifferent and passive in proportion to their coldness."[29]

Here, in James, is a perfect picture of the workings of magic detection. What is the status of truths acquired by this means? The beholder is in a state of assurance[30] in which belief needs no confirmation by evidence, nor any procedure that could benefit by evidence. Such a degree of assurance might be an aid to the policeman or the witch-hunter but makes the effort of actual investigation pointless. Religious assurance and psycho-intuitive methods are cousins and are potentially fatal to the detective genre.

Compare Hume, writing at a time when religious truths (what we now call intuitive perceptions) were taken for granted as having the same status as empirical discoveries. Whereas the task of James was to explain intuition from within a rational context, Hume's task was to explain rationality (find its limits) within an intuitive context. He wished to know, for example, whether polytheism or monotheism was the more primitive (culturally prior). He described the condition of the "raw and ignorant multitude" as taking for granted ordinary experience but being astonished by the novel and monstrous, whereas to such a "barbarous, necessitous animal (such as man is on the first origin of society)" the regular and uniform and familiar did not excite scrutiny. By contrast, "if men were at first led into the belief of one Supreme Being, by reasoning from the frame of nature, they could never possibly leave that belief, in order to embrace polytheism. The first invention and proof of any doctrine is much more difficult than the supporting and retaining of it."[31] One cannot ratchet back to a numinous polytheism from a position of reasoned faith. Hume's view resembles Maigret's procedure in the same way as James describes coming to know as magic detection. Noir is a fragile alliance of science and religion, to be broken just as much by a retreat from the "hot parts of the field" as by too *much* hot intuition. But Hume's account does not help much to explain our recent encounters with the hot and dark. It is too detached, too cold and pale.

Freud's inquiry into our discontents, an inquiry by a man who considered religion to be an illusion, brings out the notion of the religious sentiment as originating in a "sensation of eternity, a feeling of something limitless, unbounded — as it were, 'oceanic.'"[32] This feeling dates from a time when the ego was not yet detached from the external world. Such detachment is the initial process of civilization and continues inexorably into frustration, disappointment, misery, and destruction. Thus is induced the irremediable antagonism between the demands of instinct and the restrictions of civilization.

What was a latency in warm knowledge becomes in the hot thriller an important locus of interpretation. The presence of this latency accounts for the sense of a larger purpose that is embedded in a noir plot. The hard-boiled detective is so because he refuses the implications of a spiritual dimension to his enterprise. In the detective genre it remains latent. It is the realization of this latency that effects the final separation of the action thriller from the detective genre.

The Classic (or Intellectual) Thriller

The action thriller is the contemporary repository of the purely warm knowledge inherited from the warm aspect of noir. As such, the Hero of the action thriller, through the transcendence of his own actions — that perfect presentness sought by Japanese martial artists — participates in the elements of spirituality also inherited from noir. But there is another variant of the thriller that carries forward some of the emphasis on rational detection found in the English Classic and the later spy story.

In *Chinatown* (1974, Roman Polanski), the fact one needs to know to connect the beginning with the end of this movie is that Mrs. Mulwray was raped by her father. The girl who was the issue is thus both daughter and sister to the woman. In the final scene Mrs. Mulwray is killed by the police when she tries to take the girl from her father/husband. The last thing the detective Jake says ("It's still possible") needs interpretation. The simplest understanding from our point of view is that the old noir corruption, pervasive evil, and probable bad end are still there, under a veneer of civilized Technicolor.

However, a comparison of *Chinatown* with *True Confessions* (1981, Grosbard) or Akira Kurosawa's 1963 film *High and Low* reveals something of what is fading from the leftovers of noir. *High and Low* has decent hard-boiled antecedents— it was based on Ed McBain's 87th Precinct novel *King's Ransom*. In McBain's novels noir elements give way to the police procedural, but the gritty realism of the hard-boiled remains and it is this that Kurosawa transforms further into a documentary affect. The same process is at work in *True Confessions*. The moneyed corruption is still there, along with the moral quandaries, the detective's status as a representative of the common man, and the discouraging sense of inevitable failure. But the mean street and the spiritual darkness are gone. *True Confessions* ends in the desert, in a sanctuary of penance and regeneration, under the glaring desert sun. Likewise, *High and Low* begins in an ominous atmosphere, but we discover at once that the existential conundrum is not there to complicate what we know (or think we know). All that initial atmosphere is quickly evaporated by a repertoire of steeply angled shots, high-key lighting, and visually dispersed action. Kurosawa uses the wide screen to divide the attention, either by distributing the action across the whole width or by positioning it at both ends, leaving the middle clear. The visual compositions are striking. They encourage aesthetic distance in the spectator. Noir requires involvement, emotional immediacy, not thoughtful appreciation and judgment. This aesthetic distance opens space for the intellectual distance that is a feature of cold (rational) knowledge.

Given the example of these films, Jake's remark might be taken instead to have a core of hope in this (temporary) ending of defeat and despair. This possibility is the essence of the Classic thriller. Being a thriller, the plot follows the structure of the action thriller we have just analyzed. But the presence of the Detective, albeit etiolated by his hard-boiled ancestry, suppresses the transcendent element and revives the hope that cold knowledge and rational detection are still possible.

Crime movies with noir references may be called gestures, or eulogies, as when the gate comes down at the end of *High and Low*, separating the prisoner forever from the everyday world. We think at once of the end of *The Maltese Falcon*. The end of Polanski's 2010 movie *The Ghostwriter* recapitulates his own *Chinatown* with a new murder that renders futile everything that came before. These movies evoke noir, but the cultural work they are doing is quite different. *Chinatown* is a nostalgic atavism. Jake's world is the world of Sam Spade but his methods are those of Holmes and Poirot. All we need to take this additional step back to the Classic tradition is to resurrect (in memory) that world in which it is possible to believe that a few admittedly flawed but well-meaning people can set the world right. Neither Jake nor Spade could do that, but Spade does clean up a little of it and gives us hope for more, while Jake accomplishes nothing except expose the wrongdoer. From this point, in the mouth of the thriller's cul-de-sac, one escape is to look backward toward the Classic apogee.

The noir gesture has its counterpart in the Classic gesture. What Scholes calls the ornate or late mannerist style[33] is on view in a number of films— *The French Connection, LA Confidential, Devil in a Blue Dress*— that have in common the mannerist method of distancing. Exotic settings, period styling, visual or referential complexity, a relish for intricate plotting, all achieve this result, which is to encourage a *noticing* attitude, a running internal commentary that gets in the way of a more direct experience. There is also the distancing that we encounter in *The French Connection* when we begin to get a true picture of the character of Popeye, as we would distance ourselves from a bad smell or someone distasteful — a detective who actually *is* himself mean. These are all instances of the difference between the spectator's involvement in noir action and in thrilling occurrences and another sort of thriller, nostalgic in character, that I will call Classic or Classic-inflected.

Blade Runner is an instance of nostalgic noir — we might call it Neonoir — with its characteristic blend of warm and cool detection. Deckard is an assassin, but to ply his trade he needs to get knowledge of those people (euphemistically, replicants) whom he is to kill. The movie returns to and renews Classic as well as purely noir elements, but despite its future setting it is a nostalgic period piece. It has been frequently remarked that this movie could not have been made before it was because the technology for an authentic rendition was not available. We may have been willing to suspend our disbelief for space opera and *Star Trek*, but the demands of nostalgic noir will not tolerate that degree of disbelief. Immersion in the spectacle is needed for the emotional force of the drama to be felt. It is this force that carries the subtext of intuition and irrational danger without which the film is not the real thing despite superficial uses of noir devices. The near-future setting made possible by this technology dissolves the main obstacle to contemporary (nostalgic) noir. That is, that while we still need noir comforts and assurances, we no longer believe in its everyday manifestations. The recognizably alien environment of future Los Angeles gives license to the behaviors and attitudes that would seem camp in the suburbs where we live.

Compare the opening scenes of *Blade Runner* with their counterparts in *The Big Sleep*. Marlowe's penetration of the Sternwood mansion is doubled by Deckard's return to police headquarters (which also resembles the spy recruitment formula) with the chief in the role of General Sternwood (or R) and then, a more exact re-creation, Deckard's entrance into the offices of Tyrell's replicant manufacturing empire. Tyrell is the General in his hothouse and Rachael is Vivian Rutledge. The similarity between Sean Young (who plays Rachael) and Lauren Bacall as Vivian Rutledge is marked: aloof, challenging, sardonic, not to mention her relationship with Deckard/Marlowe, which will close the story. As a thriller, *Blade Runner* revives the dual warmcool character of noir.

A comparison of three scenes that are explicitly about the getting of knowledge, and that take place in the traditional repository of knowledge, a library, will illustrate the fate of rational detection and its assimilation by the nostalgic thriller. We have the archives scene from *The Mask of Dimitrios* (1944), the library scene from *Soylent Green* (1973), and the records office scene from *Chinatown* (1974). In 1944, access to knowledge is primarily a question of permission and an order sought in arcane systems of classification of information. In the 1973 *Soylent Green* the privilege of access has become more closely guarded, and the process of getting knowledge out of information is a circular exegesis itself requiring more knowledge. *Chinatown* revisits *The Mask of Dimitrios* except that now information need not be ferreted out but merely stolen. Knowledge is neither reasoned nor hermetic but legitimately available to no one. Finally, in *Soylent Green* (and in the 2010 film *The Ghostwriter*), we have reached the point where the possession of knowledge *is* the crime and the ersatz detective (a succession of detectives) is convicted and executed for having it. It is the Detective who is the threat to order (admittedly a reprehensible order somewhat less desirable than the Classic caste system), and it is the criminals (multiple and institutional, as in the thriller) who restore the order.

All these places of knowledge are difficult to navigate, primarily because of a gatekeeper whose interests do not include any detection work. The archives in *The Mask of Dimitrios* are filed in code. The *Soylent Green* library is quasi-illegal, secretive. The *Chinatown* public records office is only bureaucratically public. The hermeneutic enterprise that initially is just difficult becomes a candle in the dark, replicating the shift from classic to noir. Re-lit in the spy story, it illuminates nothing — the world has passed from totalitarian black to Orwellian white. Nothing is hidden, but it's all a sham. The great fear of bureaucracy is that it conceals only emptiness. Anything useful that might turn up has to be stolen and re-hidden before it vanishes completely. With the thriller the purpose and role of the Detective in the getting and deployment of knowledge comes to an end.

6

The Neoclassic Revival

In 1962 P.D. James published her first book, *Cover Her Face*, featuring also for the first time her series detective Adam Dalgliesh. Two years later, Ruth Rendell published her first Inspector Wexford novel, *From Doon with Death*. Both of these books fell into familiar categories. Dalgliesh was a detective who worked in the manner of Poirot, and Wexford's milieu was the police procedural. Neither of these Classic formulas had ever gone completely out of fashion — the winner of the Edgar award in 1962 was Earle Stanley Gardner.

However, in 1964 it was George Harmon Coxe. Coxe published three books that year: *Deadly Image, One Hour to Kill,* and *The Hidden Key*; one of his series characters was Jack "Flashgun" Casey. Simenon was the winner in 1966 and the hard-boiled authors Creasey, Cain, and Macdonald in 1969, 1970, and 1972. John Dickson Carr, Ellery Queen, and Rex Stout were other winners during that period. None of these authors bear much (or any) similarity to James and Rendell.

On January 6, 2013, the first seven books on the *New York Times* bestseller list were crime novels, most of them thrillers. There were no crime novels on the trade fiction list. Among the mass market best-sellers the second was *One Shot* (Lee Child), in which a military investigator and a young lawyer try to find a small town serial killer. None of these books bears much resemblance to James or Rendell either.

Crime novels have a large readership. Twenty-three percent of my local independent bookstore's 740 feet of mainstream fiction is devoted to "mystery," as the category is now labeled. A large used book store has 984 feet of mysteries, one fourth of all types of fiction. The public library is 35 percent mysteries.

This adds up to about 60,000 crime novels on offer within a few miles of my house. Many of these do not resemble the books of James and Rendell.

What is different about these two authors? They are the practitioners of a new mode of mystery writing: the English Classic. In decline since 1935, the whodunit has made a comeback. Here is a list of some well-known mystery writers since 1962, chosen almost arbitrarily from my own shelves, in order of the year of their first publication.

Maj Sjöwall and Per Wahlöö (1965)	Iain Pears (1991)
Tony Hillerman (1970)	Donna Leon (1992)
Ellis Peters (1977)	Lisa Scottoline (1993)
Margaret Doody (1978)	Fred Vargas (1996)
Sarah Caudwell (1981)	Alexander McCall Smith (1999)
Elizabeth George (1983)	Qui Xiaoling (2003)
Lindsey Davis (1989)	Jacqueline Winspear (2003)
Charles Palliser (1989)	Kate Atkinson (2004)

What can we say about this list? It is incomplete. Where is Dick Francis, for instance? The list is odd in some other respects. Kate Atkinson's detective is a conflicted P.I. who doesn't much want to work, reminiscent of Phillip Trent, though more competent. Jacqueline Winspear's detective is an amateur woman whose ancestor is Jane Marple. Smith's and Hillerman's detectives remind one of the Australian author Arthur Upfield (1924) and his Aboriginal detective Bony. Ellis Peters writes about a medieval monk, another Father Brown. Doody's detective is Aristotle and Davis's a Roman. Pears and Palliser also exploit historical settings and conditions. Sjöwall and Wahlöö's Martin Beck series, and Caudwell's office of lawyers, recall the detective team of the 87th Precinct novels. George, Leon, Xiaoling, and Vargas are in the mold of Poirot and Holmes. Scottoline writes legal thrillers. Despite their exotic settings—ancient Greece, Puritan England, the Navajo reservation—these books follow a long-familiar formula, the first of the detective genre, the English Classic.

The Neoclassic sticks very close to the five original characteristics identified by Cawelti. The original Classic was very successful, as Barzun and Taylor show just in the size of their bibliography. The other formulas—psycho-intuitive, noir, hard-boiled, espionage, thrillers—have always been defined *against* the Classical. This is the story I have been telling, which has now come to a dead end with the thriller. There is an open space for new development. What explains the failure to take up this opportunity and the return instead to an old form?

And yet, if what I have been claiming about the relationship of genre formulas to cultural conditions is true, the Neoclassic cannot be simply a reproduction of the original. It must be different in ways that reflect the anxieties of our time, not those of a century ago when the Classic formula was born.

A full account of the Neoclassic will have to address four matters.

First, what is the Neoclassic canon? In the diverse mass of contemporary novels, can we pick out the common factors that will let us see how the Neo-classic works?

Second, we need an explanation of the contemporary return to the Classic formula. As we have seen, at every genre transition there is a driver that emerges from social change and is powered by the fears for the future and nostalgia for the past that change creates. We need an account of nostalgia and how it might work to suppress genre change.

Third, we need to ask how this web of factors—nostalgia, cultural work, warm and cold knowledge, the shaman, the moral quest—has created the figure of the Neoclassic Detective. What are the differences between the Neoclassic formula and its Classic parent? In what ways does it recapitulate developments in the detective formula since Classic times (such as the path from warm knowledge through noir to the hard-boiled/thriller nexus) that are perhaps both an unwanted heritage and a competition?

Finally, given this description of, and explanation for, the Neoclassic revival, can we deduce anything concerning its future? If the Neoclassic carries within it the fragments of genetic material of all the forms that are its ancestors, will this be lost in some evolutionary dead end like that of the thriller? If so, the figure of the Detective will pass on and some new cultural trope will arise to do its work, for there will always be fears and hopes out of which a genre can be created. This question will be the business of the next, and final, chapter.

In what follows I will try to show that the reasons for the resurrection of the old Classic formula of the detective genre are many, but they all have to do with one thing. This is the decline of confidence that we can achieve true knowledge and the associated rise of the belief or fear that absolutely everything is relative. My analysis at some points may be thought abstruse. It may be objected that ordinary people cannot possibly feel in their daily lives that there are any consequences attendant on such recondite ideas.

But perhaps matters are not so philosophical. Among the manifestation of our present unhappiness and anxiety I will examine the loss of confidence in our concept of the past. We remember, in a way, the wholeness of the pre-literate life, before history was created by writing and discrepant versions of the past sprang up. This is the lost world of common sense, navigable by ordinary people of intelligence, and now destroyed in a flood of incomprehensible technology and conflicting social mores. In the train of that memory of the commonsense world came the idea, once incredible and now difficult to accept, that history is an illusion and we may be trapped in the present, cut off from everything of value. We grow tired of coping with a flood of new insights: that we cannot prove something to be true, only false; that the moderating mix of warm and cool knowledge has been polarized, leaving us with the need to choose one or the other; that the conflicting mores and complicated protocols of modern life have produced nothing but universal spin and unrelenting deconstruction; that an infinitely recursive self-reference may indicate the emptiness behind our repertoire of masks; that the possibility of improvement is naïve. What story can we tell of the lost paradise under pressure of this nostalgia? A story that is not a ridiculous fantasy, but is believable, that does not grossly contradict our experience of contemporary life? How can the Detective be made to navigate both the world of the present and the imagined past and bring us true knowledge and the hope that the damaged fabric of our lives can be repaired?

Perhaps these claims are extreme. Perhaps most people don't experience their lives in this way, or feel any urgency to ameliorate these nonexistent problems. This is the hinge by which exegesis connects to everyday life. I am suggesting that in the last thirty years matters have fallen out as I suggest. Every time there is some unresolvable conflict over cultural or ethical issues; every time we are reminded of yet another ethnic or religious conflict somewhere in the world (or at home); every time we feel threatened by aliens in our midst, be they actual human immigrants, atheists, or dabblers in alternate universes; what is at stake are these issues: What really happened? What do we know for sure? Is there a solution to these troubles that we can agree on? When any one of us in the room could be guilty, where can we go for advice on what to do next? I think many people would agree that when the matter is posed in this way, these are indeed among the problems of life in our time and we remember, or think we do, a time when this was not so.

The story that speaks most directly to these anxieties is the detective story, and specifically the English Classic formula. The business of the Classic, when it was alive, was to resolve the conflicts created by inadequate knowledge, to explicate the past, to come to an agreement about what really happened, and to free civilized society of the liars and criminals who would harm it. And it was the figure of the Detective to whom we appealed to find out what happened, who was responsible, and bring the guilty to justice. Everything I have said to this point about the reasons for the continuing popularity of the detective story supports this. And it happens there is a story readymade for the purpose, to do the social work we want done: the English Classic. The formula only needs updating to make it contemporary — new mores, new social protocols, new technology, a changed class structure — to make the criminal, the crime, the motivation, the alibis, and the Detective plausibly modern. These updates are what I have described as the differences in the way the story is told that constitute the Neoclassic formula.

Neoclassic Versions of the Figure of the Detective

The Classic formula and its use of cool knowledge never entirely disappeared, of course. The Classic might be regarded as the native language of the detective genre, the received dialect that drove out and marginalized the others in the course of its maturation. The reasoning and discovery processes from which it was formed do not need further explication, nor do the nature of warm knowledge and its introduction into the formula. Moreover, the validity awarded to cool knowledge is anterior to warm, which had to wait for the general acceptance of the innovations and discoveries of Freud and others in psychology, in fictional narration such as Joyce's interior speech, and a widespread Neoromanticism of the 1930s and '40s.[1] Possibly at an earlier period of shamanistic thinking, the medieval prominence of religious thought or the Romantics' interest in the emotions could have produced a detective story based on warm knowledge, but other conditions were missing, those analyzed in the first chapter on the prehistory of the genre. With the ground prepared it remained to work out how a story based on cool knowledge might be told, and it is this technical problem that in readers' and critics' minds justifies the award to Poe as the originator of the genre, which we have seen is only partly true. Until it was fully worked out how to tell this sort of story, until there was less need for such a story, until new ideas in logic, epistemology, anthropology and linguistics, and in many other fields began to lend some legitimacy to a relativism people once found dangerous, there could be no Maigret. Once we were willing to allow the Detective to tap this ancient root of mysticism there was no going back. Adam Dalgliesh and every Neoclassic detective after him, the murderers and their victims, the bystanders and sidekicks, had to be given this interiority in order to be at all believable.

The first and perhaps clearest difference between the Classic and the Neoclassic is the demise of the amateur detective. The authority given by the police to Miss Marple is now inconceivable, however it may have been at the time. Aside from issues such as expertise, public safety, and the intolerance under most conditions for vigilante justice, the official police simply will not tolerate encroachment on their authority by unlicensed interlopers. The amateur detective is too difficult to build a plausible story around for writers to take their time to do it. One can imagine specialized scenarios — the pressure of circumstances or simply reckless dabbling — but such stories are difficult to repeat. Obsessive dabblers do not survive. Jacqueline Winspear's Mazie Dobbs is operating in the 1920s in the heyday of amateur detection, but she is a P.I. — significantly, a *Freudian* P.I., a creature unknown to Poirot's methodical and omniscient Miss Lemon. These days Miss Marple's doings in St. Mary Mead would not endear her to her neighbors. An amateur detective who makes a living collecting terrorists would have to be working in a Third-World country.

Even the venerable P.I. has become less common. The high-handedness of Lew Archer is simply not believable. Complaints would be made, the practice stopped, and his license taken away. If not, some morally corrupt conspiracy of tolerance between the police and the detective would be required that would unacceptably taint the whole Detective enterprise. Equally hard to explain is the simple absence of police interest that is a typical feature of the hard-boiled plot. Is it really believable that there could be a string of murders and neither the police nor the press would notice or care?

The decline of the P.I. works against the noir and hard-boiled formulas, which depend on the Detective's status as outsider. There are, however, some insiders besides the police who are available. The use of lawyers and forensic accountants are instances. Lawyers as detectives have a long history, but a quasi-P.I. such as Perry Mason is not now viable, nor is Mason's employment of the thuggish Paul Drake, as he appeared in the early films. Mason himself in those films was portrayed as a bit sleazy and disreputable.

Another factor is the enormous improvements in technology — improvements from the police point of view, at least. These have invalidated a number of plot elements and forced changes in plot structure. The advent of the computer is one such improvement. Enlarged and detailed databases, the sharing of data, computer modeling that greatly speeds up tedious fingerprint identification and the work of the police artist, access to files such as bank records and the ability to sort through massive accumulations of government paperwork are all examples of changes wrought by the computer.

The computer has also introduced a new category of crime, which has brought with it one new opportunity for the unofficial expert — the hacker. Any hacker useful to a detective story has expertise that others, particularly the police, do not have. It has taken a while, however, for writers to acquire enough expertise themselves to portray a serious hacker, much as certain science-fiction plots remained ludicrous long after the science was there to support them, and science fiction movies were held back by a need for a film technology that could create stories like *Blade Runner*. It is widely said that Lisbeth Salander, Steig Larsson's creation in *The Girl with the Dragon Tattoo* (2005), is the first really convincing hacker, a type of lone rogue who by that time was already in fact extinct.

New communications technology, the cell phone and e-mail particularly, have also forced structural changes in the detective story. Long delays for messages to be sent and received, while important things are happening that can now be prevented, have made certain plots obsolete. Detectives no longer walk anywhere, though it is harder than it was for them to get a taxi. The amazing frequency of newspapers, mail delivery, and train departures that are a feature of the Holmes stories have disappeared, but in the modern detective plot these have been replaced by other, even faster practices. Calling for help or on-the-spot information was never possible before the cell phone.

DNA testing and other forensic methods, fallible as they may be in real life, have expanded the range of the possible in the gathering of material evidence. So has the proliferation of security cameras and the miniaturization, telemetry, and data storage of monitoring and tracking devices, even if their legality is still in question.

More generally, an interest in science and scientific reasoning has, from about the time of Darwin, underlain interest in the Detective. When science began to acquire cachet, first in the '20s with Einstein as its metaphor and then again in the '50s as a consequence of space exploration, this prepared the ground for detective stories based on cool knowledge. Now that we have lost interest in the puzzle story, now that we demand rounded characters, plots with some psychological complexity and that include some bit of the workings of chance, conflicted motivations, uncertain self-knowledge — in fact, many of the features found in a literary novel — our tastes are somewhat at odds. A Classic story with a veneer of warmth is one possibility. A tale of cool knowledge tainted in its acquisition by warm prejudices and assumptions is another, but rare. Contemporary detective stories have to work out some response to this quandary.

If we try to classify contemporary novels that might qualify as Neoclassic we encounter a diversity for which any classification seems arbitrary. Most authors write a variant of the Classic formula that simply takes account of the updated features I have just listed but contains a minimum of structural changes. Others are more radical. Historical detectives are a new phenomenon, along with a more aggressive use of comedy, the extension of interest in the genre beyond its Anglo-American origins and experimentation with the formula by writers who are not primarily the authors of detective stories.

Pastness and the Disease of Nostalgia

How do we come to form our ideas of what the past was like? Might it be that those ideas are not so much about the past as about the present — that we construct a past to explain the present and also as a refuge from the present? If so, then my claim that genres are transformed under pressure of events, through cultural changes brought on by those events, gets a twist. What, for example, is the case for this transformation under pressure for the hard-boiled formula?

Is it true that the hard-boiled variant was created out of its noir predecessor because the Cold War spoiled our hopes of a safer world won by a just war, substituting a hair-trigger world even less tractable to reason than before? Is it possible to identify the differences between the world of the hard-boiled novel and the noir world? The hard-boiled detective does not spend much of his time looking for material evidence out of which to construct a narrative of what happened. Rather, his time is spent interrogating people who can tell him what happened. Presumably they can tell him, but they won't unless forced to. Formerly the problem was to identify the criminal's lies among the partial but well-meaning truths told by everyone else. In the hard-boiled world nobody tells the truth unless it pays them to do so. It isn't hard to find analogues of this situation in the Cold War experience of the 1950s and 1960s. The hard-boiled detective's victory restores the world of 1946, made safe by the power of justice, protected by the strength of just men. This story only became possible after the world of 1946 was lost. The story was not about how it actually was in 1946; it was about how we thought it was.

Why, then, when the narrative of the detective genre since our first glimpse of it in the late eighteenth century has been a narrative of moving forward, of replacing or modifying each genre formula with a new one, do we now have instead a Neoclassic formula that looks backward? Why, for the first time, does the genre not invent a new formula but reconstruct an old one?

Among the motivations imaginable for looking backward in this way is nostalgia. Is this motivation operative here? One thing suggests the possibility that it is. In addition to all else, the detective story is one about a lost paradise not in need of detectives. This lost paradise is the creation of nostalgia. Nostalgia constructs history so as to contain a paradise that can be lost.

Nostalgia lies within the realm of history. The first thing to notice about it is that history is a chirographic product: unwritten, the past is not past.[2] Oral cultures remanufacture the past continuously in light of present needs. Writing down the oral narrative makes possible comparison of successive versions, thereby extracting it from a living present in which there is only one true narrative and sending it to the repository of versions we call the past. Learning to write things down creates the idea of a discrepancy. Once literate, there is no return. Once literate, everything is potentially discrepant whether or not it is written down. Discrepant things invite being sorted into true and false. This is what the Detective does, is it not?

Probably not. Even a hard-boiled detective, who wanders the crime scene turning over rocks until he finds one with the answer under it, does not go about the work without some idea of what will count as a solution. As Karl Popper pointed out,[3] hypotheses are not found and then tested for truth, they are invented and then tested for falsity. You cannot *prove* something to be true. This comports with the genre theory developed in the first chapter, in which the solution to the crime is not proved but arrived at by a dialectic of construction and deconstruction; stories are told about the crime until everyone agrees that one (the detective's) is true. This process of storytelling recapitulates for the reader the Detective's process of getting and deploying knowledge that is the basis of the genre.

There is, however, an alternate view. "I have realized," writes Alan Watts, "that the past and the future are real illusions, that they exist only in the present, which is what there is and all there is."[4] Or as Gao Xingjian says: "You should know that there is little you can seek in this world, that there is no need for you to be so greedy, in the end all you can achieve are memories, hazy, intangible, dreamlike memories which are impossible to articulate. When you try to relate them, there are only sentences."[5] Or, "The past is in the past and does not go there from the present. Rivers which compete with one another to inundate the land do not flow. The wandering air that blows about is not moving. The sun and moon, revolving in their orbits, do not turn around,"[6] which is Chinese but well might be from Heraclitus.

According to this view, history is an illusion created by memory and fixed in words. Sorting out illusory discrepancies is a pointless exercise and nostalgia is not a clinging to this or that memory but memory itself. This is the freight of civilization identified by Freud, in *Civilization and Its Discontents*, as the central paradox of our unhappiness, that out of the cultural authority by which we seek agreement on such enterprises as a true history arises the longing for our lost freedom to choose what history we want. This longing is nostalgia, a wish that it were so. Or more correctly, a wish that we could make it so.

A story reifies that wish. Stories are pre-historic. They are all already true. There is no such thing as a discrepant story. They exist in affective time; that is, time as we experience it, not as we measure it. Affective time is incommensurable with the order and the nature of events. Here is Jaques Lacan's contribution to the discussion. It was because of Lacan's desire to reform psychoanalytic practice that the nature of the self-reflective subject needed to be elucidated. In Lacan's view, the subject cannot fully reconstruct his own story because the story cannot include its own affective event horizon. Both the beginning and the end are missing from his consciousness. Autobiographies are created and ordered affectively: the events of one's life exist only because of the futile struggle to drag them out of the past, only insofar as each one can be hooked to the one before. The mental ordering and selection that are required to tell one's story is the very light by which the past can be seen.[7]

This view of history does not contradict the other one, in which the true story is not proved but agreed upon. It calls into question the nature of the story itself, turning it into a series of events ungrounded at both ends, invalidating any solution to the crime as no more than an artificial closure of a story that can't be closed.

The most intransigent statement of this problem is Popper's, in *The Poverty of Historicism*.[8] Popper states that to seek the laws of history is to fall into superstition. He says that the course of events is unpredictable, a claim I take to be stronger than that of chaos theory concerning the butterfly in Brazil's implication in the typhoon in Tokyo. The course of events is not uncomputable because causal complexity prevents us mortals from knowing exactly how events are connected. Popper states that events are not connected. His mathematics may be faulty, but it doesn't matter. If events cannot be narratively connected there are no stories.

But there is worse. Popper, in his concept of piecemeal engineering,[9] which he proposes as an alternative to utopian thinking (that is, an obsession with solutions), does suggest a way of getting on without ends or means. Piecemeal engineering resembles the narrative procedure of one thing after another. That is, we can give some reasons why Fred married Ginger even though we thought it a bad idea at the time, before it all went south and Fred took those pills, but *it doesn't add up to anything*. It's not a syllogism. It's tinkering. Bricolage. Our dislike of this claim, Popper points out, is due to our fondness for holistic thinking.[10] We tend to think that if two people are murdered under similar circumstances there must be a common factor at work, something that has tripped up many a reader of detective stories.

If we accept the claim that history is created by the telling of it, it would seem that history is not a mode of knowledge but a practical instrument for solving present problems.[11] Further, if history is a socially constructed story about the past then the claim that events are connected in such-and-such a way is just that: a convenient story. The solution to a detective story is not provably true but only agreed upon; in reality it solves (closes) nothing, is justified only by expediency, and the putative knowledge on which this solution is based is not obtained by either cool or warm reasoning but by trial and error. *Tinkering.*

In *The Clockwork Muse: The Predictability of Artistic Change*[12] Colin Martindale does away with even this rump analysis in favor of a law-like, statistically manageable process. We see Romanticism, or some other system, cropping up again and again in new costumes. We see that artistic movements have a characteristic life cycle. People's needs are few at bottom, astonishingly few when one steps back from the baroque individual, and our repertoire of means for satisfying these needs is small, possibly meager. Martindale puts a Freudian lens to these needs, which allows him to measure the recrudescence and decline of "primordial content"[13] across artistic periods, media, and styles. Presumably one could substitute a Marxist lens, or some other ideology, and produce a similar pattern but with the contributors in different allegiances. As a style becomes played out, in Martindale's account, its practitioners thrash about more and more frantically in search of a replacement, a new stimulus and an escape from habituation. Heterogeneity increases. A new paradigm appears, everyone flocks to the victorious hero's camp, and the order of normal art is restored.

Martindale's account is the one I have been giving of the process of change in the detective genre formula. We can point out the correlation between social crises and genre shifts, we can suggest why a particular crisis might have made a particular genre variation unstable, we can point out the ways in which the outcome of the crisis fits the new genre variation. We cannot claim that the genre is the *product* of the crisis. The genre exists *in* history. History is only a plausible account of what may have happened.

Nostalgia claims otherwise. The piquancy of the lost paradise story is the evident discrepancy between the present and the imagined paradise. To explain this discrepancy we must believe that the account of this paradise is a true one and that the loss of it was fated, inevitable. The story is circular. That the paradise was lost is evidence for our present fallen state, and our fallen state explains why the paradise should be lost. Nostalgia pretends that the present state is an inevitable outcome of the past, whereas all that has happened is that we have made a decision to be nostalgic and justified it with a story about the past invented for the purpose. My deconstruction of the nature of history was intended to show the falsity of the claims of nostalgia and at the same time the falsity of any claims about transcendental truths underlying the detective genre formula. The formula works the way it does because we want it to work that way, and the Detective is an iconic figure because we have need of such a one. *Nostalgia is a disease of history.*

An exemplum, from *The Once and Future King:*[14]

"If I were to be made a knight," said the Wart, staring dreamily into the fire, "I should insist on doing my vigil by myself, as Hob does with his hawks, and I should pray to God to let me encounter all the evil in the world in my own person, so that if I conquered there would be none left, and, if I were defeated, I would be the one to suffer for it."

"That would be extremely presumptuous of you," said Merlyn, "and you would be conquered, and you would suffer for it."

"I shouldn't mind."

"Wouldn't you? Wait till it happens and see."

"Why do people not think, when they are grown up, as I do when I am young?"

"Oh dear," said Merlyn. "You are making me feel confused. Suppose you wait until you are grown up and know the reason?"

"I don't think that is an answer at all," replied the Wart, justly.

Merlyn wrung his hands.

"Well, anyway," he said, "suppose they did not let you stand against all the evil in the world?"

"I could ask," said the Wart.

"You could ask," repeated Merlyn.

He thrust the end of his beard into his mouth, stared tragically at the fire, and began to munch it fiercely.

The elegiac tone here emanates from Merlyn, who knows how all this will turn out, but also from our identifying with (and approving of, abetted by the very Merlyn) the Wart's unrealistic idealism. That, we say, is how great things get done. What we overlook is that, unlike Merlyn, we don't know how things will have turned out. Elegy is the affect of nostalgia, just as story is the affect of time. And just as affective time is incommensurate with any claims for a true history, so is affective nostalgia incommensurate with any rival account of the way things were. What saves the little story about Wart and Merlyn is its refusal to come to conclusion, its willingness to leave us munching our beards.

We have seen that each variant of the detective genre gives an account of its predecessor in the changes it makes to the formula. Can we say that these accounts are nostalgic? This question has particular relevance for the Neoclassic detective story because unlike the other variants we have encountered, this one turns back to an old variant, the lost paradise of the Classic.

John Rawls, in his remarks on the utopian fantasy,[15] identifies Hegel's view of alienation as helpful. Very simply, the source of alienation is the dialectic itself, the process by which thought systems modify themselves and coalesce. The desire to end the dialectic and be complete, the longing to give up consciousness and enter the Tao, is the origin of the lost paradise story. Alienation is a belief that paradise is unrecoverable. Alienation and nostalgia are identical, the one defeated and the other hopeful, and the cure, as we have seen, lies in a decision to reject the utopian fantasy and become reconciled to the world as it is.

Against the Hegelian view of nostalgia are the ideas of Svetlana Boym, who speaks of nostalgia as homesickness.[16] She divides the emotion into two methods, which she terms *reflective* and *restorative*, by which we give shape and meaning to longing. "Reflective nostalgia dwells in *algia*, in longing and loss, the imperfect process of remembrance," while "restorative nostalgia puts the emphasis on *nostos* and proposes to rebuild the lost home and patch up the memory gaps." People who seek restorative nostalgia "do not think of themselves as nostalgic; they believe that their project is about truth. This kind of nostalgia characterizes national and nationalist revivals all over the world, which engage in antimodern myth-making.... Restorative nostalgia manifests itself in total reconstructions of monuments of the past, while reflective nostalgia lingers on ruins, the patina of time and history, in the dreams of another place and time."

Following Hegel, we would say that the Neoclassic project is in bad faith and doomed. Following Boym, we would say that the figure of the Neoclassic Detective is restorative, an instance of reconstructive, anti-modern myth-making.

Whichever is the correct view (if correctness is a viable notion here), we now have a fuller account of how genre change can be driven by social change, and we are in a position to query the Neoclassic canon and eventually to ask whether the present state of the genre has a future.

The Making of the New Classic Detective

In analyzing every genre formula I have asked the same questions. Here is a list of them.

On whose behalf is the Detective working?
How is information turned into knowledge?
How are clues assembled into a narrative?
How are the clues acquired?
Is the Detective himself at risk?
What is the effect of subsequent murders on the solution to the first one?
How is the solution revealed?
What social issues does the crime reveal?
What are the roles of the Detective, the criminal, the bystanders?
How is the story told? Is there a Chronicler?
In what ways does the story resolve social tensions and affirm common values?
In what way does the story explore the limits of the possible?

This is a long list and I am not going to work through it top to bottom. But there are some striking features of the Neoclassic that need to be pointed out: the changed status of the Detective exemplified by the demise of the amateur, the changed balance of warm and cold knowledge exemplified by the long-delayed creation of the female detective, and finally the failure of the attempt to adapt an old genre tradition to present needs.

First, the Neoclassic Detective's status is no longer that of a person outside society but has been rolled back to its position before the noir shift, that of a person with standing in society but an outsider to the local group. As a consequence, neither the group nor the enclosing society can be thoroughly corrupt. This would tar the Detective also, especially as the Neoclassic Detective is often cast as a policeman. This would bring disrepute to the institutions of social cohesion. In the Neoclassic story only some persons can be seriously wrong.

We see this in the almost universal feature of the detective's quarrel with a superior officer. The reasons for this vary. The detective is insubordinate, prone to create political debacles, uses extralegal methods, or is simply personally unacceptable. This last reason is used often to add a by now specious gender tension to the story—Jane Tennison in the long-running TV series *Prime Suspect* is an example. This gender tension is part of a perceived need to humanize the detective, to provide vulnerabilities (nearly all detectives seem to have trouble with their relationships), disabilities, unusual tastes (Dalgliesh the poet), money troubles, hectic family lives—whatever will decrease the emotional distance between the detective and the reader. This strategy is inherited from noir. Poirot is given his little foibles and we are treated in the course of the stories to a growing friendship with Japp as we

learn more about Japp's difficult wife. But it is with Maigret and the introduction of warm knowledge that we begin to encounter the detective's everyday life partly because with the new intuitive methods the story needs to let
us in to how the detective thinks. Again and again we will see that the Neoclassic's features are recycled aspects of old forms. The Neoclassic, in fact,
recapitulates the whole history of the genre.

The Amateur

The demise of the P.I. and the amateur and the return of the police detective is partly due to the increasing intolerance of society toward vigilantes,
and the difficulty of unofficial persons to get access to the facts, the crime
scene, police technology, and a whole host of privileges once accorded the
Classic detective. It is impossible to imagine now that a busybody like Marple
or the *droit de seigneur* snooping of an aristocratic Wimsey would be tolerated.
The present solution, if for some reason the author wants an amateur or
unofficial sleuth, is generally to retreat to the ratiocinative thriller, in which
a tyro can be sucked into any situation one chooses and then must extricate
himself from it. Roman Polanski's film *The Ghostwriter* (2010) is an excellent
example, but structurally this plot is little brother to *The Ipcress File, Ashenden,*
and others in what is a different tradition, the spy story. The old P.I. ruse of
being called into the case because the police must be kept out of it is no longer
very plausible, but there are some openings for unofficial detectives particularly in cases where there is no crime in the usual sense (Precious Ramotswe
restores harmony), the whole thing is too shadowy to seek help (Woody Allen's
Manhattan Murder Mystery), the crime falls within the potential detective's
expertise (e.g., accounting fraud) and when exposed can be safely turned over
to the police, or the investigator is simply a skilled snoop with chutzpah such
as a news reporter, an old trope from the days of print news. All of this only
serves to further constrain the Neoclassic detective's outsider status, rendering
it essentially nil, in fact, and so disables the detective's role in soothing our
fears for the integrity of the social fabric.

The same impulse to humanize the detective applies also to his (or her —
we now have gender parity in the genre) associates, the bystanders, and sometimes the criminal as well, but particularly the victims. There is a marked
Neoclassic taste for gaudy crimes, or for the murder to occur far enough into
the story to have given us time to feel the tragedy of our new friend's death.
The story also benefits by a new source of suspense as the reader wonders
who will be killed and is invited to play detective on this preliminary problem.
Notice that this feature invalidates the Classic function of the second murder.
We are in the noir world again, where the narrative distance between we readers and the Detective is minimized. And we can now suggest that this distance
is minimized because we want a more intense, emotionally involving story,

because we have come to believe that this is the right way to tell stories, and because there has been, in most things, a subtle shift in what we consider to be the locus of knowledge. Knowledge is no longer *out there,* waiting to be discovered. What is out there is information. The detective does not discover the truth; he manufactures it. This is a disturbing idea. The best way to neutralize it is to allow us access to the detective's thinking, so that we will come to feel that the detective is trustworthy and that we are in good hands. With this narrative strategy the old one in which the reader joins the narrative midway, recapitulating the detective's work of reconstructing previous events, can no longer be used. This is a considerable narrative loss. The detective, when he reconstructs the past, exposes the faulty interpretation of events that led to his being called in to begin with, and opens the case to being solved. The reader, when asked to do this same reconstruction, is likely to get it wrong. This is what the Classic wants to do—create surprise and satisfaction in the dénouement when the mistaken interpretation is exposed.

The professionalization of the Detective, the interiority demanded by new standards of storytelling, a change in how we think knowledge is acquired, an altered functionality for all of the traditional genre roles serves to make the superficially Neoclassic story more resemble literary mainstream fiction. These changed emphases mute the puzzle that was a central feature of the Classic and create a hospitable environment for features from the literary novel, blurring the line between the two. This is not a happy development for some readers who like the genre just *because* it works differently from mainstream fiction and does different social work.

I will take the Detective herself as an example. The Classic detective was not at personal, physical risk. This risk was made a threat in noir. In the hardboiled plot the risk was offered in bad faith — we fear it, only to be told that the Detective is in fact invulnerable. This bad faith is withdrawn in the spy story and the intellectual thriller. We have become accustomed to all of these narratives. All of them require a bond of feeling from the reader to the detective. Stories that do not offer that bond are perceived as artificial. Multiply these forced changes through the whole detective genre and you get something like an intellectual thriller dressed in Classic clothes.

Let's look at some other forced changes. We wish to introduce some sympathy for the victim, and at the same time create a more psychologically complex criminal worthy of such a victim. As these two figures are elaborated in their new roles to create a tragedy it is probable that they will become entangled with each other, introducing a moral ambiguity and relativism many readers will find disturbing. They will find it so because what they are seeking is exactly relief from this anxiety. But if the story is clearly divided into white and black hats this will seem cartoonish, damaging the psychological realism we were seeking.

A very good way to justify this widening gap is to make the crimes more horrific, eliminating any possibility of a nuanced response. A now-common feature of the Neoclassic is the presence of unlikable, difficult, even deranged characters in important roles. If the Detective is to be opened up to human failings and mistakes, these failings can now be serious—succumbing to a desire for revenge, getting the wrong man out of an obsessive need to complete the case, and so on. In the Classic formula such mistakes would have to be recovered eventually in order to preserve our respect and the genre's sense of justice. And so it goes around: for each relaxation of a demand (for justice, for unambiguous moral values, for unconflicted personalities, for intimacy)— a relaxation driven by a search for greater realism — we have to make other changes (the crimes more horrific, the criminals more twisted, the victims more pitiable, the bystanders more interfering, the chronicler more untrustworthy) so that the story is still able to resolve tensions, affirm existing attitudes, and assimilate social changes. The more the characters' roles become entangled the more difficult this becomes.

We also notice in the Neoclassic a new prevalence of sidekicks, or at least of confidantes. The Classic sidekick was not unknown, of course. But Captain Hastings, be he Poirot's *mon ami*, cannot be admitted to real intimacy, which would compromise the detective's Classic apartness. It is significant that Marple does not have a sidekick — in a way, she is herself the sidekick — in order to break down the distancing effect of the Classic tradition. Harriet Vane was Peter Wimsey's protégée and acted as a sidekick for a brief moment, but a true love interest harks back to Phillip Trent's difficulties with objectivity. Now the opposite prevails. Sharon McCone is married — although her husband calls her McCone and their collaboration is sporadic — and the sidekick can be the entrée to the detective's personal life.[17]

The Neoclassic sidekick opens up possibilities for distributed detecting. Sidekicks might be able to go where detectives can't or have needed social skills. Inspector Lewis, the former sidekick to Morse, now has a sidekick of his own who is an Oxford graduate and can serve as Lewis's guide in that inbred place. Sidekicks might be working-class or of a second-class ethnicity and so be an avenue for exploring issues of class and prejudice that might have nothing to do with solving the crime.

The Female Detective

As we saw at the beginning, warm knowledge was thought (and still is thought) to be the special province of women. The humanizing strategies of the Neoclassic are ideal for a woman detective and the need for official standing closes off the old subordinate role. One contribution of the Neoclassic has been the creation of a range of serious female detectives and generally to soften or remove the anti-feminist tone traditional to the genre.

An earlier version of this character, in the late thirties, was distributed between two types: the Pert Dame and the soft woman with a hard heart, as exemplified in two movies, *Private Detective* and *Nick Carter, Master Detective*. An important matter raised by this early manifestation of the woman detective is the issue of a subordinate role. In neither of these movies is the woman a sidekick, but nevertheless in both there is a man, the supposed real detective, to whom the successful solution is attributed in the end. This situation could be undermined by giving the apparent sidekick an ambiguous gender, officially a woman but in role and behavior a man, with a gender-neutral name such as (in these two movies) Lou and Jinks.

But here a problem arises. Only one of the traditional roles for a woman is available for this purpose: the Pert Dame. But the whole concept of the Pert Dame is defined against the man in whose shadow she can be pert. Ultimately there is no solution but to grant the woman full status as the Detective. We began to find this out in the early '80s with (among others) Sarah Paretsky in her character V.I. Warshawski. What is necessary is not to do away with the soft character (the Lush) but to harden the Dame's shell by the same method as Sam Spade used in his speech to Brigid O'Shaughnessy at the end of *The Maltese Falcon* when he tells her why, despite some things said and done, he is sending her over: for honor, that which he owes to his dead partner no matter what sort of sleaze Miles Archer was, and prudence, that which he owes to himself, to thrust off the fetters that this woman would use to confine him. It hurts, but Brigid O'Shaughnessy is going to jail. When the Dame can talk this way we have the beginnings of a female detective who can set gender issues at naught.

It is important to note that Paretsky (with Sue Grafton, Marcia Muller, and others) was not the first to grapple with this problem, nor does the change pass exclusively through the hard-boiled. P.D. James's Cordelia Gray (*An Unsuitable Job for a Woman*) in 1972, Amanda Cross's Kate Fansler beginning in 1964, Miss Marple and Harriet Vane in the '30s, and several nineteenth century characters of note mentioned in earlier chapters are all in search of other solutions. By 2004 the modern female detective was sufficiently established to be parodied in the film *Sky Captain and the World of Tomorrow*, in which the characters Frankie and Polly fission the established union back into its original parts: the Dame and the Lush.

Until very recently the movies have shown their conservative, mainstream nature with the softer variant of the Detective. Kathleen Turner played V.I. Warshawski in 1991 and a worse affect and body type could hardly be imagined. This was a clever lightweight, not a bloodied kickboxer. A character like Kay Scarpetta, half hotshot lawyer and half forensic detective, has never been filmed. Instead we have remakes of *Mission Impossible*. The only representative of warm and cold at the box office until now may be Marge Gunderson in *Fargo* (1996). Lisbeth Salander in *The Girl with the Dragon Tattoo* (2010) is a new amalgam of every characteristic invented so far — not a side-kick but a colleague, iron-hard and vengeful with hidden vulnerabilities, a brilliant hacker and thrilling action hero. She is an inverted Marge. What changed in the fourteen years between these two characters? Two wars, the rise of international terrorism, 9/11, a recession, corruption and foolhardiness in the banking industry, an oil spill in the Caribbean, and many other things to turn the hopefulness of one into the rage of the other.

The Uses of Nostalgia

Here is the contemporary warm/cool problem. The cool Detective has to be smart and rational and expert at something the culture considers brainy — hence lawyers and scientists. The warm Detective needn't now be hard-bitten, and probably ought not be, but she can't have an intuitive, empathic streak without also being a little tough and emotionally resilient. In the detective artist — Sherlock Holmes and hardly anyone since — warm and cool were not just balanced but blended. The contemporary detective artist has several faces, not one: Dalgliesh and the poet, the competent sleuth with his dysfunctional private life, the Navaho Jim Chee who is polluted by death, Martin Beck increasingly disabled by his own increasingly decrepit society. The hard-boiled detective would have delivered a smart little sermon and got on with the work. Is it because dissimulation and surreptitiousness, circumspection, and hidden knowledge are now part of our everyday experience? Or is there a more general cause, that we have begun to be suspicious about knowledge — what it is, how to get it, who has it, what to do with it? Knowledge is to detectives as wood is to carpenters. To become suspicious that "uncovering" is actually retelling or reinventing by people with other (possibly nefarious) purposes is one thing. To think that everything we suppose we know is just a story, that we are hollow people who disappear when our masks are taken off,[18] is more than just universal spin and unrelenting deconstruction. Women are familiar with this. Philosophers and scientists are familiar with this. Has this suspicion become common property, and we are now advised that safety lies not in a judicious mix of warm and cool — the detective artist — but in the fight-or-flight dialectic of the thriller? Is this one of the sources of Neoclassic nostalgia?

I have remarked on the link between the need to humanize the detective and the tendency for crimes to become more lurid. Stories about women detectives in particular tend to move toward the sensational. It isn't just men who sexualize these stories. The sexualization of a genre already inclined to psychodrama, fertile ground seeded by the psycho-intuitive tradition, turned our attention from cool detection toward the gruesome or morally shocking crime, the sordid histories of the participants, and the daily crises and depressions of the detectives. Sexualization foregrounds the body and the always embodied emotions. Men and women both are expected to display sensitivity to these matters. The readiest indicator of the true suspect in the Neoclassic is the character who fails to do so.

Consider the by-play between Lynley and his sidekick Havers, which takes up so much of the time in this mystery series by Elizabeth George. They behave like a mismatched married couple. Lynley, who is married below his station to the working-class Havers, conducts unhappy liaisons on the side with a woman who purports to be his real wife, while the female half of the detective family becomes more and more possessive, doing such things as setting the metaphorical bed on fire and complaining about not having a life, ultimately engaging in unauthorized independent detection. Watson was occasionally invited to think for himself, but never like this. The two of them (Lynley and Havers) are then deployed to avenge a female victim, a revolting child murder or a prostitute ripped to pieces, which brings all these sexual attentions to the fore and complicates (or even disables) the detecting. Somewhere in our increasingly complex social lives, the welter of conflicting mores, and confused protocols may lie another of the sources of Neoclassic nostalgia.

What would a low-temperature detective be like? A tough-love mom? You can't take the crime out of the genre, or the association of crime with violence. Insofar as feminine means not macho, would a sage, a person of quiet power who will protect us from the worst evils, a nonviolent person who must be provoked to action and never uses more than the minimum force, qualify?

Precious Ramotswe, Alexander McCall Smith's Botswanaian detective, might be such. Pre-Precious, the low-temperature Detective was an unusual but not unheard-of variation on the genre. Judge Dee comes to mind, the Zen detective pair Grijpstra and De Gier, and Pennac's Belleville novels featuring the domestic comedy of Monsieur Malaussène, who solves crimes by inadvertence, dogged persistence, and networking. But to get people to sit through a *film* of this sort would require that the usual attractions be replaced by something like a looming threat, and at once we are back in the territory of the thriller, where knowledge serves primarily to protect the endangered detective. And of course, if that detective is a woman this will be all to the good for the box office.[19] Under present conditions the Neoclassic will tend to the sensational and end in the thriller, by a different route than noir but with the same consequence: the dispersal of the tradition.

The *Prime Suspect* series, Mizejewski reminds us, "never allowed us to forget the grimness of [Tennison's] job, her life, her choices. We frequently saw her alone in her flat, or cut off from colleagues, or without a friend to celebrate a triumph."[20] Sgt. Havers isn't any better off. This may be a statement about routine female experience, but many modern male detectives live similarly. We never really cared whether Poirot was *happy*. Unhappiness was a property of other people and a temporary consequence of the intrusion of violence, which the detective was supposed to fix. Like sex and suspense, grimness seems to be one of the strange attractors of the Neo-classic. There never was nor ever will be any safe normalcy in these stories. The Detective uncovers, learns facts, but it makes no difference. What's the point? It's *the Detective* who is, who has to be, the story.

Misejewski suggests another cultural cause for this generic drift toward either the domestic psychodrama or the thriller:[21] the legacy of the mysterious woman, the femme fatale, Milton Caniff's Dragon Lady in *Terry and the Pirates*. This cultural icon is made up of two qualities: the Bad Girl and an "inscrutable aura and shadow." These are not the exclusive property of the woman, of course. Spade has them. What Spade doesn't have is the right gender. Nobody thinks twice about bad *boys* and mysterious, devious *men*. They're all over the place, whereas a fatal femme detective is a bizarre idea, a female Fantômas. Either it's a pose to be discovered in the end so that the plot can melt away in universal domesticity, or we are being asked to sanction a social violation.[22]

A judicious comparison might reveal something about this. If we set side-by-side an embodiment of Poirot by David Suchet (*Lord Edgware Dies*, 2000) and an exactly contemporaneous film about the meeting of young Conan Doyle with the model of Holmes, Dr. Joseph Bell (*Murder Rooms: The Dark Origins of Sherlock Holmes*) what do we see?

The difference between these two is that in the neo-Holmes, the murderer (O'Neill) needs very little motive beyond a twisted concern with purity. This is because the *mise-en-scène* attributes so many criminal and degenerate qualities to the society in which he (the murderer) is embedded that his behavior is strongly over-determined. Whereas in the well-lit Poirot society of polite detection, this social corruption is unheard of and the criminals go off the rails one at a time. The Poirot murderer is a deviant from, not a representative of, his society, and to drive him to murder requires many strong and complicated experiences. This is a major reason for the escalating gruesomeness of Neoclassic murders. If the 2000 Conan Doyle model were to be followed we would be in the realm of noir. The 2000 Poirot allows us to have it both ways—cool detection in a hot world. Here then we have yet another of the sources of nostalgia. Our experience of the society in which we live is irrefutably that of the Conan Doyle; we wish it were Poirot's.

For both sleuths (Poirot and the proxy Holmes) a number of characters are cast up as possible malefactors. In Poirot's England we know only one of them did it; in the rethink of dark Edinburgh any one of them could have.[23] The new-made Holmes story is constructed like a thriller, as are most contemporary stories that are not comedies or nature documentaries. The Poirot story is built on a society now vanished. Poirot is not battling irrationality as such, only a particular instance. A contemporary invocation of this vanished world, such as Robert Altman's *Gosford Park*, would have to present itself as historical fiction or include a strong dose of irony to be taken seriously. Altman's troupe soon enough emigrates from this two-faced world to inhabit the less self-referential nostalgia of Elizabeth George and P.D. James to follow the ordinary Neoclassic practice.

When we assent to these stories we set aside our relativizing skepticism about agendas, constructions, social objects, meta-narratives, and so forth so as to enjoy a night out — no worries, no morning after. Nostalgia is at work. The same motive drives the thriller — the fear of the creeping hegemony of relativism that complicates the concept of knowledge with unwanted sophistication and spoils the belief that ordinary people can operate the world without Higher Learning. The thriller sneers at this; the nostalgic revival bemoans it. Most of the time we are willing to accept Hume-Foucault relativism so long as skepticism about knowledge and human perception of the phenomenal world does not degenerate into cynicism and amorality. The fear of such a degeneration is what inflamed the arguments over existentialism and humanism[24] in the years of the original noir and is one of the drivers of our present nostalgia. Then, the assurances of Sartre (and others, despite conflicting alliances) were simply shouted down. As in all repressive families, this only made things worse. It won't do to underestimate either of the parties to this struggle, which resembles, intellectually and culturally, that between the Impressionists and the *Academie* in France of the 1860s and '70s. The Neoclassicists have a serious grievance with the world, which can be reified and assuaged by the Detective. The trope of the Detective has served in this role for now over a century.

It won't do, however, to draw this classicizing nostalgia with too few lines. For instance, as between the Poirot of the Edgware and Ackroyd stories, note such common features as the interest in clocks. But a shadow has darkened the Ackroyd tale that is not there in the more purely classic Edgware puzzle. Both of them turn on timing, but time in Ackroyd is infested with feelings about lateness, missed opportunity, and inevitable decline. Time in the Edgware puzzle is only the ticking of a well-running machine, a toy. Both victims have knives sticking out of their necks. Edgware is discovered face down; Ackroyd is face up, the fact of his horrid deadness exposed. Tongues click over Edgware's body. We hear about missing money. There are some cool observations by Poirot and one of those "open and shut case" remarks by Jaap, as well as some detached hatred exposed by several parties as if hatred were reasonable and common. This is not the way the Ackroyd goes. The difference between the two charts the direction in which the classic tradition is to be modified to make it more plausible for a contemporary audience. *The Dark Origins of Sherlock Holmes* is the predicted result. In our time, wherever we find hopes for the improvement of humankind (however unlikely) and a wish for objective knowledge of the world, we are in the presence of nostalgia. But this nostalgia is hollow. In our time it would be difficult to publish an effective drama without psychological explanations for everything, especially the childhood traumas in which we indulge ourselves. The result is darker than the sunny, original Classic.[25]

I cannot conclude this topic without mentioning one case in which nostalgia can be turned to positive effect. My example is Juan José Campanella's film *The Secret in Their Eyes* (Argentina, 2009). Campanella's work requires some exposition, but the point here is that nostalgia actually drives the plot, and in doing so exposes itself as an obstacle both to the solution of the crime and to the detective's own happiness. We begin with an old, unsolved crime about which a retired detective is trying to write a novel. He consults a colleague, a woman who was his superior at the time and with whom we learn he was in love. In the main part of the film a double investigation is recounted, intercalating the original inquiry with the new one. In the course of this both the detective and his colleague come to regret that they did not acknowledge their earlier love. We also learn that the man thought to be the murderer, who was convicted but then released by Agentinian Security to serve their own purposes, was in truth the villain. But we also learn that the husband of the dead woman, unable to overcome his grief, has captured the murderer and held him in solitary confinement for twenty-five years, as he would have been but for the intervention of Security.

None of the formal elements of this story are new. The present-day detective serves as his own Chronicler, filtering the story just as Watson would. His method is intuitive, as Maigret's was. There is what appears to be a Classic second murder, when a friend of the detective is assassinated by men who have mistaken him for the detective. Then, the detective does not solve the crime. Incorrectly, he doubts his original solution; meanwhile another man sees and acts on the truth. However, this supposed truth, not supported by any objective evidence, may in fact have been wrong, and the obsessed husband's incarceration of the supposed murderer is the real crime. This is the actual second murder as explicated by Todorov and introduced here in the discussion of the English Classic. At this point the detective's original construction of the crime, deconstructed by him during his second investigation, becomes congruent with narrative time and is reconstructed by the viewer, only to have the story deconstructed at once by the true detective. This leaves the original detective in the position of only another bystander. The fabric of society is in Neoclassic fashion sufficiently knitted up to allow the two lovers to finally unite.

Nostalgia provokes the second investigation. Throughout, nostalgia hides the truth. Nostalgia for a lost love warps the purposes of the detective. It is only when nostalgia is cleared away and the obsessed nostalgia of the true detective is revealed that everyone, including the viewer, is released into the present. The past is finally in the past. Neoclassic practice has been turned against itself to expose the futility of Neoclassicism's response to our contemporary anxieties.

Neoclassic Variations

A Neoclassic detective story might go this way: A Detective and his Sidekick are investigating the murder of X. They disagree on how to proceed; D deplores S's heavy-handed methods. Then D is murdered. S takes over the investigation and the narration. This second murder (of D, coming after the apparently connected murder of X) complicates matters rather than simplifying them. S discovers that D may have been a spy, a double agent himself responsible for X's death. Investigations at the scene of the second murder reveal that D had been waiting for someone but instead was himself attacked, and when he attempted to escape was brought down by a second person in his path. There is reason to suppose that D was lured into this trap by a Woman, probably the person who was destroying his marriage and made him a security risk. Then W is implicated in the murder of X, also, and to discover the identity of the second person, who had been lying in wait for D, becomes urgent. At this point, S comes under pressure to stop the investigation. When he does not, he finds himself also at risk of his life, probably from W, but who is she working for? To save himself, S begins a frantic interrogation of possible suspects in the murder of X, hoping to stay ahead of W long enough to find a credible counter-threat ... and so on. Perhaps such a story, ludicrously complex and combining as it does so many successive versions of the Detective, would not be recognized as a Neoclassic. A little analysis using the tools that have been developed here, however, will show that it is. Are there actual novels presenting similar interpretational challenges?

At the beginning of this chapter I remarked on the number of writers presently working in the Neoclassic mode and attempted to sort them in some meaningful way. One category was the standard or mainstream formula. Being mainstream, we would expect to find a high proportion of the practitioners here, and to find continuity with the never-quite-severed family genealogy. As exemplars, we might choose P.D. James, whose writing career began in 1962 with *Cover Her Face,* and the Martin Beck series by Maj Sjöwall and Per Wahlöö (1965–1975). For a younger author we might look to Lisa Scottoline, whose first novel was published in 1993, or Donna Leon (the Brunetti novels beginning in 1992).

P.D. James's credentials are impressive. Commander Adam Dalgliesh is an original in the great flood of high-ranking police detectives since, each packaged with the necessary partner. The progression of Dalgliesh's partners is instructive. He began with two sergeants and then was given a detective chief inspector. Both Dalgliesh and Massingham are difficult men, moody and clouded as to their true feelings, Massingham with the hard shell and Dalgliesh the hard core. Massingham eventually leaves the force for the House of Lords and, after some interim occupants, is replaced by a woman, Kate Miskin. This progression, aside from being socially meticulous, offers opportunities for the various melodramas and romantic stories that are a necessary part of the Neoclassic to tell a more psychologically realistic story, along with the lamentable troubles of the Detective himself. Dalgliesh gets SARS at one point. The stories are impeccably traditional: the crime, the disruption of the social fabric, the invocation of the Detective, the second murder and the series of red herrings, the emergence of the truth and the dramatic revelation. Less flashy than Holmes, Dalgliesh proceeds just as Holmes did — acute observation on which an inference chain can be built, systematic validation of shrewd guesses, consolidation of the reconstructed series of events with material evidence firmly linking the Detective's reasoning to the criminal's guilt.

Lisa Scottoline's stories about the lawyer Mary DiNunzio are structured within the same tradition. DiNunzio is a woman and a lawyer, not an actor nor a role to be found in the Classic but perfectly ordinary now, and a typical accommodation. The genre, no longer hospitable to amateurs like Miss Marple and wary of too heavy a diet of police inspectors, has found dramatic possibilities in professions ordinarily associated with crime such as forensics, forensic accounting, and softened-up versions of the hard-boiled P.I. such as Kate Atkinson's Jackson Brodie. This thread of continuity runs right through the genre from its beginnings. In 1942, for instance, at the height of noir, Cyril Hare published *Tragedy at Law* with the same coupled knights, Inspector Mallett and Francis Pettigrew. Eight years later, Robert van Gulik began his series of Judge Dee stories about a seventh century Chinese magistrate by translating and — significantly — updating the ancient collection *Dee Goong An*. He then went on to write his own novels about Dee, the first of them in Japanese. Dee has the usual partner, a long-time retainer named Sergeant Hoong, and two loyal assistants, Ma Joong and Chiao Tai, whom Dee rescued in an early story (*The Chinese Gold Murders*) from a life of rural banditry. Despite the exotic setting and Confucian legal system, these stories conform as well as James's to the Neoclassic pattern. A similar pushing at the Neoclassic envelope can be found in Janwillem van de Wetering's pair Grijpstra and De Gier, introduced in 1975. (Van de Wetering was Dutch but wrote in English and published in the U.S.) Here, in place of Dee's Confucianism, we have two policemen whose way became more Zen with each new novel, as their author worked out how to manage this unlikely combination. But the stories proceed normally by the ordinary means of ratiocinative detection and reach the expected solution and closure.

There is a continual search in all genres for new characters who can play the roles required, part of the effort to avoid going stale and also a marker for the response to social change that I have been exploring in this book. Some genres are more rigid than others; detective fiction is one of the more fluid, as we have seen. A great many versions of the Detective have been tried out, particularly during the formative period up to 1920, and also recently, when the sharp increase in readership has propelled "mysteries" to the second-largest category of published fiction. Changing out detectives, however, does not alter the vehicle in any fundamental way, no more than changing the tires on a car, or more radically, turning it into a dragster running on alcohol. The Navaho policemen in Tony Hillerman's novels solve crimes in the usual way, though the elements of religion and spiritual practice open up the story to cultural issues that would not otherwise be available. There are also opportunities for new sorts of crimes such as defilement, and new sorts of criminals such as ghosts and evil spirits.

As we saw in the case of Father Brown, gods and spirits may be destructive of the premises of detective fiction. They spoil the prospect of actually detecting anything, since supernatural beings are inscrutable and their actions are ungoverned. The usual procedure in which the Detective is brought in to explain the unexplainable is time-tested and applies in the Navaho case as well. The challenge whenever the detective story is transported from its native Anglo-French environment is to be faithful to two mistresses, the genre and the culture in which it is embedded. My conspicuously male metaphor for the problem suggests that it is not a matter of exotic locales. I have already looked several times at the cultural and procedural issues posed by female detectives, issues that have not gone unnoticed by scholars. Any social group presents this difficulty. Walter Mosely was in this position when he proposed a black detective operating under Jim Crow laws. Easy Rawlins is not believable to whites as a man of knowledge. When he decides to become a detective he has to make his living on blacks gone missing and similar problems that are much duller than murder. But the problem has been seen as how to assimilate the character to the story, not how to change the story to fit the detective. It is the story that carries the freight of the genre, not the Detective. The task is how to reinterpret the Detective to accommodate the story, which is itself changing in response to social needs.

Historical detectives are no different. An odd case such as Margaret Doody's use of the Greek philosopher Aristotle changes nothing. Lindsey Davis's Roman detective Marcus Didius Falco, or Ellis Peters's medieval Cadfael, differ little from Marjorie Allingham's Albert Campion, required by his respectable family to use a pseudonym so as to disguise his disreputable hobby, a disguise about as effective as the Lone Ranger's mask.

Raymond Chandler's famous complaint about the quality of writing in detective novels marks a shift in the literary standing of the genre. Of course it is formulaic — that is true of all genres. It is part of the definition. But as the possibilities for the use of genre formulas suggest themselves to authors who are not writers of detective fiction and are more likely to flout the rules, new venues for change arise.

Carlo Emilio Gadda (*That Awful Mess on the Via Merulana*) came in for some contempt from Barzun and Taylor in their *Catalogue of Crime*. "A good example," they called it, "of what happens when a serious novelist takes up crime and detection in ignorance of the genre. The crime is there, but the detection gets lost in the pursuit of human confusion and understanding. This great work of modern Italian literature gives us a holdup, then a brutal murder, but neither crime is solved while we get realism, satire, and a picture of Rome under Mussolini c. 1927."[26] Barzun and Taylor do not consider whether Gadda may be exploring problems of life under fascism, using realism and satire to explain arbitrary violence, uncertainty, and deformed values, which the detective Francesco Ingravallo mitigates by the very example of his own humanity. Barzun and Taylor's view of the detective genre is too narrow, constrained by the English Classic formula.

This brief review by the *Catalogue of Crime* tells us a number of interesting things. It implies, first of all, that the real authors of the genre, those who know the rules, are not serious writers, a curious remark from someone who thought it worthwhile to compile a list of 874 pages, with an index of nearly one hundred pages, of something not serious. It also implies that the business of a writer of detective novels is to conserve the practices of the past, not institute new ones, a task as futile as trying to prevent new words from being born. That detection has had nothing to do with the ancient "pursuit of human confusion and understanding" is, we have seen, the negation of the entire rationale for the genre, without which there would be no need for a Detective, a self-destructive folly. Barzun and Taylor assert that the crime is not solved, which is untrue. The problem is that the solution is trivial and sordid, typical of everyday crime, and is slipped into the midst of other events, spoiling the desired closure. And finally, realism, satire, and history are apparently not acceptable components in a detective story, which rather argues against Marlowe, Rumpole, and Cadfael. They complain that Ingravallo's name is not spelled consistently, ignoring the existence of cultures in which this is common, but more significantly that the book begins with the declaration "They called him Don Ciccio now," which serves notice that consistency will not be an important feature of this book. Consistency — predictability — is necessary to cool knowledge. Its absence tells us something of what problems in the getting and deployment of knowledge we can expect to see addressed.

The telling remark, however, is the two words "gets lost." Detective stories are being treated as trivial pursuits like crossword puzzles or Ouija boards, both invented in Christie's time. To ask that stories about serious issues like murder and crime be separated from the societies in which they occur and treated as games made up of pieces that can get lost has become repugnant to us. This repugnance plays a role in a great many features of the Neoclassic. Gadda's book in any case is not a direct attack on the premises of the genre, unlike C.P. Snow's *A Coat of Varnish*, which concludes that the crime is unsolvable and urges us to give up the attempt and get on with seeking out love and human warmth instead. In fact, the submersion of the crime and its investigation in *That Awful Mess* are exactly what it is claiming about what we can know, which is a great deal provided we are not too fastidious—just the point Karl Popper and others were making about science and history sixty years ago. This is an essential insight for the reinvention of the figure of the Detective.

The trajectory of Donna Leon's Commissario Brunetti is an illustration of this. As the books have accumulated they have become less and less interested in detection, that is to say of the punctilious sort preferred by Barzun and Taylor, and have interested themselves rather in Brunetti himself, his life, the life of Venice, events, interior thoughts and feelings—all the paraphernalia of the quotidian. This not a matter of bad faith, as when we are told Dalgliesh is a poet without being given any of his poetry, or that Lynley has woman troubles without seeing anything of their origin and continuing life.

Leonardo Sciascia's books are another illustration of this matter of getting lost. Sciascia was deeply involved in the struggle to contain the mafia. His novels—*To Each His Own, The Day of the Owl, Equal Danger,* all crime novels and nearly all of his work that has been translated—could hardly fail to provide a deep context for this. It is embedded down to the smallest matters. The crime is the origin of the book, but equally important is the way it is investigated, with sidling steps, delicate probes, which itself tells us something about the knowledge sought, the possibility of success, the people and the cultural context that create the knowledge.

Iain Pears's *An Instance of the Fingerpost* (New York: Riverhead, 1998) is another step in the same direction. Pears, an art historian and author of a series of clever mysteries of art crimes (the first is *The Raphael Affair* [New York: Harcourt Brace, 1990]) attempted something much more ambitious than these in his historical novel set in the early years of the Restoration of Charles II. This intricate book uses four narrators, two of whom were actual persons but none of whom could properly be called the detective, though the fourth one does provide the solution. The book's erudition is deep enough to have spawned study guides, and also enough to create a detailed experience of how life may have been lived in the mid-seventeenth century. One review praises it thus:

> One of the pleasures of reading *An Instance of the Fingerpost* is the opportunity it affords to become a kind of amateur expert on daily life in Restoration England. And it is not just the physical world that is resurrected. Pears has steeped himself in the reading and the attitudes of the period, so that his characters, in their lives and confessions, embody its rich contradictions, its entwining of superstition with the spirit of new learning, of religion with politics, of politics with violence. Here we glimpse the world through 17th-century eyes and through the medium of a language that is, for the most part, a convincing equivalent of 17th-century English."[27]

As a detective novel this book is as far out of the norm in both content and structure as Gadda's, and yet it is recognizably Neoclassic. All the elements are there, but exfoliated to such a degree that they may be hard to recognize.

Carlos Fuentes, the author of the immense, baroque historical novel of New Spain, *Terra Nostra* (1976), followed up with what seemed to be a political thriller, *The Hydra Head* (trans. Margaret Sayers Peden [New York: Farrar Straus Giroux, 1978]), as baroque as its predecessor. A bureaucrat finds himself caught up in the assassination of the Mexican president. He loses his identity — there is talk of his never having had one in the first place — and is hunted down in the usual way of the thriller. There is a vast conspiracy based in the Mexican oil cartel, and a master spy of uncertain intent, with undertones of Kafka and Dostoyevsky. We never do find out whether the assassination plot succeeded. The end of the bureaucrat is no more enlightening: "'I give up, I give up,' he said with a calm delirium that the skull-faced man observed with curiosity. 'Who is it who has this power, this power to change lives, twist lives at his whim and make us someone else? I give up'" (282). Here is the contemporary problem of knowledge in naked reality, set in a world of political power, wealth, and cynicism that has become all too familiar. The detective detects nothing. In the end he is not even sure of his own identity. He has been invoked — snatched up — not to repair the torn fabric of society but to help tear it farther. There is a gross disparity between him and his adversaries. He is one of the little people, a toy of forces beyond his control or comprehension. Here we are approaching the boundary of the genre, which I will explore in the last chapter.

Finally we must confront Vladimir Nabokov. Many of his books contain crimes—*Lolita*, of course, but also *Transparent Things* (1972), *Pale Fire* (1962), and *King, Queen, Knave* (1928, in English 1968).

Pale Fire is a long poem by a fictional John Shade. We are given the poem entire, together with annotations by Shade's neighbor Charles Kinbote, who acquired the manuscript on Shade's death. A large part of the story resides in the notes. As we piece it together (the story can be read linearly or hypertextually) we come to suspect that Kinbote is actually the deposed king of Zembla, pursued by the assassin Gradus who has killed Shade by mistake. And yet it also appears that Gradus, Zembla, and the whole story are Kinbote's mad invention, down to an artificial language created for the inhabitants of the fictional Zembla.

Here every premise of the detective genre is undermined. We are uncertain as to what is the crime, or even if one has been done. Whatever has happened, the self-identified detective may also be the criminal, detecting himself as in Robbe-Grillet's *The Erasers.* The status of the criminal is equally uncertain. Kinbote poses as the threatened bystander while at the same time he is clearly the Chronicler — perhaps the only absolutely clear thing in the book — who has so radically filtered the narrative that the reader is obliged to play detective himself. To put the reader in that role clarifies the genre structure somewhat. There are plenty of clues, which we can extract by careful reading, on which we can build several inference chains to form a narrative of what happened, but there is no way to resolve matters and ground one of the chains in evidence, discarding the others. (The problem with the reader-detective is that he can't conduct his own independent investigation. He can't collect new evidence, only manufacture it, and he can't force confessions from any of the suspects.) This final state of uncertainty is as radical a commentary on human knowledge as any to be found in literature, yet at the same time fully within the mandate of the detective genre.

Do authors such as Gadda, Robbe-Grillet, Fuentes, Nabokov, van de Wettering, Leon, Pears, and others point to the future of the genre, or to an elegant dispersal into the larger realm of fiction? Is their work an alternative to nostalgia or only a more complicated version of it? Do they give us any clue as to the next transformation?

It is impossible to answer these questions, of course. In the next, and last, chapter I will speculate on some possibilities.

7

Metaphysical Modern

The narrative of this book has been about successive changes in the detective genre and the figure of the Detective from his earliest manifestation at the turn of the nineteenth century to the present. Two hundred years of continuous evolution of the Detective have led us finally to its decadence in two forms: the thriller, eviscerated of all the qualifications for a detective story, and the Neoclassic, blocked from growth by nostalgia. What I want to ask now is whether a renewal in possible. To decide that, we need to know (or guess) what social work will be needed for which the Detective is suited. We are by now familiar with the possibilities for this cultural icon or figure, the Detective. What new variations might we look for?

My hypothesis is this: that stories of the type that I will call Metaphysical Modern will arise from contemporary questions about truth and evidence. At issue are the reliability of the knowledge we have of the phenomenal world, memory and the dubious claims we make about ourselves and others, doubts about the foundations of psychology and personality, the spectacle of spirituality assailed by materialism, morality by cynicism, community by individualism. This is a huge package of questions—quite enough to justify calling in the Detective to straighten things out. The fear that the Detective can address and ameliorate is the product of these questions. The fear is the prospect of absolute relativism, the transformation of thought into dogma, of cold knowledge and rationality gone amok.

I am not claiming that the suppositions about the future are correct, only that they are plausible enough to warrant an attempt to imagine a Detective who knows nothing certain, whose discoveries are all uncertain, who is *a priori* unable to assign responsibility or blame, who possesses no general knowledge and thus cannot come to any reliable conclusions whose inference chains are necessarily valid. Is it possible to imagine a criminal enmeshed in a complexity of event and purpose that forbids us to say without qualm that he is guilty? Is it possible to imagine a society that is in doubt as to what is a crime? Is it even possible to form a sequence of events into a story when all possible stories are formed out of the immediate and perishable contingencies of their telling?

I am not asking whether these conditions are actual or true, whether they state the condition of society accurately. What matters is whether ordinary people, people who are consumers of detective stories, *fear* they may be, or become, the case. If this is so, can the Detective help? The Detective whose business is knowledge and its use, including its right use and the human dignity and self-respect that comes with the right use of knowledge? Is there any use in a detective story in which there is no crime, in which there is a detective who is unable to discover anything about what seems to have happened, in which nothing is concluded and for which there is no response?

It would seem that a reimagined genre might have to tell stories like that, just as Poe reimagined the warm Gothic tale, which he had already mastered, as its opposite, the tale of cool reason. Not to reimagine the genre now, to wish futilely for conditions to be as they were, is to risk ossification, applying cures for now-imaginary diseases.

It might be shown that the pressing nature of these questions is one reason for the neoclassic revival.[1] It is a failed strategy, popular as it is, because it goes nowhere. The Metaphysical Modern as I conceive it will follow the opposite strategy of confrontation. Failure is probable. In fact, failure may prove to be the story.

Twin Peaks is a notorious example. Seeming unable to get a grip on any coherent story, it seemed to wander off, and its audience left with it. Most people do not much like this sort of thing. The Metaphysical Modern has not yet matured into a tradition, and audiences don't yet know what to expect. The trouble is, these stories are resistant to genre comforts. There is a deeper problem, however. The Metaphysical Modern detective detects nothing. Clues remain clues, not linkable to form a coherent causal sequence. A satisfying story is not just one thing after another. In some cases even the crime is problematic. The basic conditions for a detective story, which were laid out at the beginning of this book, would seem not to be satisfied. The Detective has either disappeared or been transfigured into a radically different figure. Which is it?

The problems posed by the Metaphysical Modern were given a philosophical shape in the 1980s with the spread of French thinking in semiotics, which spread to or was cognate to thinking in related disciplines. The problems already in progress in those disciplines were not exotic. In communications, for example, the question was how to reconstruct inevitably garbled messages. In anthropology it was how to understand another culture without contaminating the findings with the one's own culture-bound thinking. In linguistics it was to explain how speakers successfully learn to construct messages out of the brain's mere potential.

In literature, history, and other fields it was how to interpret texts, whether written or experienced, that seemed to have no fixed meaning, but only what was attributed to them or extracted from them by self-interested critics.

The implications of this thinking have been profound. Many people, not only intellectuals, have begun to fear that we have no common purpose, but are doomed to endless arguments over unresolvable matters of personal belief. In detective stories, it seems that there is no evidence with which to identify the criminal, and that failing any resolution of the story, or in the parallel real world modeled by the story, we will fall to massacre and warfare and so become the criminals ourselves.

Such doubts upset the security of a society just as the discovery of a murder at Styles did in 1919. Any such disruption of the social fabric invites the intervention of the Detective. Radical relativism must be cured, the Detective is cautioned, lest the contagion infect common sense, truth, morality, and all values. Unfortunately, this sets the fox among the chickens, for the Metaphysical Modern Detective has a very different objective.

The problem as seen by the Detective is not how to resolve doubts but how to live with them. How can some useful form of rationality be preserved under conditions of uncertainty, where every fact is only probable and every conclusion suspect and open to negotiation? What solution is possible when evidence is variable from time to time and place to place and even a consensus on what counts as a crime is unavailable? The Detective, it appears, has entered a metaphorically quantum world in which the attempt to establish rationality is irrational, in which the Detective multiplies the worries and fears he was meant to allay. Evidence evaporates, clues fission, knowledge destroys the knower. The criminal becomes the detective who detects himself. Is it meaningful any longer to speak of the Detective?

One can make two responses to this. If you regard radical relativism as a threat to be countered, then we can interpret that threat to peace and order as the disruption that invokes the Detective. This is a conservative and traditional genre strategy — when we modify a tradition we do so only just enough to go on with it. To implement such a strategy would be to devise a suitably resonant metaphor linking the crime and the metaphysical problem. Radical relativism will have to be taken seriously if it is to be satisfyingly rejected. Taking such a philosophy seriously is something many people are not prepared to do.

Not to take relativism seriously would be to reject that philosophy as the source of our fear and discouragement. In making the science fiction television series *Doctor Who*, its creators evidently pondered Arthur Clarke's dictum that any sufficiently advanced technology will seem to us to be magic. Accordingly, the Doctor gives up an attempt to explain what he is doing and makes only nonsensical explanations for how things work or don't work, or simply brushes off explanations altogether. This may be a justifiable and even honorable procedure for the detective story, but it isn't helpful.

Ignoring or covering up the problem is also not a good basis for a detective story. The more effective strategy begins by taking the premises of relativism for granted and setting out from there to rethink the genre. A detective story that can absorb these premises is what we are looking for. A useful model might, for example, reverse the premises and take "irrational" relativism to be threatened by a more naïve realism. The Detective's job would then be to restore "disorder." Eco's *The Name of the Rose* could serve as an example. In this novel the detective succeeds (or might have succeeded) in bringing the contents of the secret library into the light and exposing the monks' hidebound thinking. In the end, the peasants, sick of the whole business, rescue a few good people and burn the rest to the ground, Aristotle and all. A similar model — actually a caution — would be Borges's infinite library, containing so much knowledge that it contains none at all, requiring the Detective to proceed by picking and choosing, constructing the case as he goes until someone guilty turns up.

Is it really possible to tell a satisfying story with such bizarre scenarios?

A Preliminary Problem: Learning the Language

In dealing with this problem the movies have some natural advantages. The grammar of film, such as it is,[2] lacks tense — everything depicted is always already present. Past and future are only weak conventions supported by some editing practices, which the viewer may easily misinterpret. This presentness is an advantage. The continuous present of the visual track makes it possible to move the spectator forward through the narrative by depictions of the "same" character or the "same" object (such as an automobile) on repeated occasions, creating a sense of story out of what is actually a mere sequence of images. Meanwhile the plot[3] is by this technique being seriously ambiguated by suggesting that they are not, in fact, the same object or event.

Written stories have the opposite problem. There are no bodies in literature.[4] To exist, a person requires a body. Bodiless characters do not have the continuity that makes us living beings recognizable to ourselves and to others as time goes on and we change. In the movies time does not go on unless it is made to, but bodies, though illusory, are not a problem. In stories, time does go on, even in the simplest sense of turning the pages, while bodies (and thus characters) are a problem. Physical continuities in fiction have to be purposefully created and maintained or the story will be unintelligible. It would be just a collection of interchangeable names, actorless actions, and thoughts without identifiable thinkers.

In the movies there was never this problem with bodies until a few film-makers found out how to call physical continuity into question and so to irretrievably ambiguate the plot. Metaphysical Moderns do not have innate solutions. Solutions have to be manufactured out of the fug of meaningless-ness that beclouds systematic thinking. What the metaphysical Detective does is to offer an explanation or discover a resolution that is satisfying without being definitive — that is, without concern for loose ends. The metaphysical Detective does not uncover the truth, which is impossible, but rather finds a resting place in the continuous flow of events.

In this, the Metaphysical Modern closely resembles our contemporary conception of what it is to live a life. Lives do not end; they stop. The goal of a "good death" is to contrive to stop at a point when honor and dignity are in the ascendant. What happens after that is (simply) another story. These stories are what we tell ourselves to make sense of who we are and what has happened to us. Thus, a multiplicity of equally believable stories is very unset-tling. This unease is what permeates Kafka's detective stories — in *The Castle* and *The Trial* K tries to find out the truth but is unable to detect anything because every story (in Kafka) is false, and when *everything* is false then every-thing is at the same time true.

Perhaps it would be useful to reiterate in plainer terms the problem posed by radical relativism. The worm in the apple is subjective (that is, warm) knowledge. Once it is admitted that people can legitimately differ on the truth, if there is no way to verify the facts (let us call them facts for the time being) or to adjudicate the disagreement, then the discussion will be all downhill and will smash on the rocks, won't it? Everyone will be right about everything. Maigret knows. Who is to prove him wrong?[5] He collects what he purports to be reasons, browbeats the suspect with them, gets a confession, and asks us to close the case. And because we are all in cahoots with Maigret to have the case closed, so it is. We can see this story every night on the news.

But if one does not weaken and refuses to confess out of pure stubborn-ness there is nothing more to be done. A thorough-going relativism is a frontal attack on rooted knowledge — on fixed truths, and on unproblematic com-munication about what once passed for truths. From the relativist criminal's point of view, once Maigret makes up his mind there remains only the pure flame of conviction, which burns away all dross. This is a recipe for totali-tarianism.[6] The path to this state of affairs (a state philosophers have been puzzling over for a long time, even if the rest of us have only just arrived) is fairly easily traced.

We begin (there are other entry points) with Frege's attempt to found mathematics on the elemental concepts of number and succession, and with the now-discredited positivist construction of objectivity as that which is independent of sensation, intuition, and memory. Husserl reformulated this—a collection of objects (such as numbers) defined by a rule, known as a set — as a puzzle in epistemology by asking not what a set is but how the idea of a set could arise in the first place. With a set, one becomes conscious of things together, and also conscious of the possibly arbitrary act of grouping them together. The notion of a group will ultimately fail. Such a thing as the infinite continuum of real numbers is not a set because it cannot be made present to the mind by considering the things in the set one by one. Instead, we can imagine this thing only as a whole. Because the parts cannot be enumerated it is without parts. The infinity of subsets is the same. And so on.

Logically (rather than physio-logically), this is how film works. The frames aggregate as a whole in the mind, although a film is actually only one thing after another, twenty-four things a second. Smaller wholes then aggregate with each other (forming such objects as the conversational two-shot), becoming larger and larger as the context of similarity develops, until we have the whole film present to the mind as a single entity. If one then attempts to go back and break up this entity into frames, it vanishes. It's like trying to explain why a joke is funny.

This line of thought seems to require the existence of mental objects. These are not directly (objectively) verifiable. To imagine them is the major step that admits sensation and intuition as modes of knowledge, taking their places alongside reasoned thought. To then abandon them, there being no evidence for their existence, is to abandon the whole enterprise. Reluctance to take that step is the major step toward acknowledging the contemporary condition of radical relativism. Warm knowledge drives out cold.

No film creates its whole grammar from scratch. However, the necessity for the viewer to construct the story out of the units and relations provided by the filmmaker means that when things do not go as expected (the diction and semantics are unfamiliar) it is as if the movie were speaking a foreign language. The spectator must be educated in the particular semiotic system in use — that is, become visually literate in the "language" of this particular movie. A simple example is that to understand a detective movie it is necessary to wait until the meaning of the individual scenes is interpreted at the end by the detective. To be always asking what happened is to show one's ignorance of the language.

Shared semantic units, that is, our willingness to grant that they are similar, that they form a set or family, are the basis of genre. Such a claim as "belonging to the family of noir movies" will be a variable definition that depends on the local grammar in use. This same dependency applies to any bit of film whatever, beginning with two frames in sequence. This is what makes it possible to construct a cohesive movie of indeterminate meaning, a movie that clearly belongs to some family of movies without being able to say exactly what the members of the family are.[7]

A "film" is whatever a spectator who is literate in the language in use *calls* a film. What one analyzes is not the film any more than the score is the music. Rather, what one does is to become literate enough to read that film in performance, and what the film does is to assist in this. Learning to read the film creates the film. Every viewer creates the film for herself, using a literacy in a set of other films that person has seen. The same is true of written fiction, a situation Joyce exposed in its starkest form in *Finnegan's Wake*. So-called postmodernist novels have yet to grapple with this. Or perhaps it is that no author has been found who can make the reader *want* to grapple with it.

What may be called "the modern synthesis" is an accelerating process of extrapolating new grammars. As these become more complex, we learn to read what was formerly obscure or unintelligible. So: what is meant when I say that the thriller is the graveyard of the detective story? What is meant by saying that the languages inherited by the thriller are too impoverished to provide much scope for expression? Is it that the gene pool of a species has grown too small to allow any further speciation?

Yes, that is what is meant.

Some Examples

Last Year at Marienbad

To many people this may be the most boring movie of all time. Two anonymous people spend a lot of time looking at each other. The sound track is ... *tinkly*. There is evidently something between these two, X and A, but we do not have the energy of events—violent events demanding an explanation, secrets demanding to be exposed — needed to invoke the Detective. *Nothing happens.* Instead, we have this smothering reality of incomprehensible apparitions, unresolvable delusions, besetting impotence, and one solitary fleeting clue: A drops her glass and it breaks on the floor. Before and after this we have for a narrative only one thing after another, with no means of interpreting anything, in the most epistemologically bare-naked place imaginable.

This is the setting of the Metaphysical Modern mystery. This is the world we fear, the modern form of the Classic world of order and security disrupted by an inexplicable crime, the noir society of meager responses to pervasive corruption, the anarchy of the thriller against which our proxy heroes can only lash out, and the obsessive mudras of the Neoclassic. It this movie, *Last Year at Marienbad,* we are thrust ourselves into the unwanted role of Detective, absent anyone else to play it, with no way of constructing the past. The one clue of the broken glass, standing in for the Classic second murder, leads nowhere. We sense the presence of an inscrutable Other, an epistemological black hole that absorbs meaning and gives none back. This woman A and the man X have some connection — possibly an affair, or so X thinks, but A will not confirm this. She admits nothing. Her eyes, the turn of her head, reveal only the wariness women show for a potential stalker. Unresolved and unresolvable, the story just stops.

This is our situation, to which a rejuvenated detective genre might speak, against which a reinvigorated Detective might stand and utter the words *"Thou shall not pass!"*— calming the crisis.

X's situation is that, so long as A has the power to withhold meaning, the drama is dependent on the power relations between two competing viewpoints: the anxious, dependent one — X, and ultimately, us— and the natural force, A, the patient one who is content to let meaning reveal itself, if it will. But the pressure, the need for a solution, builds, and A cracks. A wine glass slips from her hand and shatters on the tile floor like a gunshot. Now the situation is reversed. A becomes the anxious one, needy for a resolution, dependent on X to provide it. Presumably, this dharma battle could be continued indefinitely. In reality, no one, neither we nor the characters, has the stamina for this.

The arrangement of the components of this detective story are thus: we (the viewers) stand in the role of the Detective; the crime is suppositious; the criminal's identity is fluid. There is the expected second murder, which provides the existential link between the past as constructed by the witnesses (us) and the present as reconstructed by the Detective (also us), and as it should, this opens a new inference chain leading to the solution, but the "solution" is only a stable state of infinite repetition. We, the witnesses, form an erroneous interpretation, which in our role as Detective we are forced to revise — a common experience. However, that interpretation proves to be false also, and we are shuttled back to the role of witnesses. After several revisions we conclude in frustration that we are unable to understand — also a common experience, but one that is contrary to the function and purpose of the detective story heretofore. Finally, there is a Chronicler through whom we have access to the story — which is the camera.

Because in a Metaphysical Modern there is a pervasive doubt as to whether cold knowledge is reliable, and the contamination of warm knowledge by personal interest is assumed, the Chronicler's role is peculiarly important. Watson does not tell the story as Holmes would like (as Holmes repeatedly points out), because he does not know what Holmes knows. We get a filtered and, from Holmes's point of view distorted, narrative, but we are recompensed by a better story. The drama and suspense are a product of Watson's ignorance. The same is true of the Metaphysical Modern's Chronicler, except that we will never be enlightened as to how the unfiltered story might go. And since we and the Detective are one in the same, the consequence is that there can never be a true or final solution to the crime. The Chronicler gives us the illusion of objectivity and then cruelly takes it back.[8]

Given stories like this, rolled up like hedgehogs, it would not be surprising if they were rare. But if I am right about the social work that we now would ask a rejuvenated detective story to do, perhaps the problem is not the story but the dearth of authors able to tell it well. What is needed is not a script doctor with a knife but a new Arthur Conan Doyle.

Novels

With the Classic story in hand it was possible to see what might be needed to produce it. In the case of this mostly hypothetical new formula of the Metaphysical Modern, we can only guess what factors might prove to be important.

Let us look at Gertrude Stein's *Blood on the Dining-Room Floor*, probably written about 1937.[9] On the surface this is an English Country House setup: a small gathering isolated in the country, the mysterious death of one of their number. But as with *Marienbad*, the reader is deputized as detective, a number of possible crimes are laid out, along with a selection of clues, and then we are invited to select from this buffet the bits that we want to form a narrative of our own. The result is a puzzle drama much like the satisfactions of the Classic, but lacking the solution. Alain Robbe-Grillet's *Les Gommes* (*The Erasers*, 1953) is another early example.[10] Special Agent Wallas is sent to a town in the provinces to look into a murder said to have occurred there. Wallas wanders through the town, observing and collecting indications. In the end he himself commits the crime he is supposed to be investigating. This is somewhat the opposite of Stein's story. The ending is there, as well as the business of detection, but the one doesn't lead to the other correctly. In retrospect it can be thought through, but the circularity of it frustrates that sigh of relief when the criminal is revealed and all the questions are answered.

A yet different strategy is to allow the investigation to melt away through an accumulation of details or digressions, which become more significant to the detective than the solution. Examples of this are C.P. Snow's *A Coat of Varnish*[11] and Carlo Emilio Gadda's *Quer Pasticciaccio Brutto della Via Merulana*.[12] In Snow's novel, the detective is a friend of the murdered woman. His investigation is inconclusive and is soon submerged in his feelings for his dead friend and in human issues such as the nature of evil and the evasion of punishment. Gadda's novel is one of those ever-expanding and never-comprehensive surveys of a entire culture, in this case, Rome. Detective Ingravallo investigates two crimes: a burglary in an apartment on the Via Merulana and the murder, several days later, of a young woman in another part of the same building. This woman is a relative of Ingravallo's. Contradictory and elusive clues quickly multiply; the investigation proliferates into every corner of Rome (including its many dialects, all of which are reproduced in the novel, making it very difficult to translate). The story becomes a vast, profound allegory of Fascist Italy in 1927, impossible of solution, though a somewhat trivial one is finally provided.

Other examples are the Grijpstra and De Gier novels of Janwillem van de Wetering,[13] and the Inspector Barlach novels of Friedrich Dürrenmatt.[14] Grijpstra and De Gier present the problem of how to investigate (that is, write) a genuine crime story from within a Zen philosophy. Many of the features of Zen —for example the illusion of the material world, the gateless gate of enlightenment, the koan thought process— make the pursuit of clues, logical reasoning, and the need for a solution seem pointless. Inspector Barlach, in *The Judge and His Hangman* and *Suspicion*, navigates a territory in which the relationship between crime and justice is uncertain; as in *The Erasers*, Barlach's investigation of one crime provokes another, resulting in a circular, Möbius-like tale.

Vladimir Nabokov's *King, Queen, Knave* [15] concerns the aborted drowning of a man by his wife and her lover, the woman's betrayal of her lover, and her death from pneumonia brought on by exposure to the cold while she was trying to commit the crime. *Pale Fire* contains within it the story of an attempted assassination and a resulting comic pursuit that ends in the mistaken assassination of one of the two authors of the novel, provoking in a way the creation of that very novel by the other author. Both of Nabokov's books use this self-generating and self-destructing plot to create a picture of people who are easily manipulated, who surrender their moral judgment and become gradually dehumanized. Both are genuine detective novels, combining features of all the novels I have mentioned. All the same, Nabokov regarded both the crime and its investigation as embedded in a society contaminated by the same problems that the detective story has always confronted. Because the stories' elements are reversed —first the investigation, then the crime— it seems as if the criminal is the victim of his (her) crime rather than its cause. Because the reader serves in the role of detective, as we begin to understand the true arrangement of these matters we find ourselves complicit in the crime to come, in effect protecting the crime against society.

More Films

Film is an ideal medium for the Metaphysical Modern. *Twin Peaks*, for example, is a perverse cousin to *Les Gommes*. Laura Palmer dies. An operative named Cooper investigates. Months pass. Nothing happens. Then Cooper is murdered. While Robbe-Grilet's Wallas is plodding and stolid, Cooper is baroque, but neither investigation *seems* to go forward by any principle other than happenstance. Not so. Philosophical points are being made, but they cannot be apprehended on first encounter. *Twin Peaks* had the advantage of being a series and having a whole season to establish its *raison d'être*, but it did not succeed. At the time, we did not have sufficient experience with the problem it poses.

Celine et Julie vont en bateau (1974) and *Les fableaux destin d'Amélie Poulain* (2001) are another instructive pair. Both of these movies manufacture crimes out of their heroines' imaginations. Celine's concerns a dream world that has intruded itself into the everyday one, and a house that passes back and forth between realities, in which suspicious things happen. There is some urgency about getting to the bottom of this that is not explained. Amélie's object of interest is smaller than a house — a photo booth, in which an unknown man takes pictures of himself that he then tears up. In the course of the investigation Amélie plays the role of criminal herself, stealing her father's garden gnome and metaphorically tearing it up by sending it to various exotic places from which it sends back *gnomic* messages. More significantly, she constructs a narrative roughly parallel with that of the photo booth man in which *she* is the mysterious figure who challenges a man (to whom she is attracted) to discover who she is. Both of these movies utilize detective tropes, which are fitted into zany goings-on that, if they are not irrational, certainly have nothing of the cold lucidity of an English Classic.

The City of Lost Children

There are two narratives of detection (along with much else) in this 1995 French movie. The major one concerns the efforts of a carnival strongman (named One) to find out who is stealing children off the streets, including a street orphan One had adopted. The other narrative concerns the question of who is the father (the Original) of a family of clones — who as it happens are the nephew(s) of a brain-in-a-bottle also at the bottom of the child-stealing racket. These children are wanted for their dreams, something the brain doesn't have.

The dreamworld is significant in all five of these movies. In *Les Gommes* by its absence, a vacancy that is an important story engine. The interpenetration of the phenomenal and imaginary worlds, their porousness to each other, is the means by which rationality is separated from its ordinary context of materialist realism and objectivity without sacrificing the detective structure. These worlds are purposeful, causally structured ones in which actions have largely predictable consequences. By demonstrating that an infinity of such worlds can be constructed, the Metaphysical Modern has enlarged the field of its predecessors in the same way that noir opened new possibilities to the exhausted Classic tradition.

The detective tropes run deep in *The City of Lost Children*. Once we begin to assemble a cogent story out of these strange and manic happenings, it becomes possible to extract a conventional noirish plot built on the thematic ground of threats to the family, the identification and defeat of these threats, and the reconstitution of the survivors into a restabilized and rebonded group.

In one segment we see one of those moments when new evidence causes some old encounter to assume new significance. The evidence in this case is provided by a sentient dream that seeks out its dreamer. With that dream One (the detective) realizes that the children he seeks are being kept somewhere in the City's harbor, protected by a mine field, and suddenly an earlier remark about a tattooed man reveals the next step in the search. We learn of One's insight through a voiceover reminiscent of those moments in the Dalgleish and Mirren stories in which the spectator is given a scrap of the detective's thoughts. One, however, is not naturally or professionally reticent as those police inspectors are. He is simply inarticulate. Within that constraint, conversations with Miette (his Watson) function as they did in the Holmes stories, to present to the spectator a rational procedure with nothing hidden. There follows a standard police routine of questioning all of the City's tattoo artists.

A Preliminary Assessment

Again we have Robbe-Grillet, the *éminence grise* of the Metaphysical Modern. *Trans-Europ-Express* is a detective story rather in the way that *The Singing Detective* is (or that *Babette's Feast* or *Fried Green Tomatoes* are cooking shows because they have characters in them who are cooks). We have here novels and movies that create themselves through characters who determine the premises of their own stories. It's an Escher trick, or one of those cartoons

TABLE 7. A SEQUENCE OF POSSIBLE METAPHYSICAL
MODERNS, MIXED NOVELS AND FILMS

1927	*King, Queen, Knave*	Nabokov
1937	*Blood on the Dining Room Floor*	Stein
1950	*The Judge and His Hangman*	Dürrenmatt
1951	*Suspicion*	Dürrenmatt
1953	*Erasers*	Robbe-Grillet
1956	*That Awful Mess on the Via Merulana*	Gadda
1962	*Last Year at Marienbad*	Robbe-Grillet
1962	*Pale Fire*	Nabokov
1966	*Trans-Erop-Express*	Robbe-Grillet
1974	*Céline and Julie Go Boating*	Rivette
1979	*A Coat of Varnish*	Snow
1990	*Twin Peaks*	Lynch
1995	*The City of Lost Children*	Caro
2000	*Memento*	Pearce
2001	*Amélie*	Jeunet
2001	*Mulholland Drive*	Lynch
2004	*Eternal Sunshine of the Spotless Mind*	Gondry

in which a hand draws a body for itself. The prototype of this may be Pirandello's *Six Characters in Search of an Author*. Why is *Memento* backwards? Because if you have a memory of something to which you want to connect a causal chain you have to start at Now. If you don't attach one end of the chain to this capstan you will not be able to raise the anchor. We create the past out of ourselves and then demonstrate the felicity of our invention with a lot ofPolaroids we took of how it was done. The sequence illustrates the decay of one's sense of self. Yet each one of these books and movies is an authentic detective story. The detective works out what is happening and tries to do something about it. The Classic rules are followed more or less, in part to make the story easier for us to negotiate. There is a crime, a criminal, a narrative confidante, and a collection of innocent bystanders. The Detective is invoked with the familiar charge to provide an explanation and restore the status quo ante. There are clues, conclusions are tested, the criminal is identified, and the whole business follows Todorov's double narrative structure discussed earlier.

Of the movies in the list it is *Mulholland Drive* that — predictably, given the director David Lynch's *Twin Peaks* — is the least engaged in this process of retrospective self-justification. Lynch is like a potter who, having decided to use a wheel, resigns himself to making a round pot, but sees nothing to be gained by theorizing roundness— nor if later he decides to paddle the round pot square. The others are more complicit with the film and with us and offer some ameliorations. The spotless minds even come to relish their own artificiality.

Thirteen Conversations About One Thing

A close look at this movie from 2001 suggests the attribute that these self-creating, self-consuming movies have in common. At every point in the story the whole thing has always already happened. We can't find out what is going on by taking events one at a time, as experienced. Because in film "one at a time" is the only way in which we can experience events— the consequence of a continually now — there is no external vantage from which we can watch the thing going on. We never have anything but memories, which are only ours *now*, and we will never figure out what happened because nothing happened. It only happens.

In this movie five stories are entwined in the narrative. Each story is presented in plot order, but the individual pieces are interpolated into the sequence of the others. Since the stories are not simultaneous but do intersect there is a major disjunction between spectator time, narrative time, and story time. That this movie is immediately comprehensible and fairly easily decoded indicates how visually literate we have become. Still, one suspects at the end that, as in *Mulholland Drive*, there has been some temporal slippage and that, strictly speaking, we do not come out after we went in. For most viewers this is not a question to be answered in the theater. It requires making a lot of notes.

In the case of *Thirteen Conversations* there is a crime — the unmotivated or accidental pedestrian death — but there is no murder. The murderer, however, does not know this, and goes through a process of self-discovery, accusation, conviction, and penance. The dead woman, meanwhile, who is not yet dead, descends from her initial happy ignorance to bitter knowledge. Intending to kill herself, she is saved by chance. A stranger smiles at her. If she had stepped in front of that car as she first intended she would have become the dead woman in truth and the conclusions reached by the murderer would come true. He would become the actual murderer he supposed himself to be. The movie is thick with repeated images that both help the spectator to read it and reinforce the material of events — determined by chance or obscure causes — and the false sense of security we have in cause and effect. There is the sheet that earlier was a shroud for the car that killed the temporarily dead woman — and a shroud for her, because for a moment the parking garage looks as if it might be a morgue — and the white shirt with a hole in it that blows away with her happiness and occasions her re-death. There is the doll's head with one eye closed, to be opened when wisdom is attained. And so on. In a different conversation a student is unthinkingly killed by his unhappy professor, who takes away hope. There is a sort of chorus, a third conversation in which a man assaults a coworker only to suffer the consequences himself. But in all these there is apparently no detective, no investigation, no discovery. In fact, all these people are much the viewer's inferior in perception and understanding. They are feckless victims of happenstance who could save themselves but rarely do. We are the ones who explore these people's mean streets, assembling evidence obtained from the movie into a story that explains them all and reveals who is responsible for the death of happiness.

The Metaphysical Shift

With many, perhaps most, of the Metaphysical Moderns discussed so far, though they are detective stories, it does not seem very promising to try to read them as such. *Thirteen Conversations* has all the attributes of a Metaphysical Modern, but have we encountered a crime movie about knowledge that we *cannot* read as a detective story? Does this mean that the only promising path that might have led to a renewed genre is in fact a dead end? Have we crossed a stile and wandered out into a muddy field and ended in an ancient circle of stones, purpose unknown?

Perhaps not. The essential elements *are* there, those elements that we have encountered from the time of Sherlock Holmes. There is a crime, a victim, and there are innocent bystanders. The roles are mixed, it is true, and the solution does not conform perfectly to the Rules, but all this amounts to is that these stories are not so easily decoded and that the cultural work they are doing is contemporary, not the now-familiar concerns of earlier times. Whether these stories will *continue* to be recognized as detective stories is another matter. It may be that we will find another classification that fits them better, and then the Figure of the Detective will have indeed run its course.

However, whether they are recognized, and will continue to be recognized, as detective stories is not quite the problem. What I said was that it does not seem very promising to try to read them as such. Earlier in this chapter I discussed the need to learn to interpret the language these books and films use — to read them. I have identified a complex of modern problems that I think are a plausible set of materials that might drive a shift in the genre toward the metaphysical. But there are surely other literary forms that could do this work. Readers could make this shift. But would they?

When I listed the essential elements of the detective story just now there was one I left out: the Detective. It will also be noticed that the Detective is also missing from many of the examples of the Metaphysical Modern that I analyzed, and was hard to spot in many others. In these cases I believe that they should be read with the reader in the Detective's role. This active complicity of the reader in constructing the story is a common device in contemporary fiction and should not in itself be unfamiliar. The most (or worst) that might be said is that that complicity is part of the blurring of the line between genre and mainstream fiction (which Barzun and Taylor deplored in the case of *That Awful Mess on the Via Merulana*). It may be that the metaphysical shift concerns the transference of the Detective's functions— the quest plot, the getting and right use of knowledge, the balancing of warm and cool thinking, exploring the boundaries of the possible, assimilating social changes and resolving the resulting tensions between the anxiety of change and the affirmation of existing attitudes, and all the paraphernalia of detection itself.

A very little thought is needed to see that these functions are already the functions of the reader *in the act of reading*. The author invokes the reader to discover the crime and repair the damage done by the criminal. The reader constructs the narrative and builds an inference chain, which is then grounded (validated) by the new evidence of the second murder. And now it becomes clear what the real trouble is. In taking on the Detective's role the reader has had to abandon her own. Many of the satisfactions that come from detective stories arise from the reader's attempts to keep up with the detective in interpreting the evidence. More importantly, it is this experience that the reader has of constructing and reconstructing the significance of events under the guidance of the detective, through the medium of the story finding that fears

TABLE 8. NOIR AND HARD-BOILED DETECTIVES
AND THE READER AS DETECTIVE

Noir Detective	Hard-Boiled Detective	Reader as Detective
Defends individuals against attacks by corrupt society.	Defends himself against self-interested individuals.	Many detectives, each acting alone to defend himself against fear.
Clues assembled into a narrative by experience and wisdom.	Clues accumulate but are not assembled into a narrative.	Clues are selected and interpreted so as to form an acceptable or intelligible narrative.
Clues acquired by testimony, sometimes forced, sometimes by guile.	Clues emerge through persistent, indiscriminant pressure.	Clues acquired through reading and inference.
The detective is the most endangered of all.	The detective's invulnerability is repeatedly tested.	The detective is not physically threatened.
Subsequent murders only increase the violence and the urgency.	Additional murders are part of the milieu and have little effect on the resolution.	Subsequent murders invite reinterpretation of the inference chain.
The detective's narrative construction is confirmed only by confession, which is the only reliable access to truth.	The detective is presented with a narrative when the criminal is exposed and confesses.	The detective's narrative is confirmed when events in the story seem to validate it.
Solutions are generally local and partial and the aftermath provides only solace.	Solutions are personal, ameliorating nothing and providing only narrative closure.	The solution is never conclusively confirmed and always subject to revision. The narrative closes when doubts are assuaged.

can be accommodated, tensions relaxed, and a reasoned life is still possible, which gives the detective story its endurance. These things are also the source of the Detective's power. The reader cannot play both roles at once. When the reader is asked to participate in the detective story in this way there is no longer anyone to tell the story to. This may be well for the mainstream novel but as a detective story it won't do. The task of the Metaphysical Modern is to recover the reader and to let that reader back into the story.

The right-hand column of table 8 tells us that the metaphysical detective is really a literary critic attempting to form a coherent and satisfying interpretation of the story, but one that can never be conclusively validated.

If this is an acceptable description of the workings of a Metaphysical Modern detective story, it is not surprising that many people find it unsatisfying. An unusual degree of self-confidence and a familiarity with late twentieth century literary and film narrative practices is needed. Why are these heroic efforts needed? What is at stake here? This question may not have a definitive or easily recoverable answer, no more than the solution to the story itself. But the fact that the detective story is being hammered into these new shapes suggests that *something* is at issue. The fact that this challenging alternative to the Neoclassic and the intellectual thriller is not very popular may simply be that we have not yet learned to write a good one. There are many successful tales of despair conquered and doubts laid to rest. It is easy to see, when the problem is put this way, that the really important difference between the Neoclassic and the Metaphysical Modern is that the first presents the reader with a solution and the second provides the means for the reader to come to her own conclusions.

In the early Modern period we made a now-irrevocable Faustian bargain when we decided to test the limits of rational inquiry. One cultural code for this is the (pre-existing) good scientist/bad scientist pair that can be found throughout fiction and the movies. By now it would be anachronistic to portray empirical inquiry as a benign enterprise. To do so would be as blithe and foolish as the attitude toward atomic warfare and the effects of radiation that we once paraded and that can be seen in the 1982 documentary *The Atomic Café*. At the same time, we are so deeply committed to technological solutions for almost everything that a straight-faced portrayal of the pundits of rationality as evil loonies would class us with the people who see little green men, talk to trees, or channel Osiris. Empirical inquiry is the source of both hope and despair, and we can no longer divest ourselves of either.

In Modernist art, this intellectual program involved the effort to find an art free of craft, that is, free of material purposes, contingencies, justifications.[16] This program was instructive and liberating and was very successful for a time, about seventy years. Current thinking in the arts has moved on, as the term *post*–Modern indicates. And now that term has itself become unfashionable. The means of cultural production are unstable. A common critical standard[17] would require amelioration at both the cool end (too little acknowledgement of the world of everyday experience is madness) and at the warm end (too much mundane reality kills the sense of magic that powers the intellectual enterprise). The need for amelioration is transparently illustrated by the movie *A Beautiful Mind*. John Nash's madness is both the origin of his creativity and is also Shiva, the Destroyer of himself. The mirror case might be *Sky Captain and the World of Tomorrow*, an amusing cartoon version of the very old Dr. Mabuse plot in which a lab geek cheats even death and through his creations brings about a hell of ecstasy without catharsis. Dr. Death's madness is the origin of his true self and the destroyer of his creativity. Neither of these situations is desirable or acceptable.

It is no longer a question of whether the Detective is coldly rational or warmly empathetic — or of whether the detective's methods are warm or cool, or of whether the detective inhabits a cool, law-abiding society or observes a warm, dark, corrupt one, or of whether we have a cool, amoral spy or a hot action hero. Regardless of their temperature, all detective stories have one necessary, essential, defining element: the getting and deployment of knowledge. The present view of what knowledge is, is that it is performative, unstable, local, inscrutable or only partially verifiable, and polluted by agendas of ideology and power — that knowledge is not a *thing*, a piece of the phenomenal world that can be picked up and put down, owned, but is a volatile product of action in the world.[18] We should no longer ask where knowledge is to be found but rather how it is created and destroyed. We can no longer ask whether knowledge is warm or cool. Now, it is neither. Before the Metaphysical Modern one might have wondered how a detective story would go in which the detective creates the knowledge necessary to solve the crime. The answer that I have laid out is that the detective, with as yet no knowledge of the crime, creates it in the act of solving it.

This formulation exposes one more objection to the acceptability of the Metaphysical Modern. It is a moral one. At the beginning I said that the Detective is engaged on a moral quest to find and reestablish the right and just. To say that the Detective creates the crime in the act of solving it appears to negate this, and to do so in a most offensive way. Raymond Chandler demanded that a story be about real crimes committed by real people for real reasons. The commonsense view would be that in comparison with Chandler's demand, this formulation is so much intellectual hocus-pocus insensitive to the plight of people caught in a web of wrongdoing — which is, in a word, *immoral.*

There is, I think, no fully satisfying reply to this argument. So long as people feel this way and until writers find a way to satisfy it, readers will prefer the Neoclassic, the Metaphysical Modern will gain no traction, relativism will be damned as nihilism, and any fears about the consequences of it will go unanswered.

The best I can say in reply is that the detective formula has always been about, along with some other things, order and chaos. The ordinary view, now I think in doubt, was that knowledge yields order and resists entropy. The Detective cannot be on the side of entropy, but might be the *sensei* who will teach us acceptance, how to let go of the striving, competition, and desire for control that power the engine of karma that keeps that wheel turning.[19]

Possible Futures: An Experimental Typology of the Detective Story

I have described a new formula for the detective story, the Metaphysical Modern, which I see emerging from the combination of new writing and films, and what I think are the social conditions for a new shift.

However, as I tried to make clear, there are some serious negatives in my hypothesis. What I have hypothesized may be true, but it may also never be popular, and wide acceptance is crucial to a genre formula. Unlike mainstream fiction, in which individual innovations are sought and valued, genre innovations are driven by solutions that are meaningful to many readers.

I now have a substantial arsenal of historical and critical claims about how the detective genre functions in both social and literary contexts. Is it possible to use these insights to build a typology of the genre that will suggest possible future directions? I think so.

As previously noted, the core, the ancestral narrative of the detective genre, is the uncovering of hidden knowledge. But why is knowledge hidden to begin with? Perhaps we tend to think, when we're not thinking about it, that knowledge is like time, which lives a life of its own, is sometimes encountered in the street, is away from home for long stretches, and can go missing. Time that is lost cannot be found despite our panicked searching, but is sometimes involuntarily remembered, perhaps on encountering an old photograph.[20] Memory works in us like a movie, selecting elements and editing them into an intelligible narrative that we watch, sitting in the dark, bemused spectators. Is knowledge like that, liable to be lost and found like a dime on the sidewalk? Where is it when it's lost? Does it hide in a crack like a lizard?

Perhaps knowledge is a domestic arrangement with a human partner, where the human is the stay-at-home for whom knowledge earns the daily bread (or brings home the bacon). We might then imagine a philandering knowledge, keeping house with another and producing a secret family of ideas.

Knowledge is hidden, we say. But that reifies it as a *thing*. Better to talk of secrets. Secrecy requires human agency. Secrets are created when people *hide* things. This runs counter to the notion that knowledge is simply *out there* waiting to be found, discovered, picked up: that secret knowledge is a natural phenomenon, that secrecy is a property of knowledge.

Secret knowledge is as old as human and perhaps hominid psychology.[21] There are secrets because there are people who don't want something known. This is the paranoid Fafnir scenario: like Fafnir, like a dragon's gold, secrets are under guard, protected.[22] Or, there are secrets because something has been smashed and no one knows how to put it back together. This is the Humpty Dumpty scenario, closely associated with the defeatist premise that there are only unreliable witnesses who each have picked up a piece of the eggshell and gone off with it, never to be found. Such distributed secrets are found in spy stories and certain occult tales involving wizards who scatter themselves, intending to regenerate from the bits some time in the future. The reassembly of a distributed secret is one of the Detective's methods, just as battle with the dragon is central to the action thriller.

Another possibility is that there are secrets because the right people haven't been asked (the purloined-letter scenario) or the right questions haven't been asked of them (the lost-in-the-fog scenario). These are mostly scripts of inadvertence or bumbling, but they include also the honest witness who can't come forward (he's in jail, or dead), won't come forward (he's timid or ashamed), or doesn't know he's supposed to come forward. All of these variations can be found in the Holmes canon, and the idea of something purloined and then hidden in plain sight was of course taken from Poe's story of that name. There is also that familiar person who will tell the truth if necessary but would just rather not, a major plot device of Jane Austen's novels.

What does all this amount to? Is it that we can't get a sight of what we want to know because there are people in the way? It is like trying to get a clear view of the Sistine Chapel ceiling amongst the horde of tourists, of Mt. Fuji through the clouds, of Mont St. Victoire when the painter clears away old conventions of seeing. The detective story is about how to get these things out of the way.

Perhaps. But perhaps it is the *mountain* that is in the way — the mountain that keeps us from catching sight of what we really want to see, which is all the curious and strange things made of the mountain by the tourists, mountaineers, armchair travelers, and great artists who encounter it. The detective story is about drawing our attention to the right things.

Perhaps, given these clues, we ought to consider the knower rather than what is to be known. We might look at the balance between active and passive resistance — how knowledge is extracted from people (various cool dystopias or surveillance schemes) or the warm communication of relationships. We might look at the balance between people and things, where only things are queried (the perfect police procedural, very cool) or only people (the perfect insight of Nero Wolfe without Archie, very warm). There is the cold view that everything that happens to us is an accident (perhaps we ought to call such a view frozen) and the hot view that in order to know about people you need to know about people, because people mess up everything they meddle in. One becomes tired of an inquiry that never ends because the act of looking into something changes what you're looking into, as is the case with the Metaphysical Modern. It's hard to say whether quantum detection[23] is warm or cool. Warm if you're frustrated or feel trapped, cool if you've solved that koan.

Here is an inventory of options. One would be the personal involvement of the detective, which as we have seen has tended to drift away from objectivity, illustrated by a sequence from *Inspecteur Lavardin* (the problem is personal, a prior relation to a suspect, or as in *Trent's Last Case*) to *Prime Suspect* (the problem is general and social) to *Memento* (the problem is existential). Another element would be the resistance of the corrupt and unforgiving world, which is the tension between noir and transcendental morality. Here

TABLE 9. THE DEPLOYMENTS OF KNOWLEDGE

	Pessimistic	*Optimistic*
The problem is intrinsic.	It is impossible that we should understand (*Mulholland Drive*).	Matters are driven mostly by accident, so do the best you can (*Minority Report*).
The problem might be overcome.	But won't be because corruption will always be the stronger (*The Spy Who Came In from the Cold, Gorky Park*).	But might be because thoughtfulness and hard work are sometimes effective (*Tinker Tailor Soldier Spy*).
The problem is not the solution but the power to enforce it.	Might makes right (not an acceptable premise for a mainstream movie)	Power will not necessarily be in the wrong hands (*The Pelican Brief, The Hunt for Red October,* and thrillers generally).

an illustrative sequence might run from Jane Tennison or Rick Deckard, who are official or quasi-official representatives of society and implicated in its structure, to private investigators such as Jake Gittens, to people (or non-human machines, as in *Avatar* or the stories of Stanislaw Lem) entirely outside human society.

Let's make two columns, then, with hopeless conditions on the left and more affirmative situations on the right. The causes of the problem will form the rows.

This way of organizing the question also brings out the rough correspondence between the three rows and the three plot types worked out earlier. The bottom row is the Fafnir scenario (the knowledge we need has already been dug up but it is guarded by the dragon); the middle row is the Humpty Dumpty one (we already have the knowledge we need but it's broken into little pieces); the top row corresponds to all those attitude-induced difficulties caused by the fear that it's all a sham, that what passes for knowledge is just glittery stuff. The columns are knowledge-centric, the rows are socio-centric.

Can a new crop of stories be genetically engineered from these possibilities? The socio-centric rows in the table compose the two tasks of the Detective, which are to get knowledge and to deploy it. Effective deployment requires power. Let us make two Cartesian planes, one concerning knowledge (the columns) and one concerning power — that is, the deployment of knowledge — (the rows), and correlate them according to the various forms of the Detective into a three-dimensional field. All of the possibilities for the detective story will be found within this field.

Each plane has two axes. On these diagrams the x-axis is horizontal and the y-axis is vertical.

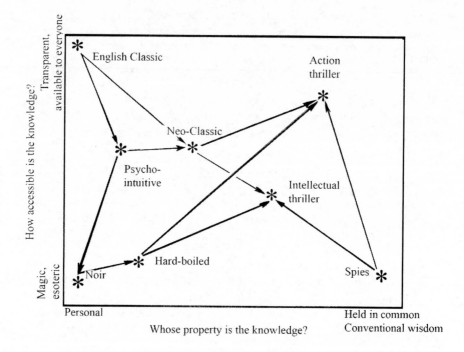

Figure 1. The Cartesian Space of *Knowledge* in the Detective Story

On the plane of knowledge (fig. 1) these two axes are as follows:

The x-axis: Whose property is this knowledge?—the extremes being (at the left) knowledge that is entirely personal, unknown to anyone else, and at the right, knowledge that is common property or conventional wisdom.

The y-axis: How accessible is this knowledge to others?—the extremes being, at the bottom, knowledge that is magic (hopelessly esoteric), and at the top, knowledge that will inevitably be found out.

On the plane of power (fig. 2) the two axes are as follows:

The x-axis: Who wields the power?—the extremes being (at the left) personal power that is used entirely by whim, and (at the right) the power of the masses.

The y-axis: How possible is it to change the situation?—running from hopeless to changeable.

On each plane, arrows indicate the direction of change. On the plane of knowledge (fig. 1), for example, the position of the English Classic at the far left tells us that all English classics are single-person, personal dramas. The problem is caused by one individual and rectified by another. The Classic's position at the top tells us that knowledge is available to every rational person. When the English Classic admitted warm knowledge the genre moved toward

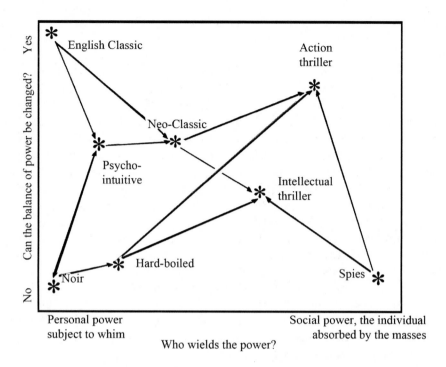

Figure 2. The Cartesian Space of *Power* in the Detective Story

the other end of the scale, where knowledge is bound up with emotions and intuitions that are personal and inscrutable to others. The direction of the arrow indicates that change always follows this path. The cool Classic cannot admit warm knowledge.

On the power plane (fig. 2) the English Classic is located in a similar position. That is, the criminal acts alone with no social entanglements— he is not a puppet — and all crimes are theoretically preventable or at least expiable.

On both planes there is a movement of the Classic downward, comparable to the move of the psycho-intuitive, except the Neoclassic also moves farther to the right. The Neoclassic detective is less self-sufficient both in his ability to discover the truth and in his power to act. The Neoclassic detective does not work alone but for some institution, such as the police or a law firm or something more outré such as, in the case of Margaret Doody's Aristotle, a school, the Lykeion (Lyceum).

The x-axis on the plane of knowledge runs from personal (knowledge is obtained afresh by individuals) to knowledge held in common. The epitome of common knowledge is the spy story. Everyone knows what the spy knows— it is inherent in being sent on a mission when those in power know what they want done, and the targets know also, and so can take steps to defend themselves. The spy's job is to find out how to deploy that knowledge to the desired end, an expedient task that is accomplished using mostly magic detection — testimony sought and elicited by trial and error and suasion rather than evidence. Increasing the proportion of transparency in the acquisition of knowledge — greater use of evidence acquired by deduction rather than testimony acquired by force — and an increasing tendency for personal motivation (the spy works for himself rather than an agency) moves the spy story toward the center where the intellectual thriller lies. Leaving out the personal knowledge and motivation moves the spy story toward the action thriller — the action hero has no special knowledge of the situation he faces and has no personal, transcendent concerns, merely survival. We all know what the hero has to do but not, until the last moment, how he will do it. This is a requirement for suspense, an essential ingredient in the action thriller. When the hero is given his mission there will usually be a feint toward a personal motivation — honor, patriotism, revenge, lust — but this is erased by the survival imperative with which he is presented by his opponents. The hero may seek opportunities to engage in these gladiatorial contests in order to exercise his skills, as in some martial-arts movies. This is part of the spy heritage. Most confrontations, though implicit in the mission ("should you choose to accept it, Mr. Phelps"), are not provoked.

As did the English Classic, noir dramas also tend to drift toward the center, transforming themselves into hard-boiled stories and from there into one of the two varieties of thriller. English Classics and spy stories are the original forms of their genres, out of which the succeeding formulas grew. For the thriller the situation is just the opposite. Each form of the thriller has three influences, but no succeeding formula. They are dead-ends.

As the detective genre has aged, the sub-genres have drifted toward the center. Contemporary detective stories are a blend of Neoclassic, neo-noir, and intellectual thriller, neither warm nor cool, public nor private, concerned equally with the actions of individuals and groups, with attention less exclusively focused on the detective. Detective stories have become more like the mainstream novel. There is one dimension yet to consider. If the planes of knowledge and power are superimposed on one another as the opposite faces of a cube (fig. 3) some new relationships can be seen.

There is (or could be), for example, a diagonal line running from the English Classic on the plane of knowledge to the spy story on the plane of power. One can imagine a fuzzy area in the center of the cube, a cloud, where we might find another sort of detective story. What would such a story be like? It would be one of transparent social knowledge — conventional wisdom, statistical outcomes — and of totalitarian public opinion: the hive. The rules of behavior in such a society are easily altered but changes are not determined

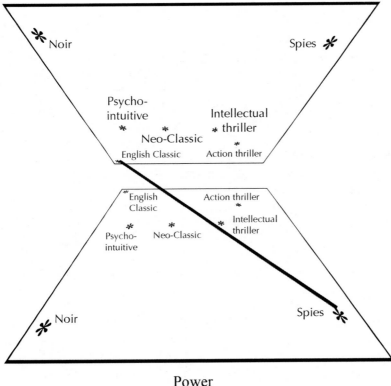

Figure 3. The Relationship of the Layers of Power and Knowledge

by individuals: it is a world of arbitrary and unforseeable direction, a dystopia. This is repellent and stony ground for a detective story. The action thriller encroaches on this region and it is not a surprise that dystopian stories do tend to be thrillers in which the hero faces a conspiracy or social coercion, susses out the situation by the use of detective methods, and then protects himself or escapes (or fails to) by instinct and physical skills. A detective in such a story might find it impossible to know what a crime was, be without authority to act, work in a completely incrutable world closed to both deduction and intuition. The film *Memento* would be an instance of this, or *Soylent Green*.

But there are detective stories of this sort that are not so intractable and bleak. We saw in the case of *13 Conversations About One Thing* what happens when a story moves at all deeply into this area of chance, nonlinear and apparently causeless occurrence. Genre elements— the identity of the detective, the gathering of evidence, the construction of a story and then a plot out of the initial narrative fragments, the discovery of the criminal and the domestication of the crime — become tangled and uncertain and the boundary is blurred between the story and family of detective stories. Such stories may be difficult to read as *detective* stories, but our examination of some of them, Modern Metaphysicals, shows that not only can they be so analyzed but that the effort to do so brings insight into what this extraordinarily malleable genre is capable of.

What story does the diagonal running from the thriller on the plane of knowledge to noir on the plane of power suggest? Thrillers, by contrast with the Classic, tend to have mobs of villains backed by an infinity of supporters, but like the Classic, the hero always succeeds and enjoys substantial moral support (not always apparent at first), which generates valuable help at crucial moments. Thrillers are full of hope — not always realized, sometimes bitter — which goes some way to accounting for their popularity. But if we match the thriller's transparent knowledge with noir's solipsism and bleakness we get a different story entirely, a tale of suspense where we know at the outset that the hero will die but we don't know how, and that the mission will fail with unimaginable consequences. But before we judge too hastily, there is a worthwhile story something like this— the sacrificial quest. How would *The Lord of the Rings* have been changed in its premises if Frodo rather than Gollum had fallen with the ring into the Crack of Doom, or if the point of view had been Gollum's? The higher powers that seem to govern such Greek tragedies as Gollum's would disappear, but the grandeur and moral heroism of reaching for transcendent Good would remain and, through sacrifice, become more astonishing. We see something of this when Frodo, exhausted from his ordeal, passes over to the Uttermost West. Frodo becomes a Christ-figure.

Moreover, if Sauron were to have prevented the loss of the ring, Frodo's quest would not have been invalidated. The resulting apocalypse is the backstory of many a science-fiction epic and alternative history such as the victory of Hitler. The Hero loses his life but becomes a model for the survivors, and new little quests spring up like daffodils in the spring. The solace of a malicious god is more acceptable to most of us than an indifferent one.

But how are these stories *detective* stories? Where is the figure of the Detective? These stories seem to be about the getting and deployment of knowledge, incorporating a mix of warm and cool thought; they are about crimes that disrupt the social fabric and solutions that repair it; they do the social work of externalizing, explaining, and calming our fears; they show us how unwelcome change might be accommodated — but many stories do this. All the great, lasting stories do this. The ancient need for stories arises from our ability to think these things. But there is a hole in the middle. There is no *detective*.

Detective stories can, or could, be full participants in the company of the immortal. The present offers this chance to someone. The old, tired genre formulas have been cleared away, and no longer obscure the view. Consider the anti–Metaphysical. Either no one would have a clue and nothing would ever happen, or that man who is always bleating, "It's an open and shut case," would be right. Or consider the reversal of the detective's role. In the anti–Metaphysical plot the detective would be the oppressor, the man of superior knowledge who uses it as the representative of an illegitimate ideology of sin and expiation, an oppressor to whom is opposed, who can be opposed by, no one. Who is to take the role of criminal, someone with insufficient information and lacking the knowledge to say what it all means? In the universe of ordinary matter the criminal is after power or money or revenge and is crippled by a hubris that prevents him from realizing his deficiencies. In the anti–Metaphysical on the other side of the mirror it would seem that we common folk are the criminals.

Does anyone want stories like this? Do we have a choice but to take up the challenge to reimagine the Detective?

Conclusions

What shall we make of this excursion through the history of the detective genre, which we undertook so as to better understand the peculiar cultural authority of the figure of the Detective?

One possibility has been left unexplored. Since the early '80s, claims have been made that the digital and social media will create new art forms with new purposes differently positioned in society. Forty years on, these claims are beginning to seem plausible, but no one has produced an authoritative example.

Given the complete opaqueness of the future of storytelling (since it is one of the oldest and most indispensable human activities, we can assume it *has* a future), it would be impossible to predict a future for the digital Detective. So many of the conditions for the genre could change, as our exploration of the planes of knowledge and power shows, that we will probably not have new detective stories recognizable to us. Or perhaps some other story form will arise that speaks to the getting and deployment of knowledge and does the same social work. This succession of genres is common, after all, and is as natural as the succession of forest trees of which Thoreau wrote:

When, hereabouts, a single forest tree or a forest springs up naturally where none of its kind grew before, I do not hesitate to say, though in some quarters still it may sound paradoxical, that it came from a seed.... In all the pines, a very thin membrane, in appearance much like an insect's wing, grows over and around the seed, and independent of it, while the latter is being developed within its base. Indeed this is often perfectly developed, though the seed is abortive; nature being, you would say, more sure to provide the means of transporting the seed, than to provide the seed to be transported. In other words, a beautiful thin sack is woven around the seed, with a handle to it such as the wind can take hold of, and it is then committed to the wind, expressly that it may transport the seed and extend the range of the species; and this it does.[24]

Appendix

Chronological List of Films Mentioned in the Text

Year	Title	Detective	Actor
1931	*Dangerous Female*	Sam Spade	Ricardo Cortez
1932	*Secrets of the French Police*	François St. Cyr	Frank Morgan
1933	*The Kennel Murder Case*	Philo Vance	William Powell
1935	*The Casino Murder Case*	Philo Vance	Paul Lukas
1935	*Lord Edgware Dies*	Hercule Poirot	Austin Trevor
1936	*Secret Agent*	Richard Ashenden	John Gielgud
1937	*Pépé le Moko*	Inspector Slimane	Lucas Gridoux
1939	*The Hound of the Baskervilles*	Sherlock Holmes	Basil Rathbone
1939	*Nick Carter, Master Detective*	Lou Farnsby	Rita Johnson
1939	*Private Detective*	Jinks	Jane Wyman
1940	*Calling Philo Vance*	Philo Vance	James Stephenson
1941	*The Maltese Falcon*	Sam Spade	Humphrey Bogart
1944	*The Mask of Dimitrios*	Cornelius Leyden	Peter Lorre
1946	*The Big Sleep*	Philip Marlowe	Humphrey Bogart
1959	*The Hound of the Baskervilles*	Sherlock Holmes	Peter Cushing
1961	*Last Year at Marienbad*	X	Giorgio Albertazzi
1963	*High and Low*	Chief Detective Nokura	Tatsura Nakadai
1965	*Alphaville*	Lemmy Caution	Edward Constantine
1965	*Murder on the Orient Express*	Hercule Poirot	Albert Finney
1966	*Trans-Europ Express*	Elias	Jean-Louis Trintignant
1967	*Bonnie and Clyde*	Frank Hamer	Denver Pyle
1968	*The Thomas Crown Affair*	Vicky Anderson	Faye Dunaway
1971	*The French Connection*	Popeye Doyle	Gene Hackman
1972	*The Godfather*		
1973	*Soylent Green*	Detective Thorn	Charlton Heston
1974	*Celine and Julie Go Boating*	Julie	Domenique Labourier
1974	*Chinatown*	Jake Gittes	Jack Nicholson
1976	*The Seven Percent Solution*	Sigmund Freud	Alan Arkin
1981	*True Confessions*	Tom Spellacy	Robert Duvall
1982	*Blade Runner*	Rick Deckard	Harrison Ford
1982	*The Hound of the Baskervilles* (mini-series)	Sherlock Holmes	Tom Baker
1983	*The Hound of the Baskervilles*	Sherlock Holmes	Ian Richardson

Year	Title	Detective	Actor
1985	*Young Sherlock Holmes*	Sherlock Holmes	Nicholas Rowe
1986	*The Singing Detective*	Philip Marlow	Michael Gambon
1987	*LA Confidential*	Jack Vincennes	Kevin Spacey
1987	*The Untouchables*	Eliot Ness	Kevin Costner
1988	*The Hound of the Baskervilles*	Sherlock Holmes	Jeremy Brett
1988	*Without a Clue*	Sherlock Holmes	Michael Caine
1990	*Twin Peaks*	Dale Cooper	Kyle MacLachlan
1991	*Fried Green Tomatoes*	Evelyn Couch	Kathy Bates
1991	*Prime Suspect*	Jane Tennison	Helen Mirren
1993	*Adventure of the Egyptian Tomb*	Hercule Poirot	David Suchet
1993	*Manhattan Murder Mystery*	Woody Allen	Woody Allen
1994	*Pulp Fiction*		
1995	*The City of Lost Children*	One	Ron Perlman
1995	*Devil in a Blue Dress*	Easy Rawlins	Denzel Washington
1996	*Fargo*	Marge Gunderson	Frances McDormand
1999	*The Sopranos*		
2000	*Memento*	Guy Pearce	Leonard Shelby
2001	*Amélie*	Amélie Poulain	Audrey Tatou
2001	*A Beautiful Mind*	John Nash	Russell Crowe
2001	*Gosford Park*	Inspector Thompson	Stephen Fry
2001	*Mulholland Drive*	Betty Elms	Naomi Watts
2001	*Thirteen Conversations About One Thing*		
2004	*Eternal Sunshine of the Spotless Mind*	Joel Barish	Jim Carrey
2004	*Sky Captain and the World of Tomorrow*	Sky Captain	Jude Law
2009	*The Girl with the Dragon Tattoo*	Lisbeth Salander	Noomi Rapace
2009	*The Secret in their Eyes*	Benjamin Esposito	Ricardo Darren
2010	*The Ghostwriter*	Ghost	Ewan MacGregor

Chapter Notes

Chapter 1

1. Let me give an example. The Detective is coextensive in time and place with the narrative of Bohemia, and both share a common origin in the bourgeoisie and its creature, the industrial revolution. The first part of Elizabeth Wilson's *Bohemia* (New Brunswick: Rutgers, 2000) is an excellent book on the origins and varieties of Bohemia. Matthew B. Crawford explains, in his book *Shop Craft as Soulcraft* (New York: Penguin, 2009) how industrialization and alienation from work in both blue-collar and cubicle work go hand in hand with intensification of a desire for rationality and meaning. Siegfried Geidion's *Mechanization Takes Command: A Contribution to Anonymous History* (Chicago: University of Chicago Press, 1948) remains the best introduction to the industrial revolution. Lines of argument such as this deserve fuller treatment, but to give it would take us too far from the main question.

2. The best information on the gender of readers is the Bowker Consumer-Focused Research Report, which is proprietary. I infer my assertion from the facts that 25 percent of the market is for mysteries (second most popular category after romance) and 65 percent of the books are bought by women. By comparison, romance accounts for 54.5 percent of the market, and 93 percent of readers of romance are women (http://book square.com, Aug. 4, 2009, accessed Feb. 4, 2010, and *Publisher's Weekly* trade statistics). A general, non-statistical account of women readers is Kathleen Klein, ed., *Woman Times Three: Writing, Detectives, Readers* (Bowling Green, OH: Bowling Green State University Popular Press, 1995).

3. Much of this is taken, directly or indirectly, from one of the founding texts of the now huge literature on the Detective, John G. Cawelti's *Adventure, Mystery, and Romance* (Chicago: University of Chicago Press, 1976) and especially chapter 4. Subsequent theorizations of the genre are many, mostly derived from Cawelti's.

4. In the late 1920s Ronald Knox, a member of the Detective Club, formulated on behalf of the club a set of rules that were a reduction of the more general genre requirements. These have come to define the English Classic. As with all such codifications, the Rules appeared toward the end of the life of the thing to be defined. The English Classic Detective ossified and was replaced by subsequent formulas, but all these formulations must satisfy the enabling conditions. Knox's rules will be found in my third chapter, on the English Classic.

5. Holmes's Watson is of course the best-known. Before Watson I find only one instance, in Poe (1841 and 1845). Poe's Chronicler, however, is unnamed and no attempt is made to humanize him. We know a great deal about Watson, and have ample means to test his honesty and reliability, whereas we take Poe's Chronicler on faith. It is interesting that we do so, without irony.

6. The concept of a crime is a fluid one. The war crime, for example, is a recent notion dating only from the Hague Convention of 1899 and 1907 and refined at Nuremburg after 1945, although the ideas on which it is based are of course much older. The codification of the concept begins with the Geneva

Convention in 1949. The writing of Hannah Arendt on Nuremberg is basic reading. Susan Sontag's *Regarding the Pain of Others* (New York: Farrar, Straus and Giroux, 2003) might also be recommended.

7. See for example Norbert Elias, *The Civilizing Process*, trans. Edmund Jephcott, rev. ed. (Oxford: Blackwell, 1994), 233–236, in the section "State Formation and Civilization." And of course Montesquieu's *De l'esprit des lois* (1748).

8. This formula continues to be employed. Examples from the later history of the genre include Emma Tennant's *The Last of the English Country House Murders* (1976), and also the surprising *Blood on the Dining-room Floor* (Pawlet, VT: Banyan, 1948) by Gertrude Stein.

9. Not at first she, possibly because the requirement of rational thought was felt to be fatally limiting in the same way that a blind detective (Max Carrados) or a seriously neurotic one (Monk) is thought to represent an insurmountable difficulty. This is of significance to a conflict much broader than feminism, that between (cold) rationality and (warm) emotions in which the Detective plays a large role. Presently, however, there is no dearth of female detectives or studies of them. Carla Kungi, *Creating the Female Detective* (Jefferson, N.C.: McFarland, 2006) and *Women Times Three* (note 2).

10. Daniel Cordle, *Postmodern Postures: Literature, Science, and the Two Cultures Debate* (Aldershot: Ashgate, 1999).

11. Famously, C.P. Snow's two cultures. A compendium of documents of the time confirms that the original argument between Snow and Leavis was over the validity of two forms of knowledge, the objective/rational and the instinctual/emotional (*Cultures in Conflict: Perspectives on the Snow-Leavis Controversy*, ed. David R. Cornelius and Edwin St. Vincent [Chicago: Scott Foresman, 1964]). Our current position is to assert that the difference between the two cultures is in their characteristic ways of getting and using knowledge, out of which is constructed the reified, supposedly a priori division of knowledge into kinds.

12. For an explanation of story time see Umberto Eco, *Six Walks in the Fictional Woods* (Cambridge: Harvard University Press, 1994). It is, in summary, the order and sequence of events as they occur in the story. These events may be rearranged for the purpose of telling the story; this is narrative time. Holmes's Dr. Watson, typically for the Chronicler, generally begins in narrative time but shifts to story time after a sentence or two. To scramble the events of the story would be to obscure the chain of reasoning that is the rationale of the tale.

13. Many plots, from Austen to Trollope, turn on a lack, or a failure, of communication between characters. They flirt with the arbitrary and their resolution is far too transparently in the hands of the author, and an author trying to play a bluff hand against drama.

14. Originally London: J. Roberts. Restored edition, with introduction and notes, by Geoffrey M. Sill (Stockton, N.J.: Carolingian, 1973). The subtitle reads: "*The Reason of their being so Frequent, with Probably Means to Prevent 'em. To which is added, three short treatises; I. A Warning for Travellers: With Rules to know a Highwayman; and Instructions how to behave upon the Occasion. II. Observations on House-Breakers: How to prevent a Tenement from being broke open: with a Word of Advice concerning Servants. III. A Caveat for Shop-keepers: With a Description of Shop-Lifts, how to know 'em, and how to prevent 'em. Also a Caution of delivering Goods. With the Relation of several Cheats practiced lately upon this Piblick. Written by a Converted Thief. To which is prefix'd some Memoirs of his Life.*"

15. Rzepka, 53–54.

16. Edward Bulwer-Lytton, *Pelham*, 1818, ed. Jerome McGann (reprint, Lincoln: University of Nebraska Press, 1972). My remarks are taken from Heather Worthington, *The Subverting Vision of Bulwer Lytton* (Plainsboro, N.J.: Associated University Presses, 2004), 54–59.

17. Cawelti, *Adventure, Mystery, and Romance*, 77.

18. The alternative strategy is to use force, essentially torture or blackmail, to obtain facts or confessions. Always common, forced discoveries are particularly characteristic of hard-boiled stories and the thriller. Force is not non-rational but anti-rational, and the detective's disdain for its use is a good marker for the Detective icon.

19. Later in the development of the genre this practice will be considered illegitimate,

as not fair to the reader. Holmes gets away with it first because his solutions are filtered through Watson, whom it is acceptable to mystify, and second because he justifies it rationally, famously remarking that it is a mistake to theorize in advance of the facts. When the use of a Chronicler fell out of fashion it became a problem of how to maintain suspense without retreating to the magical behavior of Cuff.

20. I will have more to say later about this second crime, which became a structural feature of the English Classic.

21. A term of opprobrium used at the time to mean sensual as well as shocking. The sensational novel was felt to be deliberately provocative, and the epithet was intended to brand these books as scandalous. Of course, they sold very well.

22. This quotation and the remarks following are paraphrased from the introduction (pp. 18–20, 28) by Natalie M. Houston to the 2003 edition of Braddon's novel (Toronto: Broadview Literary Texts).

23. Gaboriau constructed his stories as Poe did, but Gaboriau's were episodic as suited to serial publication in newspapers. This form of publication also encouraged authors to continue their stories for as long as possible, as do modern soap operas for the same reasons.

24. The relationship is structural, and my comparison should not be taken at face value without a more detailed examination. Pudd'nhead is a long way from hard-boiled; it's Twain himself who might be called that.

25. In later chapters I will explore the post-war neo-noir and Neoclassic forms. The existence of a neo implies that the original is moribund. The new version is not always in the line of development, however, and such will be the case.

26. Described on the Fantômas web site: "The opium-smoking, male-drag donning, death's-head-tattooed daughter of Fantômas, Hélène is a bad girl at least half a century ahead of her time. She and Fandor harbor an unrequited passion for each other, but since he is the sworn enemy of her father her loyalties are forever divided. Fandor's association with the stiff-necked Juve doesn't help, either. And if Fandor is indeed the son of Fantômas, their love is incestuous!" This gives some idea of the over-the-top style of the tales (Robin Walz and Elliott

Smith, *Fantômas*, http://www.fantomas-lives.com/).

27. Note that the word *wimp* dates from the early twentieth century. It is just plausible that Zangwill used this as the detective's name with intent. Constant is probably also named with intent, considering Zangwill's positive attitude toward the working class. The "Bow" of the title is a rough working-class district in the East End. One of the earliest even slightly effective police forces was the Bow Street Runners, set up in the mid-eighteenth century by the novelist Henry Fielding.

28. "Propaganda by Deed: The Greenwich Observatory Bomb of 1894," Royal Museums Greenwich, available online at http://www.rmg.co.uk/explore/astronomy-and-time/astronomy-facts/history/propaganda-by-deed-the-greenwich-observatory-bomb-of-1894, accessed May 29, 2013. There is also Henry James's *The Princess Cassimasima* (1886).

Chapter 2

1. Doyle backdates the story by nine years, to 1878. Is there any significance to this? It must be the only thing in the Holmes canon not yet examined by the exegetics. The story, so-called, is actually a novella, the tale proper being glued to a second tale of Mormon vengeance, the back-story to what we have just read. The existence of this superfluous melodrama set in a "Country of the Saints" might suggest that Doyle did not yet have a mature understanding of the detective formula, but he was in fact susceptible to this sort of exotic adventure all his life. The conflict between these two genres and the inclination to pair them, the one serving to temper the other, captures the central polarity and source of iconic power of the Detective. What Doyle learned to do only imperfectly was to fully integrate the two narratives, not accomplished, as we shall see, for another half-century, and then by Raymond Chandler at the cost of a substantial transformation of the genre itself.

2. Tolkien's *Lord of the Rings* and *The Hobbit* are, by contrast, not extensible at all, nor are his fellow-Inkling's Narnia chronicles. These are finished, bounded tales. The best one can do is to use the given material to tell another story of the same type. A bet-

ter illustration of the open character of the Holmes canon would be Batman (in the original incarnation).

3. Not everyone, of course, likes him. Chandler called him an "attutude" who made a dozen quotable remarks. He is, in the view of some, an aloof, arrogant, bipolar character with addictive behaviors and no friends or sex life. But such contradictions are true of anyone worth knowing and no bar to his humanity. Indeed they are part and parcel of it.

4. Abduction was first used in its logical sense by C.S. Peirce in 1879 (Thomas A. Sebeok and Jean Umiker-Sebeok, "You Know My Method: A Juxtaposition of Charles S. Peirce and Sherlock Holmes," in *The Sign of Three: Dupin, Holmes, Peirce*, ed. Umberto Eco and Thomas A. Sebeok, 11–54 [Bloomington: Indiana University Press, 1983]).

5. That the confession is a requirement of the French sense of what is just bespeaks a different story structure and explains Inspector Maigret's use of intuition as evidence prima facie rather than simply an indicator of undiscovered evidence is supportable. This innovation will be explored more fully later.

6. Theodore M. Porter, *Trust in Numbers: The Pursuit of Objectivity in Science and Public Life* (Princeton, N.J.: Princeton University Press, 1995), 220. This is found in a discussion of scientific community, affirming the tension between cold and warm.

7. Porter, *Trust in Numbers,* 217.

8. G.K. Chesterton, *The Man Who Was Thursday* (New York: Sheed and Ward, 1975), 45.

9. Chesterton, 123.

10. At the very end of *The Man Who Was Thursday* Syme invokes the power of love in the person of "the girl with the gold-red hair, cutting lilac before breakfast, with the great unconscious gravity of a girl." This notion's sisters are in Lawrence, Yeats, Joyce and thousands of other conscious and unconscious authors.

11. Probably very few of our decisions are made entirely on the basis of evidence. Our long interest in the figure of the Detective suggests a wish for more reasonableness in human affairs.

12. Marjorie Nicolson, "The Professor and the Detective," *Atlantic Monthly,* April 1929, reprinted in Howard Haycraft's col-

lection *The Art of the Mystery Story* (New York: Simon & Schuster, 1946), 110–127.

13. Which would cause the reader to identify too closely with the character and so remove that character from the list of suspects. Rather a different practice from our own authors, for whom such an identification would offer an irresistible opportunity to prey on the reader's weakness.

14. "Einstein" being the representative scientific bugbear of the time as "Darwin" is of ours; this from p. 119 of the Haycraft version.

15. Michael Gilbert, *Smallbone Deceased* (New York: Harper, 1950), 84.

16. See Porter, "Objectivity and the Politics of Disciplines," in *Trust in Numbers,* 193–199.

17. The best short exposition of the career of Romanticism is, in my opinion, Jacques Barzun's *Berlioz and the Romantic Century,* 3rd ed. (New York: Columbia University Press, 1969), 1:370–381. My comments on the subject can be traced to Barzun.

18. Less violently stated by Tzvetan Todorov, "The Typology of Detective Fiction," in *The Poetics of Prose* (Ithaca: Cornell University Press, 1977), 42–52.

19. Pierre Bayard, *Who Killed Roger Ackroyd?* trans. Carol Cosman (New York: New Press, 2000).

20. Untainted examples are not that obscure, of course. Kafka's *Trial* comes to mind.

21. Michael Cohen, *Murder Most Fair: The Appeal of Murder Fiction* (Madison: Fairleigh Dickinson, 2000), 35.

22. Cohen, *Murder Most Fair,* 36; Ian Ousby, *Bloodhounds of Heaven: The Detective in English Fiction from Godwin to Doyle* (Cambridge: Harvard University Press, 1976), 21–24.

23. The English Classic tradition is usually dated from 1913 and E.C. Bentley's *Trent's Last Case.* Trent fails. He is brought down by love and all those humane qualities thought inimical to the stylized English tradition of Poirot and Wimsey.

24. Willard Huntington Wright, "Twenty Rules for Writing Detective Stories," *American Magazine,* September 1928.

25. Yes, Poirot is present in the story, but as is always the case as a proxy for the reader. The real detective is the author's proxy, the

narrator, because it is the author who knows the right answer. A more complete exposition of these relationships will be found farther on.

26. Omitting the atypical *Valley of Fear*, half of which has nothing to do with Holmes and detection, and the last collection on the grounds that Doyle may have by that time become too self-conscious about Holmes and tweaked him to fit the reputation he had acquired.

27. A thorough linguistic analysis of the Holmes canon has been carried out by Mark Lu Shengli in his master's thesis *Sherlock Holmes as a Romantic Detective: A Stylistic Analysis of Holmes's Use of Language* (National University of Singapore, 2009).

28. The raw score is for feeling over thinking by 64 to 46.

29. When the word *warm* is used we should remember that it forms a dichotomy with *cool*, a metaphor for the emotional/rational pair. *Warm* does not refer to such personal qualities as outgoing or welcoming. The emotions can also be selfish and cruel. In this context, eccentricity is a warm quality.

30. This list was assembled with the help of the International Movies Database (http://www.imdb.com) and Michael Pointer's *The Sherlock Holmes File* (New York: CN Potter, 1976).

31. The séance does get into the 1939 script. Perhaps the wholly invented mummers' Christmas in the 2002 film is a functional equivalent. In 1959 the Franklin character, transformed into a silly bishop who could not possibly assent to such occult doings, blocked the whole possibility.

Chapter 3

1. Van Dine, whose real name was Willard Huntington Wright, was the creator of the series detective Philo Vance (1925–1939), an ersatz English lord affecting upper-class behavior. The American Wright in his Van Dine persona was the ironically perfect explicator of the English Classic.

2. I will continue to use this word *deduction* despite what was said about Holmes's method of guessing (abduction) because it is the conventional way of speaking.

3. I will discuss magic detection more carefully in the next chapter.

4. *On the Origin of Stories* (Cambridge: Harvard, 2009), 20.

5. James Alcock, "The Belief Engine," *Skeptical Inquirer* 19(3): 255–263.

6. This is the principle behind the idea that a writ is not served until the recipient accepts it.

7. Paraphrased from Dudley Andrew, *Concepts in Film Theory* (Oxford: Oxford University Press, 1984), 10–11.

8. In 2010 a new television version of *Murder on the Orient Express* attempted to humanize Poirot by providing him with a spiritual crisis. Doubts concerning the correctness of shielding the perpetrators are found in the text, but they do not amount to a crisis. Compare Albert Finney's 1965 portrayal, impervious to ambiguity and moral quandary. Christie's text occupies the normative middle ground of convention and moderation.

9. Simenon's Maigret is the great exception to the Detective's dismal personal life. Maigret's uxorious marriage, middle-class life, and love of ordinary pleasures are integral to his way of thought, as we shall see.

10. Raymond Chandler expressed a notable ire toward Philo Vance.

11. The procedural is a story in which the crime is solved by a systematic thoroughness that eventually invalidates every solution but the correct one; it has been favored in stories turning on the breaking of an alibi. The insight of Holmes or Poirot does not enter into the procedural.

12. Examples from the movies would be *The Pelican Brief* and the Indiana Jones trilogy.

13. Randall Collins in his book *The Sociology of Philosophies: A Global Theory of Intellectual Change* (Cambridge: Harvard University Press, 1998) puts the optimum number of competing systems at three or four. Two few and they fission, too many and they fuse. The English Classic occupied a position analogous to that of Confucianism, growing more stagnant, resistant to change, and hence more vulnerable as it aged.

14. This novel is often called hard-boiled, but the true hard-boiled genre variant is a post-war invention that follows different conventions and does different cultural work. The novel has the affect of hard-boiled but in most respects obeys Classic rules.

15. The Pert Dame, the Lush, and female detectives will be discussed again in the following chapters.

Chapter 4

1. This argument is taken from the first pages of Kern's fifth chapter, on emotion (Stephen Kern, *A Cultural History of Causality: Science, Murder Novels, and Systems of Thought* [Princeton: Princeton University Press, 2004]).

2. Eventually, solutions to the problems of filming a detective story were found, but movies until the early fifties were better suited to gothic melodrama and mystification. Contrast the dark tone and foreboding of the Basil Rathbone Holmes with the brighter Charlie Chan movies—the cooler Chan required an excessive verbalization of the detective's thoughts to make the story intelligible.

3. The M'Naughten Rules date from 1843 and were derived from British law. These were in use until the 1950s, when a more lenient American version came into use.

4. My schema is based on an article by William J. Coburn, "A World of Systems: The Role of Systematic Patterns of Experience in the Therapeutic Process," *Psychoanalytic Inquiry* 21 (2002): 656–677. The idea of open form comes from the poet Charles Olson.

5. Here it is necessary that I acknowledge an objection that has been present in my argument that changes in the genre are a response to social change. First, my practice of justifying claims for past conditions by pointing to their outcome in the later times is an instance of "whig history." This term was coined by Herbert Butterfield in 1931 *The Whig Interpretation of History* and argued by historians and scholars in a very wide range of disciplines since. Second, to argue from the existence of social attitudes to their manifestation in the detective story and then to explain features of the detective story by reference to social attitudes is a circular argument. Until now I have discouraged these objections by staking my claims about social conditions on common currency and easily defended by reference to a very wide range of sources. In this instance I may cite three. Morris Dickstein's *Dancing in the Dark: A Cultural History of the Great Depression* (New York: W.W. Norton, 2009), Richard J. Evans, *The Coming of the Third Reich* (London: Penguin, 2003), and Inga Clendinnen's *Reading the Holocaust* (Cambridge: Cambridge University Press, 1999). In the introduction Clendennin writes, "I have known about Nazis for as long as I can remember. The outbreak of World War II very nearly coincided with my fifth birthday, and in the next few years I lived with the uneasy dread that the two events were obscurely, fatally connected" (1).

6. The first Maigret stories were translated into English in the early thirties, but there were no more until 1939.

7. Dashiell Hammett, *The Maltese Falcon* (reprint, New York: Vintage, 1992), 215.

8. Page references will be to the 2000 reprint (Kelly Bray, Cornwall: Stratus).

9. See chapter 1, note 11.

10. Susan Rowland, "The Wasteland and the Grail Knight: Myth and Cultural Criticism in Detective Fiction," *Clues* 28(2): 46, 53.

11. This is quite untrue; the book is clearly not a satire. The judgment is indicative of Barzun and Taylor's commitment to the ratiocinative formula. Their hostility to Carlo Emilio Gadda's *That Awful Mess on the via Merulana* is another example: "A good example of what happens when a serious novelist takes up crime and detection in ignorance of the genre" (Jacques Barzun and Wendell Hertig Taylor, *A Catalogue of Crime,* expanded ed. [New York: Harper and Row, 1989], Entry 1394).

12. Barzun and Taylor, *Catalogue of Crime,* 43.

13. An excellent bibliography, giving also the details of the first French publication, is *Maigret Bibliography,* http://www.trussel.com/maig/maibib.htm (accessed Jan. 24, 2012).

14. Pierre Assouline, *Simenon, a Biography,* trans. Jon Rothschild (New York: Knopf, 1997), 86.

15. Assouline, *Simenon,* 340–357.

16. In French he is a *commissaire.* In English he is demoted to inspector.

17. Assouline, *Simenon,* 89.

18. Marlowe (in *The Big Sleep*) denies that he is a detective and implies that a shamus is something much humbler. To imagine Marlowe as a humble man is difficult, but he certainly does not overesti-

mate himself, and we ought to take the denigrating word gumshoe (which he does not actually use), together with the shaman, as composing the whole concept.

19. As to be a detective was not, there being abundant enough examples in the noir and hard-boiled canon to support this claim.

20. Rowland, "The Wasteland and the Grail Knight," *passim*.

21. Pulps were so called from the cheap wood-pulp paper on which the magazines and books of these popular authors were printed. Hammett, Gardner, and many others of this period were first published in the pulps, the most famous being *Black Mask*. Pulp readers, mostly working class, wanted action and were impatient with cerebration. Hammett, Chandler et al. did not so much as invent the process as explain how it worked in a context that would appeal more to middle-class readers (Charles J. Rzepka, *Detective Fiction* [Malden, Mass.: Polity, 2005], 181–182).

22. Rzepka (*Detective Fiction*, 179–183), citing also other authorities, makes an attempt to theorize the early hard-boiled as a rejection of history. It is a rejection of old social practices certainly, a new response to changed conditions, but so long as evidence and reasoning drive the story, no matter how feebly, we can not accept this on the fundamental ground that the whole raison d'être of the genre is to *explain* the past, not to reject it. To exorcise the past is as far as we might go at this point.

23. Raymond Chandler, "The Simple Art of Murder," in *The Art of the Mystery Story,* ed. Howard Haycraft (New York: Simon & Schuster, 1946), 234.

24. Cawelti, *Adventure, Mystery, Romance* 163–164

25. David Bordwell, *Narration and Film Form* (Madison: University of Wisconsin Press, 1985), 67.

26. The Classic tradition construes knowledge as existing in the world, external to its discoverer. Subjective knowledge raises the possibilities of private knowledge and inscrutable evidence. The noir narrative is predisposed toward subjective knowledge.

27. Modern retellings of Classic stories don't fare well unless supercharged with the narrative devices developed for the Neoclassic.

28. A series of three columns by Edmund Wilson in the *New Yorker* trashed the form as lowbrow spectacle and are undeservedly remembered. The first, on October 14, 1944, "Why Do People Read Detective Stories?" started the brouhaha and provides a sufficient familiarity with this attitude.

29. Remarked upon earlier in explicating the deviance of the 1959 *Hound of the Baskervilles*. As the argument proceeds the public role of science will play a large part, because science is now the most culturally powerful proponent of things rational and empirical.

30. There were some technical matters to be satisfied, of course. The characteristic chiaroscuro of a noir film, for example, requires fast film and lenses to work under such conditions. Such matters are commonly discussed in histories of film and in books on film narrative such as David Bordwell's—*The Way Hollywood Tells It* (Berkeley: University of California Press, 2006) and *Narration in the Fiction Film* (Madison: University of Wisconsin Press, 1985)—and John Gibbs, *Mise-en-Scene: Film Style and Presentation* (London: Wallflower, 2002).

31. The concept of virtuality as definitional in the arts was developed by Suzanne K. Langer from Ernst Cassirer's thought. Unfortunately, this idea came at the wrong time (1942) and was overwhelmed by other formulations, so that it is now taken for granted as a little too elementary.

32. Sigfried Giedion, *Mechanization Takes Command* (New York: Oxford University Press, 1948).

33. Bentley was also the inventor of the Clerihew, after his middle name, a deliberately clunky verse form. One cannot help thinking there is some significance in all these things being found in the same man.

34. Chan was based on a real detective, Chang Apana (Yunte Huang, *Charlie Chan: The Untold Story of the Honorable Detective and His Rendezvous with American History* [New York: Norton, 2010]).

35. See Maxine Hong Kingman's *China Men* (New York: Knopf, 1980).

36. The first female detectives were a Miss Gladden, in a novel by Andrew Forrester Jr., *The Female Detective* (1863), preceded by a few months by *Ruth Traill, Ruth the Betrayer*, serialized in 1862 by Edward Ellis (Judith Flanders, "The Hanky-Panky War,"

Times Literary Supplement, June 18, 2010, 14).

37. Frankie's soft spot is for the sidekick Dex. This Dex is a good example of the genius who keeps the machinery going, familiar as Scotty in *Star Trek* but going back much farther than machinery to such figures as the expert horse-coper, the maker of fantastic swords, and others. That the figure had an interesting renaissance during the years of the heroic pilot and airplane romanticism would be worthy of a study of its own.

Chapter 5

1. Douglas T. Miller and Marion Nowak, *The Fifties: The Way We Really Were* (New York: Doubleday, 1977), 159.

2. Rowland, "Wasteland and the Grail Knight," 46; Cawelti, *Adventure, Mystery, Romance,* 27.

3. Cawelti, *Adventure, Mystery, Romance,* 35–36.

4. *The Dreadful Lemon Sky* (New York: J.B. Lippincott, 1974), p. 112 in the Fawcett paperback edition.

5. Mickey Spillane, *One Lonely Night,* 1951 (reprint, New York: New American Library, 2001); Mickey Spillane, *The Mike Hammer Collection,* 2 vols. (New York: New American Library, 2001), 2:95.

6. Raymond Chandler, *The Big Sleep,* 1940 (New York: Modern Library, 1995), 5.

7. These are widely reprinted. http://writingclasses.com, accessed Feb. 4, 2012.

8. Tony Judt, with Timothy Snyder, *Thinking the Twentieth Century* (New York, Penguin, 2012), 15.

9. Miller and Nowak, *The Fifties,* 221.

10. Ibid., 15

11. Tzvetan Todorov, "The Typology of Detective Fiction," *The Poetics of Prose* (Ithaca: Cornell University Press, 1977), 42–52.

12. These terms are explicated by Umberto Eco in *Six Walks in the Fictional Woods* (Cambridge: Harvard University Press, 1994)

13. Leslie Fiedler, *What Was Literature? Mass Culture and Mass Society* (New York: Simon & Schuster, 1982), 34.

14. David Halberstam, in *The Fifties,* gives a comprehensive account of *Peyton Place,* its public reception and effect on the new paperback and blockbuster promo-

tional strategies (New York: Villard Books, 1993), 577–586.

15. Miller and Nowak, *The Fifties,* 17.

16. Ibid., 233.

17. Other second-generation authors include Donald E. Westlake (1962), Elmore Leonard (1969), Bill Pronzini (Nameless Detective, 1971), Joseph Wambaugh (1972), and George V. Higgins (1972). It is notable that most of these also had substantial careers in film and television, and that Wambaugh, with experience in the police, could write as an insider.

18. Important hard-boiled novelists of the third generation would include, with the initial dates of their careers and their series detectives, James Ellroy (1981), Marcia Muller (1982, Sharon McCone), Sue Grafton (1982, Kinsey Millhone), Sara Paretsky (1982, V.I. Warshawski), Ian Rankin (1987, Inspector Rebus), Walter Mosely (1990, Easy Rawlins), Dennis Lehane (1994), and Henning Mankell (1997, Inspector Kurt Wallander).

19. The language is Evans's.

20. John Keegan, *Intelligence in War* (New York: Knopf, 2003). Keegan makes this point throughout.

21. Ibid., 3–4.

22. The period of the Great Game in which Kim participated is an important element in the history of spying and spy novels. See Peter Hopkirk, *The Great Game: The Struggle for Empire in Central Asia* (New York: Kodansha International, 1992).

23. Paraphrased from Jerome Bruner, *Making Stories* (New York: Farrar, Straus and Giroux, 2002), 90–91. Brian Boyd, in his *On the Origin of Stories* (Cambridge: Harvard University Press, 2009), discusses the social functions of fiction extensively, particularly in part 3, "Evolution and Fiction."

24. Robert L. O'Connell, *The Ride of the Second Horseman* (Oxford: Oxford University Press, 1995), 235.

25. Allan Hepburn, *Intrigue: Espionage and Culture* (New Haven: Yale University Press, 2005), 4.

26. Hepburn, *Intrigue,* 20.

27. This and the immediately following argument are from Richard Bulliet, *The Case for Islamo-Christian Civilization* (New York: Columbia University Press, 2004), 62–63.

28. William James, *The Varieties of Religious Experience* (New York: Modern Library, 1902), 222.

29. James, *Religious Experience*, 192.

30. Ibid., 242

31. William James, *Principal Writings on Religion*, ed. J.C.A. Gaskin (Oxford: Oxford University Press, 1993), 136–137.

32. Sigmund Freud, *Civilization and Its Discontents*, trans. James Strachey (New York: W.W. Norton, 1961), 11.

33. Robert Scholes, *The Crafty Reader* (New Haven: Yale University Press, 2001), 180. Scholes's ideas on this subject go back to his book *Semiotics and Interpretation* (New Haven: Yale University Press, 1983).

Chapter 6

1. Neo-Romanticism is widely attested, as can be seen by the number of scholarly books turned up by an Internet search. The quintessential Romantic William Blake was not given a full critical analysis until Northrop Frye's first book, *Fearful Symmetry*, in 1947.

2. Walter J. Ong, *Orality and Literacy* (London: Methuen, 1982). The autobiographical process by which memory is converted into history is described by Nabokov in *Speak, Memory*.

3. Karl Popper, *The Logic of Scientific Discovery* (New York: Basic, 1959).

4. Alan Watts, *The Way of Zen* (New York: Pantheon, 1957).

5. Gao Xingjian, *Soul Mountain*, trans. Mabel Lee (New York: HarperCollins, 2000), 329.

6. Seng-Chao, quoted in Yu-lan Feng, *The History of Chinese Philosophy*, vol. 2, *The Period of Classical Learning* (Princeton: Princeton University Press, 1983), 261.

7. Mark Currie, *Postmodern Narrative Theory* (New York: St. Martin's, 1998), 83. This follows on a pungent two-page critique of sequentiality that has deep connections with story and the concept of paradise, or origins. Currie invokes Derrida's concept of supplementarity, which he glosses as a counter-logic to narrative sequence. That is, what happens next does not follow from the origin but is already contained within it; has already occurred. This is the essence of affective time.

8. Karl Popper, *The Poverty of Histori-cism*, 1944, in German (reprint, Boston: Beacon, 1957).

9. Ibid., sections 20–21.

10. "The belief ... that it is the task of the social sciences to lay bare the law of evolution of society in order to foretell its future ... might perhaps be described as the central historicist doctrine" (Ibid., 105–6). Popper goes on to question *any* law of social evolution as being only a particular historical statement. Stephen Jay Gould's argument in *Wonderful Life: The Burgess Shale and the Nature of History* (New York: W.W. Norton, 1989) is that evolution is a complex process without a predictable outcome. Humans, Gould suggests, are not the result of the evolutionary process, but only the actual outcome. A repeat of the process would produce a different outcome.

11. Which, in his defense, Popper says also of science (*Poverty of Historicism*, 55).

12. Collin Martindale, *The Clockwork Muse: The Predictability of Artistic Change* (New York: Basic, 1990). Stanley Fish's chapter on stylistics in *Is There a Text in This Class?* (Cambridge: Harvard University Press, 1980) covers this ground more thoroughly.

13. "Primordial states of mind are often marked by a timeless, dream-like quality.... References to infantile and oral themes are also common" (Ibid., 59). "Physiognomic or animistic perception ... and synesthesia ... are also marks of primordial cognition" (60). "It is Picasso and Pollack — not Giotto or Cimabue — who paint like children" (31).

14. T.H. White, *The Once and Future King*, 1939 (New York: G.P. Putnam's Sons, 1965). The quotation is found on p. 181 of my 1987 Ace reprint.

15. John Rawls, *Lectures on the History of Moral Philosophy* (Cambridge: Harvard University Press, 2000), 335–6.

16. Svetlana Boym, *The Future of Nostalgia* (New York: Basic, 2001), 41.

17. Sgt. Joe Friday's squad-mate was supposed to serve this function, but the byplay was so cold and formal that it had the opposite effect.

18. An issue raised two generations ago by Erving Goffman in *Frame Analysis* (New York: Harper and Row, 1974). Goffman believed there was a real person behind the mask. Now we may not be so sure.

19. Linda Mizejewski provides an exten-

sive analysis of *The Silence of the Lambs* along these lines, showing how the respectable victim can play an active role rather than just being tied to the tracks (*Hardboiled and High Heeled: The Woman Detective in Popular Culture* [New York: Routledge, 2004]).

20. Mizejewski, *Hardboiled and High Heeled*, 93.

21. Ibid., 91.

22. There is one movie type that will allow us to root for the bad guys: the caper flick. Here wile and guile are celebrated and there is plenty of room for a woman. In fact, the way women can generate suspicion is a positive benefit to the form. Caper flicks are inverted thrillers. They begin with the gathering of intelligence and end with the failure of the adversary in an implosion of scorn.

23. Or some, many, or all of them. This last option is that of *Murder on the Orient Express*. Taking the premise seriously that everyone did it would be Kafka. Christie's version is a gimmick. The 2010 Suchet version speeds up the story to leave room for totting up a lot of Christian nonsense concerning guilt, which is utterly foreign to Poirot's pragmatism and faith in reason. If Poirot and the story were altered in good faith, why was it done? What cultural need was being served?

24. The objection was to the Enlightenment idea of a perfectible society, which the recent war had exposed as the ideological and propaganda engine of fascism, of totalitarianism generally, and of bourgeois (we would say suburban) complaisance. The intent was not to relegate compassion, generosity, and so forth, but it proves fatally easy to think so, as our own culture wars demonstrate.

25. There is an irony here. Everyone's psychology is unique. Its nature is hypothetical. It is not evidence in the way that fingerprints and alibis are. We construct it, thus bootlegging in the very relativism and radical uncertainty we were trying to avoid. In order to prevent this result the psychological motivation must be broadly intelligible, turning the characters back into the stick figures, which the appeal to psychology was intended to avoid.

26. Barzun and Taylor, *Catalogue of Crime*, 221.

27. Taken from a review by Andrew Miller in the *New York Times* online edition for March 22, 1998.

Chapter 7

1. It would be absurd to claim that these are new questions; they go back to the beginnings of intelligent life. Why we find them to be of particular urgency just now would be a separate inquiry. I am only suggesting that the two counter-strategies of Neoclassic and Metaphysical Modern are an index of that urgency.

2. A pocket summary of thinking about this, twenty years after Christian Metz's *Film Language,* is Benjamin Rifkin, *Semiotics of Narration in Film and Prose Fiction* (New York: Peter Lang, 1994), 20–23.

3. To avoid a long digression into narrative theory we may distinguish here between *narrative*, which is the sequence of events as told, and *story*, which is those events arranged (or rearranged) in temporal order. *Plot* is the construction (by the reader, in the end) of the causal links between events in the story and is thus logically posterior to both narrative and story. One reads the narrative, constructing the story as one goes. When one understands the story only then does the plot emerge. This usage differs somewhat from the convention. David Bordwell, *Narration in the Fiction Film* (Madison: University of Wisconsin Press, 1985) Umberto Eco, *Six Walks in the Fictional Woods* (Cambridge: Harvard University Press, 1994).

4. Bernard Williams, *Problems of the Self: Philosophical Papers 1956–1972* (New York: Cambridge University Press, 1973), especially the essays "Bodily Continuity and Personal Identity" (19–25) and "Are Persons Bodies?" (64–81).

5. What makes the problem of radical relativism so intractable is the concomitant hard materialism of cold knowledge: the belief that every question has only physical origins and a purely physical solution. This is the old Berkeleyan position without God as guarantor.

6. It is also the substance of the indignation of Sartre and others over Enlightenment humanism, an indictment that has become accepted wisdom since. Humanism assumes the possibility of a perfected society. It is the business of the Detective to per-

fect matters, or at least to restore them to the degree of perfection already achieved. Before the Metaphysical Modern no detective story was, nor could be, anti-humanist. One could despair of any practical accomplishments without relinquishing the belief in a perfect community. Some would say this is why the detective genre appeals to bourgeois readers.

7. This is actually an everyday problem. It is why, for example, one cannot, in a conversation or a novel, say exactly what one means, but only suggest a family to which it might belong. One must negotiate the meaning with the recipient of the message, and the result is always a compromise.

8. There is a density of ideas here sometimes best articulated in film theory. One entry point is Seymour Chatman's *Coming to Terms: The Rhetoric of Narrative in Fiction and Film* (Ithaca: Cornell University Press, 1990). Also useful is the opening material of Benjamin Rifkin's *Semiotics of Narration in Film and Prose Fiction* (New York: Peter Lang, 1994).

9. John Herbert Gill, "Introduction," in Gertrude Stein's *Blood on the Dining-Room Floor: A Murder Mystery* (Mineola, N.Y.: Dover, 2008).

10. Alain Robbe-Grillet, *Les Gommes,* trans. Richard Howard (New York: Grove, 1964).

11. C.P. Snow, *A Coat of Varnish* (New York: Charles Scribners Sons, 1979).

12. Carlo Emilio Gadda, *That Awful Mess on the Via Merulana,* trans. William Weaver (New York: George Braziller, 1965).

13. The first of these was *Outsider in Amsterdam* (New York: Soho, 1975) (Van de Wetering writes in English).

14. *The Inspector Barlach Mysteries: The Judge and His Hangman* and *Suspicion,* in German, 1950 and 1952, trans. Joel Agee (Chicago: University of Chicago Press, 2006).

15. Vladimir Nabokov, *King, Queen, Knave,* in Russian, 1928, trans. Dimitri Nabokov and the author (New York: McGraw-Hill, 1968).

16. Glenn Adamson, *Thinking Through Craft* (Oxford: Berg, 2007).

17. Pierre Bourdieu, *Distinction: A Social Critique of the Judgement of Taste,* trans. Richard Nice (Cambridge: Harvard University Press, 1984). Bourdieu shows how such a common standard could arise. There is a considerable philosophical and critical literature on this matter, from which I cite only one: John R. Searle's *The Construction of Social Reality* (New York: Free Press, 1995).

18. There are no claims made here about the "existence" of the phenomenal world. One is free to treat experiential encounters with it as either scientific materialism or samsara, without great consequences for the issues that concern us here.

19. This is the way of Janwillem van de Wetering's zen detectives Grijpstra and De Gier. Van de Wetering, like Stanislaw Lem, has not translated into movies. Since the true response to the solution of a koan is laughter, many people may have problems with seeming to laugh off murder, child abuse, and the other horrors that plague detectives' lives, and many moviegoers and readers are needed.

20. As with Proust, memories have a different reality; there is always a sense of loss standing between them and experience.

21. Frans de Waal, *Chimpanzee Politics* (New York: Harper and Row, 1982).

22. Richard Hofstadter, "Paranoid Style in American Politics." *Harper's Magazine* 229 (1374) (Nov. 1964): 77–86.

23. The plight of Wallas in *Les Gommes* (1969) or more recently, *13 Conversations About One Thing* (2001).

24. *The Writings of Henry David Thoreau,* 20 vols. (Walden edition, Boston: Houghton Mifflin, 1906), *Essays,* 184–204, 186, http://www.walden.org/Library/The_Writings_of_Henry_David_Thoreau:_The_Digital_Collection/Essays.

Bibliography

Novels referred to in the text are listed in the index

Adams, Richard. *The Hitchhiker Quartet*. New York: Harmony, 1986.

Alcock, James. "The Belief Engine." *Skeptical Inquirer* 19.3 (May/June 1995): 255–63.

Alder, Bill. "Maigret, Simenon, France: Social Class and Social Change in the 1930s Maigret Novels of Georges Simenon." *Clues* 29.2 (Fall 2011): 47–57.

Allain, Marcel, and Pierre Souvestre (afterwards Marcel Allain). *Fantômas*. Published in book form from 1911 in Paris by A Fayard.

Anderson, Peter Bogh. "Genres as Self-Organizing Systems." In *Information Organization: Studies in Organizational Semiotics*, ed. Kecheng Liu, 214–60. Boston: Kluwer Academic, 2001.

Arendt, Hannah. *The Human Condition*. Chicago: University of Chicago Press, 1958.

Barzun, Jacques. *Berlioz and the Romantic Century*. New York: Columbia University Press, 1969.

_____, and Wendell Hertig Taylor. *A Catalogue of Crime*. Expanded ed. New York: Harper and Row, 1989.

Baudelaire, Charles. *Le Spleen de Paris*. 1869. Reprint trans. Louise Varèse. New York: New Directions, 1970.

Baudrillard, Jean. *The Mirror of Production*. Trans. Mark Poster. St. Louis: Telos, 1975.

Bayard, Pierre. *Who Killed Roger Ackroyd?* Trans. Carol Cosman. New York: New Press, 2000.

Berlin, Isaiah. *The Roots of Romanticism*. 1965. A.W. Mellon Lectures on the Fine Arts. Ed. Henry Hardy. Reprint, Princeton: Princeton University Press, 1999.

Bonfantini, Massimo A. "To Guess or Not to Guess?" In *The Sign of Three: Dupin, Holmes, Peirce*, ed. Umberto Eco and Thomas A. Sebeok, 214–60. Bloomington: Indiana University Press, 1983.

Bordwell, David. "The Detective Film." In *Narration in the Fiction Film*, 64–70. Madison: University of Wisconsin Press, 1985.

_____. *Narration and Film Form*. Madison: University of Wisconsin Press, 1985.

_____. *Narration in the Fiction Film*. Madison: University of Wisconsin Press, 1985.

_____. *On the History of Film Style*. Cambridge: Harvard University Press, 1997.

_____. *The Way Hollywood Tells It*. Berkeley: University of California Press, 2006.

Bourdieu, Pierre. *Distinction: A Social Critique of the Judgement of Taste*. Trans. Richard Nice. Cambridge: Harvard University Press, 1984.

_____. *The Field of Cultural Production*. Ed. Randal Johnson. New York: Columbia University Press, 1993.

Boyd, Brian. *On the Origin of Stories*. Cambridge: Harvard University Press, 2009.

Boym, Svetlana. *The Future of Nostalgia*. New York: Basic, 2001.

Bruner, Jerome. *Making Stories*. New York: Farrar, Straus and Giroux, 2002.

Bulliet, Richard. *The Case for Islamo-Christian Civilization*. New York: Columbia University Press, 2004.

Bulwer-Lytton, Edward. *Pelham*. Ed. Jerome J. McGann. 1818. Reprint, Lincoln: University of Nebraska Press, 1972.

Cawelti, John G. *Adventure, Mystery, Romance*. Chicago: University of Chicago Press, 1976.

Champigny, Robert. *What Will Have Happened: A Philosophical and Technical Essay on Mystery Stories*. Bloomington: Indiana University Press, 1977.

Chandler, Alfred D. *Scale and Scope: The Dynamics of Industrial Capitalism*. Cambridge: Harvard University Press, 1990.

Chandler, Raymond. "The Simple Art of Murder." *Atlantic Monthly*, Dec. 1944. Reprint, New York: Vintage, 1950 and 1988.

Chatman, Seymour. *Coming to Terms: The Rhetoric of Narrative in Fiction and Film*. New York: Columbia University Press, 1990.

Clendennin, Inga. *Reading the Holocaust*. Cambridge: Cambridge University Press, 1999.

Cohen, Michael. *Murder Most Fair: The Appeal of Mystery Fiction*. Madison: Fairleigh Dickinson, 2000.

Collins, Randall. *The Sociology of Philosophies: A Global Theory of Intellectual Change*. Cambridge: Harvard University Press, 1998.

Connelly, Kelly C. *From Poe to Auster: Literary Experimentation in the Detective Story Genre*. Philadelphia: Temple University, 2009.

Cordle, Daniel. *Postmodern Postures: Literature, Science, and the Two Cultures Debate*. Aldershot, U.K.: Ashgate, 1999.

Cornelius, David R., and Edwin St. Vincent. *Cultures in Conflict: Perspectives on the Snow-Leavis Controversy*. New York: Scott Foresman, 1964.

Crawford, Matthew B. *Shopcraft as Soulcraft*. New York: Penguin, 2009.

Currie, Mark. *Postmodern Narrative Theory*. New York: St. Martin's, 1998.

Davenport-Hines, Richard. *Gothic: 400 Years of Excess, Horror, Evil, and Ruin*. London: Fourth Estate, 1998.

Defoe, Daniel. *Street Robberies, Consider'd*. London: J. Roberts, 1748; restored edition, with introduction and notes, by Geoffrey M. Sill, Stockton, N.J.: Carolingian, 1973.

Delameter, Jerome. *Theory and Practice of Classic Detective Fiction*. ABC Clio, 1997.

Demko, George J. "Detective Fiction and Edmund Wilson: A Rejoinder (More than 50 Years Later)." 2005. http://www.dartmouth.edu/gjdemko/praise.htm. Accessed Oct. 18, 2011.

De Quincey, Thomas. "On Murder Considered as One of the Fine Arts." *Blackwood's Magazine*, 1827. Reprint, Oxford: Oxford University Press, 2006.

De Waal, Frans. *Chimpanzee Politics*. New York: Harper and Row, 1982.

Dickstein, Morris. *Dancing in the Dark: A Cultural History of the Great Depression*. New York: W.W. Norton, 2009.

Dirda, Michael. *On Conan Doyle; or, The Whole Art of Storytelling*. Princeton: Princeton University Press, 2012.

Dostoyevski, Fyodor. *Crime and Punishment*. 1866. Trans. Richard Pevear and Larissa Volokhonsky. Reprint, New York: Vintage, 1992.

Eco, Umberto. *Six Walks in the Fictional Woods*. Cambridge: Harvard University Press, 1994.

_____, and Thomas A. Sebeok, eds. *The Sign of Three: Dupin, Holmes, Peirce*. Princeton: Princeton University Press, 1983.

Elias, Norbert. *The Civilizing Process*. Rev. ed. Trans. Edmund Jephcott. Oxford: Blackwell, 1994.

Evans, Mary. *Imagination of Evil: Detective Fiction and the Modern World*. London: Consortium International, 2009.

Evans, Richard J. *The Coming of the Third Reich.* London: Penguin, 2003.

Ewert, Jeanne C. "A Thousand Other Mysteries: Metaphysical Detection, Ontological Quests." In *Detecting Texts: The Metaphysical Detective Story from Poe to Postmodernism,* ed. Patricia Merivale and Susan Elizabeth Sweeney, 179–98. Philadelphia: University of Pennsylvania Press, 1999.

Fekete, John. "Culture, History, and Ambivalence: On the Subject of Walter Benjamin." In *Explorations in Film Theory,* ed. Ron Burnett, 168–79. Bloomington: Indiana University Press, 1991.

Feng, Yu-lan. *The History of Chinese Philosophy.* Volume 2: *The Period of Classical Learning.* Princeton: Princeton University Press, 1983.

Fiedler, Leslie. *What Was Literature? Mass Culture and Mass Society.* New York: Simon & Schuster, 1982.

Fish, Stanley. *Is There a Text in This Class?* Cambridge: Harvard University Press, 1980.

Flanders, Judith. "The Hanky Panky War." *Times Literary Supplement,* June 18, 2010, 14.

Frank, Lawrence. *Victorian Detective Fiction and the Nature of Evidence: The Scientific Investigations of Poe, Dickens, and Doyle.* New York: Palgrave Macmillan, 2003.

Freeling, Nicholas. *Criminal Convictions: Errant Essays on Perpetrators of Literary License.* New York: Peter Lang; London: Peter Owen, 1994.

Freeman, R. Austin. "The Art of the Detective Story." *Nineteenth Century and After,* May 1924: 713–21. Reprinted in *The Art of the Mystery Story,* ed. Howard Haycraft, 11–12. New York: Simon & Schuster, 1946.

Freud, Sigmund. *Civilization and Its Discontents.* Trans. James Strachey. New York: W.W. Norton, 1961.

Fuller, Steve. *Social Epistemology.* 2nd ed. Bloomington: Indiana University Press, 2002.

Gates, Philippa. *Detecting Women: Gender and the Hollywood Detective Film.* Albany: State University of New York Press, 2011.

Geidion, Siegfried. *Mechanization Takes Command: A Contribution to Anonymous History.* Chicago: University of Chicago Press, 1948.

Gibbs, John. *Mise-en-Scène: Film Style and Presentation.* London: Wallflower, 2002.

Goffman, Erving. *Frame Analysis.* New York: Harper and Row, 1974.

Goldstein, Phillip. *Modern American Reading Practices.* London: Macmillan, 2009.

Gould, Stephen Jay. *Wonderful Life: The Burgess Shale and the Nature of History.* New York: W.W. Norton, 1989.

Guillory, John. *Cultural Capital: The Problems of Literary Canon Formation.* Chicago: Chicago University Press, 1993.

Halberstam, David. *The Fifties.* New York: Villard, 1993.

Hepburn, Allan. *Intrigue: Espionage and Culture.* New Haven: Yale University Press, 2005.

Hofstadter, Richard. "The Paranoid Style in American Politics." *Harper's Magazine* 229.1374 (1964): 77–86.

Hollows, Joanne et al., eds. *The Film Studies Reader.* London: Arnold, 2000.

Hopkirk, Peter. *The Great Game: The Struggle for Empire in Central Asia.* New York: Kodansha International, 1992.

Houston, Natalie M. "Introduction." *Lady Audley's Secret.* Toronto: Broadview Library Texts, 2003.

Huang, Yunte. *Charlie Chan: The Untold Story of the Honorable Detective and His Rendezvous with American History.* New York: Norton, 2010.

Hühn, Peter. "The Detective as Reader: Narrativity and Reading Concepts in Detective Fiction." *MFS: Modern Fiction Studies* 33.3 (Fall 1987): 451–466.

James, William. *Principal Writings on Religion.* Ed. J.C.A. Gaskin. Oxford: Oxford University Press, 1993.

_____. *The Varieties of Religious Experience.* New York: Modern Library, 1902.

Judt, Tony, with Timothy Snyder. *Thinking the Twentieth Century.* New York: Penguin, 2012.

Kayman, Martin A. *From Bow Street to Baker Street: Mystery, Detection, and Narrative.* New York: St. Martin's, 1992.

Keates, Jonathan. *Stendahl*. New York: Carroll and Graf, 1994.

Keegan, John. *Intelliigence in War*. New York: Knopf, 2003.

Kern, Stephen. *A Cultural History of Causality: Science, Murder Novels, and Systems of Thought*. Princeton: Princeton University Press, 2004.

Kingman, Maxine Hong. *China Men*. New York: Knopf, 1980.

Klein, Kathleen Gregory. *The Woman Detective: Gender and Genre*. 2nd ed. Urbana: University of Illinois Press, 1995.

Klein, Kathleen Gregory, ed. *Women Times Three: Writing, Detectives, Readers*. Bowling Green: Bowling Green University Press, 1995.

Klevan, Andrew. "Notes on Teaching Film Style." In *Style and Meaning: Studies in the Detailed Analysis of Film*, ed. John Gibbs and Douglas Pye, 214–27. Manchester: Manchester University Press, 2005.

Knevelson, Roberta. *Peirce and the Mark of the Gryphon*. New York: St. Martin's, 1999.

Kolb, Martina. "Review of Robert A. Rushing, *Resisting Arrest* (New York: Other, 2007)." *Comparative Literature Studies* 46.3 (2009): 545–49.

Kungi, Carla. *Creating the Female Detective*. Jefferson, N.C.: McFarland, 2006.

Langer, Suzanne K. *Feeling and Form*. New York: Scribner, 1953.

_____. *Mind: On Human Feeling*. Baltimore: Johns Hopkins, 1966–82.

Leitch, Thomas, and Barak Keith Grant, eds. *Crime Films*. Genres in American Cinema. Cambridge: Cambridge University Press, 2002.

Lemoine, Michel. *The Method of Investigation According to Maigret: A Methodological Absence of Method?* Trans. Strphen Trussel. http://www.trussel.com/maig/lemoine.htm. Accessed Oct. 18, 2011.

Leonard, Elmore. "Ten Rules for Writing." http://writingclasses.com.

Macdonald, Ross. "Down These Streets a Mean Man Must Go." *Antaeus* 25/26 (Spring/Summer 1977): 211–16.

Martindale, Collin. *The Clockwork Muse: The Predictability of Artistic Change*. New York: Basic, 1990.

Mathews, Harry. *My Life in the CIA*. Normal, IL: Dalkey Archive, 2005.

Merivale, Patricia, and Susan Elizabeth Sweeney. *Detecting Texts: The Metaphysical Detective Story from Poe to Postmodernism*. Philadelphia: University of Pennsylvania Press, 1999.

Miller, Andrew. Review of Iain Pears, An Instance of the Fingerpost. *New York Times,* March 22, 1998.

Miller, Douglas T., and Marion Nowak. *The Fifties: The Way We Really Were*. New York: Doubleday, 1977.

Mizejewski, Linda. *Hardboiled and High Heeled: The Woman Detective in Popular Culture*. New York: Routledge, 2004.

Monaco, James. *How to Read a Film*. 4th ed. Oxford: Oxford University Press, 2009.

Montesquieu, Charles de Secondat, Baron de. *L'Esprit des Lois (The Spirit of Laws)*. Paris: Barillot and Files, 1748. Place of publication incorrectly given as Geneva. Reprint, New York: Prometheus, 2002.

Moody, Nickianne. "Crime in Film and on TV." In *Murder Most Fair: The Appeal of Murder Fiction*, ed. Michael Cohen, 227–43. Madison: Fairleigh Dickinson, 2000.

Moore, Lewis D. *Cracking the Hard-Boiled Detective*. Jefferson, N.C.: McFarland, 2006.

Moretti, Franco. *Signs Taken for Wonders: Essays in the Sociology of Literary Forms*. Trans. Susan Fischer, David Forgacs, and David Miller. London: Verso, 1988.

Nicolson, Marjorie. "The Professor and the Detective." *Atlantic Monthly*, Apr. 1929. Reprinted in *The Art of the Mystery Story*, ed. Howard Haycraft, 110–127. New York: Simon & Schuster, 1946.

Norden, Pierre. *Conan Doyle*. London: John Murray, 1966.

O'Brien, Geoffrey. *Hardboiled America: The Lurid Years of Paperbacks*. New York: Van Nostrand Reinhold, 1981.

O'Connell, Robert L. *The Ride of the Second Horseman*. Oxford: Oxford University Press, 1995.

O'Connell, Stephen. *Detective Deleuze and the Case of Slippery Signs.* 1998. http://www.artdes.monash.edu.au/globe/yraks.html.

Ong, Walter J. *Orality and Literacy.* London: Methuen, 1982.

Pointer, Michael. *The Sherlock Holmes File.* New York: Clarkson N. Potter, 1976.

Popper, Karl. *The Poverty of Historicism.* New York: Beacon, 1957.

_____. *The Logic of Scientific Discovery.* New York: Basic, 1959.

Porter, Theodore M. *Trust in Numbers: The Pursuit of Objectivity in Science and Public Life.* Princeton: Princeton University Press, 1995.

Propaganda by Deed: The Greenwich Observatory Bomb of 1894. http://nmm.ac.uk.

Pykett, Lyn. "The Newgate Novel and Sensation Fiction 1830–1868." In *Cambridge Companion to Crime Fiction,* ed. Martin Priestman, 19–39. Cambridge: Cambridge University Press, 2003.

Pyrhonen, Heta. *Murder from an Academic Angle: An Introduction to the Study of the Detective Narrative.* Camden: Camden House, 1994.

Rawls, John. *Lectures on the History of Moral Philosophy.* Cambridge: Harvard University Press, 2000.

Rifkin, Benjamin. *Semiotics of Narration in Film and Prose Fiction.* New York: Peter Lang, 1994.

Roth, Mary. *Foul and Fair Play.* University of Georgia Press, 1995.

Rowland, Susan. "The Wasteland and the Grail Knight: Myth and Cultural Criticism in Detective Fiction." *Clues* 28.2 (Fall 2010): 44–54.

Rushing, Robert A. *Resisting Arrest: Detective Fiction and Popular Culture.* New York: Other Press, 2007.

Rzepka, Charles J. *Detective Fiction.* Cambridge: Polity Press, 2005.

St.-Germain, Philippe. "Orson Welles' Mr. Arkadin — A Maze of Death. Trans. Philippe St.-Germain and Steve Erikson." *Senses of Cinema* 10 (2000). http://www.sensesofcinema.com.

Scholes, Robert. "Light Reading: The Private Eye Novel as a Genre." In *The Crafty Reader,* 138–82. New Haven: Yale University Press, 2001.

Schreuders, Piet. *Paperbacks, USA.* San Diego: Blue Dolphin, 1981.

Schütt, Sita A. "French Crime Fiction." In *Murder Most Fair: The Appeal of Murder Fiction,* ed. Michael Cohen, 59–76. Madison: Fairleigh Dickinson, 2000.

Searle, John R. *The Construction of Social Reality.* New York: Free Press, 1995.

Segal, Eyal. "Closure in Detective Fiction." *Poetics Today* 31.2 (Summer 2010): 153–215.

Snow, C.P. *The Two Cultures.* 2nd ed. Cambridge: Cambridge University Press, 1959; reprint 1993.

Sontag, Susan. *Regarding the Pain of Others.* New York: Farrar, Straus and Giroux, 2003.

Strausbaugh, John. "The Novelist Who Was Also a Spy, or Not." *New York Times,* Apr. 26, 2005.

Todorov, Tzvetan. "Primitive Narrative." In *The Poetics of Prose,* trans. Richard Howard, 53–65. Ithaca: Cornell University Press, 1977.

_____. "The Typology of Detective Fiction." In *The Poetics of Prose,* trans. Richard Howard, 42–52. Ithaca: Cornell University Press, 1977.

Tuchman, Gaye, and Nina Fortin. *Edging Women Out: Victorian Novelists, Publishers, and Social Change.* New Haven: Yale University Press, 1989.

Van Dine, S.S. (Willard Huntington Wright). "Twenty Rules for Writing Detective Stories." *American Magazine,* Sept. 1928. Reprinted in *Philo Vance Investigates,* 1936.

Van Dover, J.K. *Making the Detective Story American.* Jefferson, N.C.: McFarland, 2010.

Watts, Alan. *The Way of Zen.* New York: Pantheon, 1957.

Wellmer, Albrecht. *The Persistence of Modernity: Essays on Aesthetics, Ethics, and Postmodernism.* Trans. David Midgely. Cambridge: MIT, 1991.

Wessels, Henry. "The Philosophical Exercises of Janwillem Van de Wetering.

With a Checklist of Books." *AB Bookman's Weekly,* Sept. 7–14, 1998.

Wexman, Virginia Wright. *A History of Film.* 6th ed. Boston: Pearson, 2006.

Williams, Bernard. *Problems of the Self: Philosophical Papers 1956–1972.* Cambridge: Cambridge University Press, 1973.

Wilson, Edmund. "Mr. Holmes, They Were the Footsteps of a Giant Hound!" *New Yorker,* Feb. 17, 1945.

_____. "Who Cares Who Killed Roger Ackroyd?" *New Yorker,* June 20, 1945.

_____. "Why Do People Read Detective Stories." *New Yorker,* Oct. 19, 1944.

Wilson, Elizabeth. *Bohemians, the Glamorous Outcasts.* New Brunswick: Rutgers, 2000.

Worthington, Heather. *The Subverting Vision of Bulwer Lytton.* Plainsboro: Associated University Press, 2004.

Xingjian, Gao. *Soul Mountain.* Trans. Mabel Lee. New York: HarperCollins, 2000.

Index